TROUBLED PEOPLE, TROUBLED WORLD

Troubled People, Troubled World

Psychotherapy, Ethics, and Society

Michael Briant

With a Foreword by Rowan Williams

OpenBook
Publishers

https://www.openbookpublishers.com

©2025 Michael Briant; Foreword ©Rowan Williams

An earlier edition of this book entitled *Psychotherapy, Ethics, and Society: Another Kind of Conversation* was published in 2018 by Cambridge Scholars Publishing

All external links were active at the time of publication unless otherwise stated and have been archived via the Internet Archive Wayback Machine at https://archive.org/web

Any digital material and resources associated with this volume will be available at https://doi.org/10.11647/OBP.0416#resources

ISBN Paperback: 978-1-80511-356-0
ISBN Hardback: 978-1-80511-357-7
ISBN Digital (PDF): 978-1-80511-358-4
ISBN Digital eBook (EPUB): 978-1-80511-359-1
ISBN HTML: 978-1-80511-360-7

DOI: 10.11647/OBP.0416

Cover image: Lucien Pissarro, *Ruth Gleaning Corn* (1896), https://commons.wikimedia.org/wiki/File:Ruth_verzamelt_aren,_RP-P-1950-755.jpg

Cover design: Jeevanjot Kaur Nagpal

For those I have loved

The world is washing out its stains, he said.
Young blood's its great objection.
But when we're duly white-washed, being dead,
The world will bear Field-Marshal God's inspection.
—Wilfred Owen, 'Inspection'

We are such stuff
As dreams are made on; and our little life
Is rounded with a sleep.
—William Shakespeare, *The Tempest*

Contents

Acknowledgements

I am deeply indebted to Bruce Kinsey, John Mason and David Winter, who very generously gave me so much help and advice on this book as it finally took shape. I am also very grateful to Anne Corsellis, Malcolm Edwards, Jeannette Josse, the late Peter Lomas, Kalu Singh, Srinath, Xavier Renders, Timo Storck, Norman Cohn's widow, Marina Voikhanskaya, and Peter Wadell, all of whom also read the work, or parts of it, and offered their thoughts on the evolving text. Xavier, now a child psychotherapist again, but for some years vice-rector of the Université Catholique de Louvain, urged me to write rather more about Lacan than I had originally planned, although he is a devotee of Winnicott rather than of Lacan, but the views I have expressed on Lacan are of course my own and, needless to say, Xavier is not responsible for them in any way. I also benefitted greatly from conversations with Daniel Pick and correspondence with the late Anthony Ryle. It was similar thought-provoking conversations with Chris Rowland (senior) on apocalyptic ideas and movements that convinced me that the connection between the two and violence needed more consideration than I had given it in the book's first edition. It was a pleasure to work with Alessandra Tosi and Lucy Barnes of Open Book Publishers: their professional expertise, guidance and encouragement were invaluable. And finally I'd like to thank very warmly my patients, from whom I learned so much, especially those who have allowed me to recount something of their lives in the following pages.

Foreword

Rowan Williams

The current slow collapse of what we might call a humanistic and law-governed understanding of national and international political processes, the resurgence of violent self-interest (individual and national) as an unchallengeable justification for how we act, the dominance of algorithms and impersonal probabilities in the management of individuals – all of this adds up to a set of darkening shadows over a great deal that we in the 'developed' world have taken for granted. In this moving and deeply insightful book, Michael Briant argues that we are more than ever in need of an intelligent conversation between psychiatry and social or political analysis if we are not to be fatally immobilized by the confusion that prevails in so many places. We inhabit a culture that does not help us or encourage us to *think* about *wanting*. We are tacitly urged to resist the labour of interrogating our instinctive responses to the world, of making imaginative and continuous sense of our stories; the focus is on the pressure of unthought desire here and now, with the result that the obstacles to unthought desire here and now appear as the enemy of our very selves. The radical fear that this generates pushes us into the classic dilemma (already familiar in most of the traditional spiritual systems of the world) of whether we respond with aggressive and acquisitive action so as to neutralize and absorb the enemy, or whether we deny, repress, or ignore the crisis, shutting the doors on our vulnerability or uncertainty. Both strategies produce an intensified risk of violent conflict and profound damage to self and others (including the other life forms with which we share our planet). Both decisively block the formation of durable and nurturing relations.

 https://doi.org/10.11647/OBP.0416.11

It is this risk that should make us aware of the vital importance of sustaining that dialogue between the arts and sciences of the psyche and the study of social process. As Briant notes, the claim of psychoanalysis to be a scientific discipline has drawn increasing (not undeserved) scepticism from many quarters; but—rather than letting this push us back into an impersonal or mechanistic picture of human interaction — we need to let it question some of our assumptions about what counts as 'science', what counts as 'useful knowledge'. Briant's carefully and compassionately narrated instances of what therapy actually looks like help us to see what it means to *come to know* in the process of conversation, where some sort of mutual need is allowed to slip into the light, however briefly, so that one or both persons sharing in a dialogue realize that the other knows something they have to learn. The Polish priest and philosopher, Jozef Tischner, said that dialogue begins when I acknowledge that the other knows something I need to know, something I need if I am to live well. The therapeutic encounter at its best is where that acknowledgment can be grasped and worked with.

Bring this into the context of global politics and it stands as a major challenge to where we have allowed ourselves to drift. No-one, least of all the author of this book, will imagine that a brief introduction to the dynamics of the psyche will work some magic on the world's most powerful individuals and convert them to the values of dialogical encounter. But the conversation of society goes on, like a small plant growing between apparently fixed slabs of stone; given time its roots will run deep, and the smooth surface of apparently settled and unchangeable habit may yet crack open. Books like this are a contribution to that process of rooting certain kinds of wisdom in continuing conversation— opening our sympathies by way of detailed narrative, stretching our minds with fresh models of how we think and feel. This is a seriously important and highly accessible book, whose insights could hardly be more timely.

Cardiff, February 2025

Preface to the Second Edition

Troubled People, Troubled World is the second edition of *Psychotherapy, Ethics and Society: Another Kind of Conversation*, which was published in 2018. At the suggestion of Open Book Publishers, I've changed the title to signify that this is a revised and much expanded version of the original. Two developments seemed to call for that. The first is that dark forces seem to be gathering again all over our world, menacing democracies or replacing them; there is war once again in Europe and bitter conflict in the Middle East, in Africa and elsewhere. These developments have complex roots, but many psychotherapists, whilst acknowledging that, are dismayed by the lack of any psychological insight into how they may have come about. In the first half of the nineteenth century we learned that cholera was caused by drinking water contaminated by human waste, and after the second world war there was widespread hope that we might similarly find the source of our recurring demonization and dehumanisation of others, and the cruelty and destructiveness associated with it. In an article that appeared in *Encounter* in 1962, David Astor, editor of the *Observer*, coined the term "the scourge" to refer to one of its major sources. This new edition tightens the focus on it.

Secondly, rather like Ruth in the woodcut on the cover of this book, psychotherapists glean information about human motivation in fields where we are invited to do so. Some, of course, specialise in forensic work, but even those who, like myself, do not, feel part of a long history of practitioners who believe that what we gather or learn could help prevent further outbreaks of what otherwise seems to be an incomprehensible affliction. The psychosocial measures that writers like Erich Fromm advocate, however, face both the resistance of vested interests and a fatalism that dismisses them as utopian. The subtext of the latter view appears to be that we must accept the suffering we see around us because more suffering, more cruelty and violence are generated when we attempt to do anything about it. The implication is that this is something we must stoically accept because it is human nature, but it is also human nature to try to alleviate suffering, to rectify grievances and fight against injustice. Some of those interested in these matters make a link between utopian ideas and apocalyptic beliefs, claiming, though it is not always clear, that the former are always derived from the latter and that both necessarily end in violence. A brief preface is not the place to cite examples, but if that is indeed what they think, the legitimacy of their inferences and the validity of their claims are open to challenge. I have added a more detailed discussion of these issues in Chapter 5. I have also expanded the two appendices, and rounded the book off with a postscript.

Introduction

Many years have passed since the ending of the Second World War, and it is hard for us now to imagine the feelings of those who were then stumbling out of that desolating darkness. Relief, elation, hope, grief, sadness, anger, fear, humiliation, shame and guilt were just some of the emotions, at times conflicting, that fed into an overwhelming determination, now half forgotten, that we must never allow such a cataclysm to happen again. That determination was massively strengthened as we became aware of the fate of the Jews, and of others designated 'undesirable' such as political dissidents, the disabled, homosexuals, Gypsies, Jehovah's Witnesses, and races deemed 'inferior' like the Slavs. The devastation and destruction that resulted from the fighting were one thing, but these groups were not, to use a contemptible expression, 'collateral damage', they had been singled out and persecuted well before hostilities began. For the totalitarian regimes and their puppets, they were pathogens that disfigured and threatened the purified societies they sought to create, and they needed to be expunged.

In his book *East West Street* (2016), Philippe Sands has described how lawyers came up with two concepts, 'crimes against humanity' and 'genocide', as their contribution to the efforts to ensure that the forces of evil might be kept at bay. Future perpetrators of such crimes might be deterred, they believed, if they knew that international law provided a legal framework within which they might be caught and prosecuted. However, valuable though such legal notions might be, they did not offer any clues as to the psychosocial origins of the fantasies that drove the impulse to demonise and dehumanise.

Many would assume that 'racism' might offer more, but a focus on ethnicity would leave out other important examples from this and other periods of history, and it misses, or at least does not foreground, a feature

 https://doi.org/10.11647/OBP.0416.00

of key significance common to them all: "the urge to purify the world through the annihilation of some category of human beings imagined as agents of corruption and incarnations of evil."[1] The words are those of the historian Norman Cohn, and they are taken from the introduction to one of his books. They are important because they highlight the fact that those who carried out these atrocities were not simply justifying their actions to themselves and to the world after the event, but rather that they actually saw themselves as engaged on a mission of moral or religious cleansing and regeneration.

In an article that appeared in *Encounter* in 1962, David Astor, editor of the *Observer*, referred to this as "the scourge". At the core of it he identified a "perverse morality", which led those who subscribed to it to believe that they had a *duty* to kill certain groups of people for no other reason than that they were members of those groups. Though individuals might be guilty of wrongdoing, as in any community, the groups themselves were essentially innocent, but they became the focus of virulent and vicious paranoid fantasies. The 'holocaust', as we commonly call it, was perhaps the worst example of it, but there had been other versions of it in human history and there would be variants of it in the future, though it was hard to foresee what form they might take. For Astor the scourge showed the power of unreason; it was as irrational as persecuting all left-handed people simply because they were left-handed. He argued for a rigorous, academic study of it, and played a key role in bringing this about by arranging the funding and the establishment of the Institute for Research in Collective Psychopathology at Sussex University in 1966. Norman Cohn was invited to lead the Institute because his research on manifestations of the phenomenon in the Middle Ages was widely respected and admired.

The Columbus Centre, as it became known, sponsored studies into episodes in much more recent history, and Cohn himself, alongside *Europe's Inner Demons* (1993), his much-admired study of the persecution of the witches, wrote *Warrant for Genocide* (2005), an investigation into the origins of the 'Protocols of the Elders of Zion', the malevolent myth that there was a Jewish conspiracy to take over the world. Cohn shared Astor's view that the attempt to wipe out the Jews was an instance,

---

1   Norman Cohn, *Europe's Inner Demons* (London: Pimlico, 1993), xi.

within our lifetime, of an ancient affliction which, like the plague, could be shown to have recurred periodically over many centuries.

A year or so before he died, I asked him how he had become interested in the topic. "Oh, that's easy", he replied, before telling me that he had served in Intelligence during the Second World War and had been asked to interview a former S.S. officer. During the course of this meeting, the interviewee said to him: "I know we did some terrible things, but you must understand that we had to do them to clean up society." Some time later, he was detailed to interview a KGB officer who had defected from the Soviet Union, and at one point the officer said exactly the same thing. Cohn was struck by these identical admissions from individuals who came from societies based on very different social philosophies, and they led him to think that they represented the flaring up of a psychosocial syndrome that had appeared in various incarnations over two millennia. At the moment, movements claiming the sanction of Islam are attracting a great deal of attention, but some of the most famous historical examples in the past, such as the persecution of heretics and the great witch hunt, have been Christian. One of the two fundamental teachings of Christianity, however, is "thou shalt love thy neighbour as thyself," but Vladimir Putin, another modern manifestation of Astor's perverse morality, is murdering his *en masse*, all the while parading his Orthodox piety and basking in the full backing of the Moscow Patriarch. These modern episodes believe they have the sanction of their religion, but, as Cohn's story illustrates, the guise in which they appear may equally be aggressively secular.

For many historians, any notion of a psychosocial syndrome is misconceived because they are more impressed by the differences between one regime and another. The danger of this approach, however, is that we ignore the psychological patterns or 'constants', just as the danger of the psychosocial line is a psychological reductionism which, as I demonstrate in Chapter 3, ends in absurdity. Perhaps it was because Cohn was aware of these problems that the Columbus Centre pioneered an interdisciplinary approach, drawing in historians, sociologists, social anthropologists, psychotherapists and psychoanalysts—anyone, in fact, who might be able to make a significant contribution to its concerns. The Centre also tried to avoid national bias by involving co-workers from different countries. Operating only twenty years or so after the end of the

Second World War, it tended to be preoccupied with the mass murder of the Jews: with ethnic cleansing, in other words. Yet, as we know only too well from the history of our "inner demons", as Cohn calls them, that and the persecution of people on religious or moral grounds may easily go hand-in-hand.

It is the persecution of people on religious or moral grounds that I focus on in this book. It is not, however, a comparative study of current versions of it, of the teaching that has inspired them, their organisation, funding, affiliations and so forth: there are already quite a few people writing on these subjects. Although I do draw rather heavily on one particular example in Chapter 3, I am more concerned with the deeper psychological processes that underlie this bewildering paradox. More specifically: what can psychodynamic psychology contribute to our understanding of it? Can we learn anything from it as to how we might prevent, or at least contain, the barbarism it sanctions? Can the practice of psychotherapy offer us any insights into a different, more inclusive, kind of ethics? And, if so, can we glean any guidance from it on steps we might take to further it? These are the questions that I intend to explore.

The recurrence of collective psychopathology has lent some urgency to them, yet the prevailing views about human motivation fail us when we look to them to try to fathom how groups become demonised and dehumanised or how we might counter such deadly developments. Many practitioners are very concerned, as I am myself, by the discrepancy between what we learn as therapists and the assumptions about human motivation that underlie so much current thinking about socio-political issues, dominated, as it has become, by 'Economic Man'.

What are those assumptions? And how credible is the model, sometimes referred to as 'homo economicus', that has been fashioned out of them? Let's take these questions in turn. Economic Man is a view of human nature that appears in several variants, a recent example being rational economic choice theory. However, they all boil down to the belief that we are fully conscious of the forces that govern us, and that we are driven solely by greed or fear of starvation; that we are essentially asocial individuals who gather together only out of calculated self-interest, and that considered self-interest (whatever that means) rules, and indeed should rule our relationships; that we make our own lives according to something called 'character', rising heroically, if we have it, above the constraints that those of weaker moral fibre blame for their failures, and owing little or nothing to anyone for any success we attain. If we are poor, it is because we are lazy or lack control over our basic urges and find ourselves with more children than we can afford. Poverty, from this perspective, is a moral failure.

These assumptions may be vague and contradictory, but like all such assumptions they have important implications for the way we organise our society, for anyone who subscribes to them can only conclude that attempts to reduce inequality or even maintain a safety net are seriously misguided since they would undermine the main incentives to work and encourage fecklessness. Economic Man *requires* inequality. But the thinking of much of the Left (as well as of the Right) also rests on it, for left-wing writers have commonly dismissed any other views as 'bourgeois ideology', leaving one wondering how much the speed with which 'communist' societies have converted to capitalism owes to the fact that they hold such fundamental assumptions in common.

In the early years of the twenty-first century, it is hard to imagine how beliefs such as these could be regarded as anything other than curiously archaic, and attempts to base social policy on them as anachronistic as trying to run a modern industrial economy on the technology of an era before the invention of the internal combustion engine, the aeroplane or indeed electric light. To be fair, they have been increasingly challenged, and even ridiculed, by a number of eminent economists, but their influence remains tenacious and very widespread. In 2018, Kate Raworth, an Oxford economist, published a book called *Doughnut Economics. Seven Ways to Think like a 21st Century Economist*, in which she writes:

> At the heart of twentieth century economics stands the portrait of rational economic man: he has told us that we are self-interested, isolated, calculating, fixed in taste, and dominant over nature—and his portrait has shaped who we have become. But human nature is far richer than this, as early sketches of our new self-portrait reveal: we are social, interdependent, approximating, fluid in values, and dependent on the living world.[2]

Examples of the imprint of rational economic man abound, but the following shows very lucidly the rigour with which its logic has been

---

2   Kate Raworth, *Doughnut Economics: Seven Ways to Think like a 21st-Century Economist* (London: Random House Business Books, 2017), 28.

pursued. The passage is taken from *CentrePiece*, the magazine of the
Centre for Economic Performance at the London School of Economics:

> The standard economic approach to crime is a simple one. It states that
> individuals weigh up the expected costs and benefits from a crime,
> taking into account the probability of getting caught, and participate
> in illegitimate activities only if the expected benefits outweigh the
> expected costs. If an individual is making a choice between work and
> crime, it is clear that a crucial factor will be the level of wages he or she
> could obtain.[3]

The crudity of this is breath-taking, as indeed are the questions it begs,
yet the passage points to the strength of its ideological grip amongst
those who may act as advisors to, and therefore have considerable
influence on, governments. The authors offer no evidence that they ever
interviewed anyone convicted of "illegitimate activities", nor indeed do
they define the nature of those activities. Presumably they are referring
to offences such as theft and fraud, rather than rape or sexual abuse
or murder or deliberately causing bodily harm. Having stated what
they call the "economic theory of crime", however, they go on to argue
that statistics for the rise in property crime from the mid-1970s to the
mid-1990s confirm the accuracy of the model. I cannot claim extensive
experience in this area, but two patients come to mind: a fifteen-year-
old boy with a string of convictions for stealing, and a young man who
had served a prison sentence for robbing a bank. For the former, the
thefts were impulsive and opportunistic, whilst for the latter the crime
was clearly more planned. In neither case, however, did deliberations
of the sort the economists imagine play any part at all in their thinking.
The fifteen-year-old boy had been abandoned several years earlier
by his father after an accident that had left the latter traumatised.
His mother had become depressed and withdrawn, and the boy had
initially attracted the attention of the police through his desperate, but
clumsy, efforts to get her to relate to him. He would become threatening
towards her, and the police would be called. On one such occasion he
was accused of attacking them. Although he always insisted that it was
the other way around, he was prosecuted and served time, briefly, in a

---

3   Stephen Machin and Costas Meghir, "Does Crime Pay Better?", *CentrePiece: The
     Magazine of Economic Performance* 4(3), 1999, 25–27.

unit for young offenders. Prominent in the story of the bank robber, on the other hand, was persistent parental discord. Neither individual, so far as I know, continued in a life of crime: both were actually furthering their education and endeavouring to gain qualifications when I saw them. The fifteen-year-old, in fact, contacted me several years later to say that he had written a play. Poverty had undeniably contributed to their drift into crime, for it was a drift and not a thought-through choice, and the two stories illustrate how this came about and the more complex and subtle roots the 'standard' economic approach ignores. Among the questions this approach fails to address are: why, then, does not everyone on very low wages turn to crime? Do those who refrain from theft have difficulty doing sums? Or do they lack intelligence? Or imagination? Or are they emasculated by a morality that 'standard' economics would regard as irrelevant and outmoded?

By contrast, consider the Cambridge Study in Delinquency.[4] This provided feedback on a carefully defined group of 411 boys growing up in a working-class area of London, some 95% of whom were observed between the ages of eight and thirty-two. Each individual was interviewed eight times, face-to-face, over a sixteen-year period, with the final report being sent to the Home Office, which had originally commissioned it, in 1988. Although this was eleven years before the *CentrePiece* article, the economists make no reference to it in their piece. Amongst those who became offenders, four factors were found to be significant. The first was poverty: eventual offenders were, as children, brought up in large, low-income families, living in bad housing; the second was failure at school in the form of low attainment, troublesome behaviour, hyperactivity and difficulty in concentrating; the third was unsatisfactory parenting, characterised by harsh, even cruel discipline, alternating erratically with passivity or neglect, or a setting, perhaps, of parental conflict; and fourth, one or both parents or other close relatives had criminal convictions, so criminality was to a greater or lesser degree part of the family culture. The Cambridge Study describes the main features of a "criminogenic" background, a background that essentially fails, in specific ways, to meet the child's needs. The presence of such factors, however, does not

---

4   David P. Farrington and Donald J. West, *The Cambridge Study in Delinquent Development: Long-term Follow-up Report: Final Report to the Home Office* (Cambridge: Institute of Criminology, University of Cambridge, 1988).

imply that everyone from such a background will stray into a life of crime, but the one factor that stood out as preventive was, curiously, the absence of friends at the age of eight. The authors of the study could not account for this, but perhaps the absence of company at least meant that the child was not getting into bad company. In other words, some part of the picture may be the influence of peers.

In citing the Cambridge Study, I am in no way challenging the claim that there is a link, as the economists noted, between property crime and low wages, but arguing rather that the economic model does not explain it. The Cambridge Study, for example, shows that if children are engaged in delinquent behaviour at an early age, the likelihood is that they will continue on a criminal path. According to the economic model, this would presuppose that they have carried out a cost-benefit analysis of their career prospects before they have stopped playing children's games in the playground. More worryingly, the economic model requires a division of society into rich and poor or, for the reasons I have pointed out, an underclass. In doing so, it ends up with the contradiction of requiring the relative deprivation that both the economists and the criminologists single out as a major contributing factor to the very problem they are trying to solve.

I have digressed a little to draw attention to one area in which the notion of Economic Man fails to explain something it claims to be able to explain, but its defects let us down even more dismally when we track back to the psychopathology with which I began. Economic Man has no concept of belonging or meaning, so it cannot account for identity politics. Like creatures who herd, we cling to the familiar and the group as anxiety takes hold. Where loss of livelihood threatens us, or there are challenges to internalized ideas about gender roles or sexuality, where control over our lives seems to be diminishing and we increasingly face feelings of helplessness and humiliation, we become vulnerable to those who peddle apocalyptic ideas, whether sacred or secular. Encouragement to identify with the awesome power of an all-powerful, avenging god or trust in the irresistible force of historical destiny becomes deeply seductive. The appeal of these fantasies, whatever form they take, may lie at a subliminal level, and people are more easily manipulated because of that, but they are clearly compensatory: they serve to alleviate the pain of the powerless or those who feel they have no place and no value in the world in which they may have been brought up.

Above all, however, is the perception that societies based on ideologies like capitalism, in which Economic Man plays a fundamental role, are deeply amoral because their core values are materialistic. That they are amoral is not strictly speaking true because, as I pointed out, their morality is that poverty results from moral failure, whilst for those with Calvinist leanings material success is a sign of divine approval. Those who are not religious, on the other hand, view success or failure as a reflection of virtues such as hard work, perseverance and manly courage in taking risks. Greed and selfishness are overtly embraced. For adherents of most of the world's great faiths, however, the flaunted omnipotence and materialism is deeply offensive: to see one's own worth or that of others as deriving in a narcissistic, self-congratulatory way from how rich one is or what one owns, to make that the governing goal of one's life, is anathema. But it also humiliates the 'losers', and generates a sort of 'free-floating' anger, by which I mean anger looking for a focus, or mooring.

Anger may attract individuals towards movements that exploit it and populist leaders who encourage its expression in violence towards some demonised other. Alternatively, it may take the form of individual acts of homicide or, where there is also despair, suicide. Two health economists, David Stuckler and Sanjay Basu, in a chapter of their book *The Body Economic* (2013) entitled "The Post-Communist Mortality Crisis", describe what happened in the early 1990s in the wake of the collapse of the Soviet Union. Ten million Russian men died—a massive fall in the size of the population that was spotted by the United Nations, which instigated an investigation. What emerged from that investigation was that the deaths were due to the speed of the transition from a communist economy to a capitalist one—as well as indifference to the effects that might have on those who would be caught up in it. How could it have happened? The authors tell us that, in the Soviet era, a number of towns had been established that were centred on a single industry. Such towns ranged in size from 10,000 to a 100,000 people. One would specialise in the milling of lumber, for example, another around nickel, another around coal; they were inextricably linked, the products and livelihood of one depending on the parts and products supplied by the others. There was a debate as to whether the countries that had replaced the Soviet Union should press ahead as quickly as possible with privatisation and other free-market reforms or whether the pace should be more gradual. For various reasons, the 'shock therapists', as they came to be known, won, in part because they were able to promise massive American aid. The consequences were complex and disastrous, and amongst the most devastating were the effects on the former Soviet 'mono' towns. They collapsed like dominoes one after the other and left their inhabitants without jobs, money to buy food or pay for housing, medication or access to healthcare. Hard evidence of the fatalities that followed was set out on their death certificates, examination of which revealed that many of the young men thrown out of work had perished from alcohol poisoning (or more direct forms of suicide), homicide or injuries. "Such deaths seem straightforward", Stuckler and Basu write, "men whose factories had shut down and were out of work were experiencing a high level of mental distress and anxiety, and their response was to turn to alcohol, harming themselves and others".[5] The men had also, despite their relative youth, died from heart attacks, although coroners' reports recorded that, according to the autopsies, their arteries were clean. In other words, the cause of death was stress.

Those who argued for and defended the lethal, headlong rush to introduce a market economy did so in the conviction that it would prevent a return to communism. Whether they would have been so enthusiastic if they had foreseen the death toll is hard to know, but they also believed that the quicker the transition to capitalism, the quicker people would feel the benefits. Similar arguments were used by the leaders of the former Soviet Union to justify the collectivisation of agriculture in the years following the Russian Revolution. "But you can't make an omelette without breaking eggs", was the regular reply of their supporters, just as the ideologues of neo-liberal economics acknowledge that their prescriptions will entail pain—pain, of course, for other people. On the face of it, they had carried out a cost-benefit analysis, though their comprehension of the costs was very limited. Nor were the benefits forthcoming, except for a select few: the former

---

5   David Stuckler and Sanjay Basu, *The Body Economic: Why Austerity Kills* (London: Allen Lane, 2013), 25.

insiders, for instance, who in many cases took over industries owned by the state, and instead of investing in them, stripped them of their assets, sold them, and deposited the proceeds in Swiss bank accounts. A large section of the population was plunged into poverty, and some years after the conversion to capitalism, the World Bank estimated that 25% were living on less than $2 a day, and often lacked sufficient money to buy food.

Yet, there seems to have been some foreknowledge of the suffering this upheaval would inflict and a certain squeamishness at taking responsibility for it. Stuckler and Basu quote Milton Friedman's proposal that economic decisions should be left to a computer, because it would be willing to make "tough, painful decisions". The Scottish analyst Ronald Fairbairn describes this as essentially schizoid—the intellectual in love with a system. It has to be acknowledged, he says, that sometimes this can do good, but it may also cause untold harm to millions.[6]

Economic Man not only fails to explain, but is deeply implicated in the spread of the sort of malignant ideologies I likened earlier to the plague. Yet, as a psychology, it has no empirical base. This is in marked contrast to psychodynamic psychology, which has grown out of the practice of psychotherapy, from therapists listening to their patients session after session and labouring day after day with them to understand what lies behind their actions and their sometimes obscure and difficult states of mind. Psychodynamic psychology has emerged from the insights therapists have gained in this way, though attempts to enshrine them in a theory have not always been happy, and the psychology, notoriously, has been, and remains riven, with conflict. The convictions that define it, however, are more important than its differences.

What are these convictions? The picture is very different from that of Economic Man: the belief that we have inborn or, as we might say now, genetically encoded maturational processes, and that the environment, especially the most immediate environment of parents and family, can facilitate or frustrate those processes; that we react to such environmental failures with strategies that develop into more or less permanent patterns of relationship, like the patterns of speech that form a dialect or the phonetics that distinguish an accent; that 'irrational'

---

6   W.R.D. Fairbairn, *Psychoanalytic Studies of the Personality* (London: Routledge and Kegan Paul, 1952), 21.

phenomena such as fantasies, dreams, neurotic and even psychotic symptoms can be understood in terms of those transformations, though we may be unaware of that or, indeed, of the basic, universal needs they strive to meet; and, lastly, that the patterns we develop in childhood may be inappropriate for later stages in life and create serious problems, but that because they are so deeply entrenched, they can often only be ameliorated through professional help—and not always then.

Some of the phrases I have used in the foregoing may remind readers of the writings of Donald Winnicott, but I believe that in essence they are characteristic of all psychodynamic thinking. Within that tradition, practitioners have devised their own language for the processes they observe: the language of 'projection', 'identification', 'repression', 'splitting', and so on. Such phenomena have been noted, however, for centuries. There are few more famous examples of projection than the New Testament challenge to us to check the beams in our own eyes when we are waxing self-righteous about the motes in other peoples'. And the dynamics of envy, so widely associated with the writings of Melanie Klein, have rarely been more vividly described than by St. Augustine in his *Confessions*. In 397 A.D. he wrote:

> I have myself seen jealousy in a baby and know what it means. He was not old enough to talk, but whenever he saw his foster-brother at the breast, he would grow pale with envy. This much is common knowledge. Mothers and nurses say they can work such things out of the system by one means or another, but surely it cannot be called innocence, when the milk flows in such abundance from its source, to object to a rival desperately in need and depending for his life on this one form of nourishment? Such faults are not small or unimportant, but we are tender-hearted and bear with them because we know that the child will grow out of them. It is clear that they are not mere peccadilloes because the same faults are intolerable in older persons.[7]

The same passage also draws our attention to a fact we commonly ignore: that envy may consume the 'haves' as well as the 'have-nots', and that we often overlook our more fortunate state when we see love and care being lavished on the more needy, as in our facile denigration

7   Quoted by Neville Symington in *The Analytic Experience* (New York: St. Martin's Press, 1986), 162–3.

of dependence ('the culture of dependence') and our resentment of refugees. Like the older child Augustine describes, we cannot bear to see another being nurtured: we disparage them as undeserving and perceive in them an envy which is actually our own.

Another example of an insight that can be found in the very distant past is given by James Gilligan in *Preventing Violence*. Gilligan, a forensic psychiatrist and psychotherapist, tells us that he developed his theory that violence has its origins in feelings of shame and humiliation (or the threat of them) as a result of listening to prisoners in American jails over a period of more than a quarter of a century. When asked why they had committed the brutal acts that had led to their incarceration, the invariable answer was that their victim had "dis'ed" them—slang for disrespected, shamed or humiliated. Gilligan thought he had stumbled on something new, something previously unknown, until he discovered that this is the motivation ascribed to Cain for the murder of his brother Abel in the Old Testament. The Bible makes it crystal clear: in the King James version, in chapter 4 of Genesis, verses 4 and 5, we read that "the Lord had respect unto Abel and to his offering: But unto Cain and to his offering he had not respect". Gilligan writes:

> In other words, God 'dis'ed' Cain. Or rather Cain was dis'ed because of Abel—and he acted out his anger over this insult in exactly the same way as the murderers with whom I was working.[8]

For Jungians in particular it is precisely our alienation from (or neglect of) such ancient wisdom that lies behind so much of what they call "the neurosis of our time". Whether or not we subscribe to that view, it is clear that the insights of psychodynamic psychology may be traced back to the beginnings of recorded history.

Psychodynamic psychology, nevertheless, remains extremely controversial, and one of the most controversial things about it is the idea that the therapist might learn anything from the patient. For someone like the philosopher and anthropologist Ernest Gellner, psychoanalysis (and by extension any psychology based on it) is a closed system, logically untestable, and therefore unscientific, a system that perpetuates itself through practitioners who teach their patients to think about themselves

---

8   James Gilligan, *Preventing Violence* (London: Thames and Hudson, 2001), 31.

in a particular way and trainees who come to adopt their views through suggestion. In *The Psychoanalytic Movement*,[9] Gellner derisively nicknames the model I call Economic Man "Accountant Bundleman", linking the view that we are at heart all little businessmen who base our lives on simple calculations of profit and loss with David Hume's view that we are just bundles of sensations. Gellner argues that everyone knows that this "official" view of human motivation is nonsense and that the forces that animate us are far more subtle, contradictory, and complex; and that it is the truer and more realistic insights of psychoanalysis that have been responsible for the extraordinary success of Freudian ideas, which he likens to the conquest of the Roman empire by Christianity, except that it has been much more rapid. These positions, however, seem at war with each other: the suggestion on the one hand that psychoanalysis is eyewash, and the argument on the other that it has achieved dominance because its insights are so much more convincing. But part of the problem, as anyone familiar with the field knows, is that practice varies greatly, and there is a wide spectrum of views amongst therapists as to the role of theory in their work. Gellner was in fact attacking one particular standpoint; one way of presenting it; a way we might call the classic analytic stance.

What does this involve? A key element is the idea of the analyst or psychotherapist as an expert; that this expert, when consulted by a patient, makes a diagnosis, and then treats the patient on the basis of that diagnosis, in much the same way as a physician would treat a patient in any other branch of medicine. The model is in fact the medical model— not surprisingly since many practitioners are medically qualified, and psychotherapy is widely included in the range of medical specialities offered by hospitals, clinics and GP surgeries.

Where does this expertise come from? How does one acquire it? The answer is that it derives from a long, expensive, and demanding training through which the trainee learns how to interpret material 'correctly', and that it is this skill in interpretation that 'cures'. The practitioner certainly listens to the patient, and indeed listens to a patient who has been instructed to avoid all censorship and relate everything that comes into her or his mind, however trivial, offensive or obscene—a process

---

the therapist is supposed to facilitate by refraining from judgement. However, as critics point out, such listening is listening in the light of a theory, a theory that is used to interpret all that transpires so that the 'evidence' that emerges from practice is a product of the theory and cannot, therefore, be used to support it.

An alternative view might start with the idea that 'cure' is far too crude a word to describe the relief that patients seek, and the concept of treatment almost crass. There is a person who suffers, as we all do, and a term derived from the Latin *'patiens'* conveys this, whereas words like 'client' (management speak for someone looking for some thing or some service to buy), or 'analysand' (which conjures up pictures of someone who offers him or herself up for psychological dissection or deconstruction) do not. The longed-for relief may be focused on a distressing symptom, but often that feels far too simple, for the problem may not be anything as easily identifiable, specific or discrete. Or the symptom someone brings might be clearly identifiable and life-threatening, such as an eating disorder, but the underlying problem may be about how one might feel more in charge of one's own body. Similarly, the initial complaint might be of depression, but the issue at the root of it is grief and some utterly irrational conviction that one was responsible for the death of someone dearly loved. A young man insists, for example, that he has motor neurone disease, though all the exhaustive medical checks he has undergone show that he is mistaken, but he will not be reassured. His beloved father died of it a year or so ago and he is identifying with him rather than mourning. To talk of treatment or cure in such contexts feels absurd: there are no simple answers to conflicts about those whom we love, no cure for loss, no 'fix' for life—and we should rightly be contemptuous if offered one. Therapy is not a treatment by one who is superior and 'knows' of someone who is inferior and does not know, but an agreement by two individuals to talk over, share and compare their thinking on issues that trouble one of them. If it helps, it helps because the patient is able to find something he or she needs in the relationship for his or her own healing or maturation. Carl Jung's description of the role of the therapist in that relationship seems very apt:

> If I wish to treat another individual psychologically at all, I must for better or worse give up all pretensions to superior knowledge, all

authority and desire to influence. I must perforce adopt a dialectical
procedure consisting in a comparison of our mutual findings. But
this becomes possible only if I give the other person a chance to play
his hand to the full, unhampered by my assumptions. In this way his
system is geared to mine and acts upon it; my reaction is the only thing
with which I can legitimately confront my patient.[10]

To argue that healing and growth arise from the relationship, however,
risks setting up a dichotomy between the relationship and interpretation
when, obviously, as in any relationship, what is said is an integral part
of it. Winnicott famously described interpretation as naming something
when it is on the tip of a patient's tongue: not the application of the
correct dose of theory, but a comment or intervention that leaves the
other feeling understood—as perhaps never before. This deepens
rapport, builds trust, and is ultimately liberating. Often we try to be
more specific as to what is needed: a relationship, perhaps, where the
patient feels neither invaded nor ignored, or one in which he or she is
able to feel some of the warm engagement that was lacking with one
or both parents. This has led some practitioners to talk of therapy as
an "emotionally corrective experience", which sounds contrived and
authoritarian, and carries with it the questionable implication that
there is someone who knows how to provide better parenting. The
relationship between therapist and patient is not one in which the
therapist corrects someone who is misshapen, mistaken or deficient, but
one characterised by what Erikson calls "mutuality": there is a patient
who needs a therapist and a therapist who needs a patient. Training
for the therapist is less about learning theory and how to apply it than
exploring his or her attraction to this kind of work, and addressing, in
the process, unresolved difficulties and inhibitions that are likely get in
the way. Theory, in fact, is not so much a set of verbal medicaments
to be applied at suitable moments as the accumulated attempts of
practitioners to clarify, reflect on and make sense of the things they have
learned in their day-to-day work over many years. Such attempts have
often been incomplete, inconsistent and muddled; sometimes they have
just been wrong; in many ways they resemble old maps and travellers'

---

10   C.G. Jung, *The Practice of Psychotherapy* (London: Routledge and Kegan Paul,
      Second Edition, 1966), 5.

tales, but they offer, nevertheless, the observations and reassurance of those who have travelled that terrain before. If this seems disrespectful, we should remember that it was actually the view Sigmund Freud took when he wrote in his *Autobiographical Study* (1924) that he had made many beginnings, thrown out many suggestions, but found it hard to tell whether much or little would come of them.

For those who work in the psychodynamic tradition, some of these 'beginnings' and 'suggestions' have survived to form the framework of modern therapy, notably the idea, mentioned earlier, that we can discern patterns in the relationships we set up, and that these reflect the influences that have moulded us; the interest over the last half century or so (longer in the case of the Jungian tradition) in the impact of these patterns on the therapist and their value as a source of insight into the other's internal world; and the notion that the meaning of our life experiences is only really intelligible in terms of our history. If outcome studies reveal anything, they tell us that the crucial element in healing and development is the relationship, and these heirlooms of the psychodynamic tradition offer us vital clues to understanding that.

Therapy may be as much a learning experience for the therapist as for the patient, but the information the practitioner gleans is hardly problem-free, and it is here that ideas such as transference and counter-transference are invaluable. Like highlights, they create new reliefs and cast different shadows: they illuminate connections, and enable us to gain insight. In doing so, they offer the possibility of change. Curiously, it is a process that is often derided: 'So it is all because your brother broke a flower pot on your head when you were two years old?', might be a typical example. Yet few of us imagine that peacemakers in troubled parts of the world would get very far unless they were adequately informed of the historical background of the warring parties, so how can we ridicule such awareness when we are striving for reconciliation between the conflicting parts of ourselves? Meaning stems from shared experience, and is intimately linked with belonging, with the story and context of our relationships. As Marcel Proust somewhere observes: "when we have understood, we hear in retrospect".

Hearing in retrospect is as good a description as any of the dissonances that led me to write this book. However, trying to convey the private and very subtle quality of what happens between patient and therapist not only leaves a discouraging sense of dissatisfaction, but also carries the danger that understanding becomes fixed and identity frozen in a narrative that emerged from a particular time and place. Something is distilled, yet perspectives change as time passes and other insights dawn. For many readers, if they have read this far, the very notion that a psychology that derives from psychotherapy can help us in any way with broader socio-political issues may be highly questionable. Psychotherapy tends to be written off as marginal, the realm of the 'sad', the 'mad', and the 'bad', as the tabloid press might put it. Those who seek such help, however, are often anything but unsuccessful in worldly terms. In fact, their very achievements and the unexamined values that drive them may lie close to the heart of their problems.

The argument of this book, then, if I may summarise and re-state it, is that the model of human motivation that has come to dominate our thinking about socio-political issues through economics cannot help us understand many of the issues that trouble us, in particular that of movements that cause widespread suffering in the name of moral and religious regeneration; that the model of 'Rational Economic Man' ignores key elements in our make-up or shifts them into the liminal, where they languish with the 'feminine' and the 'emotional'—and in so doing is deeply implicated in the recurrence of this ancient problem; that it is an ideology without any solid foundation; and that psychodynamic psychology, the stock of insights that therapists have acquired from their experience of listening to people can, by contrast, shed valuable light on these matters because ethical issues are the very 'stuff' of the work.

Practitioners, who scrupulously avoid being judgemental, often do not recognise this; but people who avail themselves of therapy (for all that they would deeply resent any attempt by a therapist to impose their values on them) nevertheless talk typically about matters that are essentially ethical in nature: relationships, for example, with partners, parents, children and colleagues; about love and hate, and how to cope with the conflict between the two; about envy and jealousy, anger and violent impulses, guilt and shame, sexuality, loss, belonging, meaning, and so on.

People only embark on therapy after they have come to feel that their own rational efforts will not take them any further. A highly intelligent and musically very gifted young man could have been speaking for all those who turn to a professional for help when, a few weeks into our work, he said, "I came to realise that I needed to seek another kind of conversation".

Throughout this book, I have quoted extensively from these therapeutic 'conversations', as they seem to me to be the best way of conveying the psychology and of illustrating my points. I cannot call them case histories because case histories are written from the perspective of the therapist. Nor are they oral histories because oral histories are supposed to be verbatim records of what their subjects say, although they may well be edited or angled, consciously or unconsciously by the person who collates them. To try to ensure that I was not simply telling a one-sided story, I invited subjects to check on the accuracy of my recollections, and at the same time to satisfy themselves that their identity had been rigorously disguised and confidentiality properly preserved. Intriguingly, several felt I need not have been so fastidious, and mostly they did not want me to change very much. Some had not realised that a therapist might have feelings about what had transpired, and for one or two the whole exercise may have been therapeutic, possibly because it allowed closure.

The plan of the book is as follows: Chapter 1 considers two fundamental problems that face us when we try to think about psychotherapy and ethics: that the practice of psychotherapy is based on an ethic, and the problem of free will. I suggest that Spinoza's ideas about free will may help.

In Chapter 2, I examine the division in psychotherapy between practitioners who believe we are governed by all-powerful instincts and those who believe that our most fundamental need is for relationship. In trying to fathom the sources of demonisation and dehumanisation, is the notion of a 'death instinct' helpful, or are we better served by Ronald Fairbairn's ideas about the origins and nature of schizoid states?

Chapter 3 looks at some historical examples of movements that have carried out persecutions in the name of moral or religious regeneration and studies of their psychological make-up.

Chapter 4 (Pascal's Paradox) describes one psychological model that may shed light on the inner conflicts of those who do evil in the name of conscience, and the way our inner and outer worlds interact.

Chapter 5 is concerned with the contrast between guilt and shame.

Chapter 6 tries to pull together the threads I've followed in the preceding chapters and attempts an answer to the question as to whether we can learn anything from psychotherapy about ethics. Can it help us understand the ethical puzzle with which I began? And can it offer us any guidance about a more inclusive ethics?

The conclusion, Chapter 7, briefly examines psychodynamic thinking over the past century as to the measures we might take to further humanism. It endeavours to link the findings of psychotherapists and analysts with those of medical epidemiologists, neuroscientists, and others in related fields like health economics, whose concern is with the mental and physical well-being of the community as a whole.

1. Psychotherapy and Ethics

What can we learn about ethics from psychotherapy? People who seek out a therapist are rarely looking for someone to tell them how to live, though they may press for advice if they feel troubled by some particular dilemma; yet the language of ethics figures insistently throughout the narratives that unfold. Whether we are aware of it or not, they are shaped, constrained and indeed driven by themes that anyone with even a little acquaintance with the history of ethics would recognise as deeply familiar. As practitioners, we endeavour to create and maintain a non-judgemental stance because we know we would not get very far if we heaped praise and blame on our patients, yet we are faced all the time with people who, for one reason or another, are constantly passing judgement on themselves. As practitioners we are no more qualified than anyone else to judge others, but self-recrimination (along with recrimination against others) is something we continually observe, and we have to respond as best we can. Let us go back, then, to the question with which I began and ask whether the experience can offer us any insights into, or guidance on, issues that have, for many centuries, been ethical concerns.

"None at all", one is tempted to reply, and for two compelling reasons. The first is that the practice of psychotherapy assumes an ethic: the alleviation of suffering and the value of the individual. This is implied by the very act of offering time to people who are in trouble or distress. It is an ethic, moreover, that psychotherapy shares with Buddhism, though the thinking of each about the origins of suffering and their prescriptions for lessening it differ in some ways and in others overlap. For many Buddhists, for instance, it is a mistake to dwell on the past because they believe that the past, however traumatic, needs to be transcended through meditation. Another example would be anger, in that Buddhists accept it as an emotion but doubt the wisdom of

 https://doi.org/10.11647/OBP.0416.01

expressing it as this tends to turn one into a monster. Psychotherapists, by contrast, are always concerned that anger that is not directly voiced will find more insidious ways of making itself felt: in depression, perhaps, or sulking—with all the damage these reactions do to relationships. Such differences have led some commentators to believe that the two traditions are incompatible, whilst others see them as complementary, the one offering perceptions and paths to freedom the other lacks.

It could be argued that the divergences between Buddhism and psychotherapy are derived from the slightly different focuses of the two disciplines: Buddhism has always been concerned with suffering in general, whereas psychoanalysis, for Sigmund Freud, was more narrowly about neurosis—with the modest aim, as Freud famously observed, of changing neurotic suffering into the kind we all have to bear as part of life. Such a transformation, however, might not make one a 'better' person, and Freud tended to react impatiently to any suggestion that improving someone morally might form any part of his mission. In a letter in 1915 Freud writes:

> The unworthiness of human beings, even of analysts, has always made a deep impression on me, but why should analysed people be altogether better than others? Analysis makes for unity, but not necessarily for goodness. I do not agree with Socrates and Putnam that all our faults arise from confusion and ignorance. I think that too heavy a burden is laid on analysis when one asks of it that it should be able to realise every precious ideal.[1]

James Jackson Putnam, to whom Freud's letter was addressed, was an admirer and professor of neurology at Harvard. In another letter, this time to Oskar Pfister, a Swiss pastor and lifelong friend, Freud wrote: "I don't cudgel my brains much about good and evil",[2] a view we might expect given that one of his favourite observations was that "morality is self-evident".[3] It meant a sense of justice and consideration for others, and a dislike of making others suffer or of taking advantage of them. In other words, morality for Freud was primarily concerned with social

---

1   Quoted by Ernest Jones in *Sigmund Freud, Life and Work, Vol. 11* (London: The
     Hogarth Press, 1955), 204.
2   Op. cit. 506.
3   Op. cit. 463.

relationships, whereas for the predominantly Christian culture of Middle Europe, it was supremely about sex. On that, however, Freud was adamant: writing to James Putnam on July 8, 1915 he declared: "I advocate an incomparably freer sexual life".[4]

It would be hard to imagine a clearer statement of an ethical position. The primitive conscience Freud calls the superego, moreover, is the agency that curtails that freedom. It followed, therefore, that the aim of psychotherapeutic work could be described as one of dismantling the superego and replacing it with ego, or, more simply, replacing an irrational and unexamined conscience with a conscience rooted in reason.

For all that the superego might need to be modified or superseded, its initial formation was seen as a developmental achievement. Notions of development, however, along with terms such as "maturity" and "growth", are value-laden: they all hold out some goal we are supposed to adopt, and against which we can be checked and either commended or condemned.

Take, for example, Erik Erikson's definition of maturity in terms of "genital primacy". Although many will protest that this concept is outmoded, it illustrates the problems very clearly. In classical psychoanalysis, development is supposed to proceed through the oral and anal stages to the genital phase, but the features of the latter were never as clearly spelt out as those of the earlier two. Erikson writes:

> While psychoanalysis has, on occasion, gone too far in its emphasis on genitality as a universal cure for society and has thus provided a new addiction and a new commodity for many who wished to so interpret its teachings, it has not always indicated the goals that genitality actually should and must imply. In order to be of lasting social significance, the Utopia of genitality should include:
>
> 1. mutuality of orgasm
>
> 2. with a loved partner
>
> 3. of the other sex
>
> 4. with whom one is able and willing to share a mutual trust
>
> 5. and with whom one is able and willing to regulate the cycles of:

---

4   Quoted by Peter Gay in *Freud: A Life for Our Time* (London: Papermac / Macmillan, 1989), 143.

    a.   work

    b.   procreation

    c.   recreation

6. so as to secure to the offspring, too, all the stages of a satisfactory development.[5]

An ideal is laid before us: a socio-biological one. As such, at first sight it has a lot to commend it—both for the community and for the individual. The community, it could be argued, is merely encouraging heterosexuality, and in so doing indicating the value it places on continuity. For the individual, on the other hand, there is a simple and straightforward recipe for contentment in life—where, that is, no irremediable physical or psychological impediment renders that unrealistic. For those, however, for whom such a recipe does present problems, for example a fair proportion of those seeking psychotherapy, it may well feel prescriptive and excluding. Others might object to Erikson's prescriptions as mechanistic and parochial, narrowly rooted in the values of Middle America, to which they cannot or do not wish to subscribe. By contrast, Freud himself, when asked to say what he meant by "health", replied: "To love and to work", a formula whose laconic simplicity includes those who have not been able or have chosen not to follow Erikson's path, yet have found love and fulfilment in other ways.[6] Monks and nuns, healers and artists in various parts of the world would be obvious examples. Some societies are intolerant of difference, but others, as Erikson himself observes elsewhere, manage to accommodate it and find a place of value for those who do not or cannot conform, and this, it could be argued, is paradoxically a factor in the survival and continuity of those societies.

The practice of psychotherapy may indeed be based on an ethic, but it does not follow that it is pointless to examine it: on the contrary, what we are dealing with becomes clearer and more honest when we can lay

---

5   Erik H. Erikson, *Childhood and Society* (London: Penguin Books, 1965), 257.

6   There is some dispute as to whether Freud actually used these words, but Charles Rycroft writes: "In the early days of psychoanalysis, recovery of the capacity to love and work was regarded as the criterion of successful analytical treatment" in Charles Rycroft, *A Critical Dictionary of Psych-Analysis* (London: Nelson, 1968), 179.

bare assumptions and values, follow trains of reasoning, and consider and compare some of the thinking to which it has given rise.

The second reason why people might have difficulty with the idea that we can learn anything about ethical issues from psychotherapy is that most of us feel we can only legitimately talk about good and evil, praise and blame, guilt and responsibility if we believe we are in charge of our own lives. Michel Foucault is a relatively recent example of a philosopher who, as he turned his attention to these matters towards the end of his life, said that he regarded free will as "the ontological condition of ethics".[7] In Foucault's view we do not have very much free will, and the practice of psychotherapy and the theory that has arisen from it tend to support Foucault's reckoning. Freud himself was a determinist whose work was devoted to confronting us with the origins of our mental life and ways of relating to one another in human biology, and our understanding of this organic basis has been deeply enriched and refined in recent years by developments in genetics and neuroscience. What, then, remains of any belief in our own agency? The trouble is that most of us also find it very hard to imagine living without the idea that we have free will. In practice, we have to hold people responsible for their actions, good and bad, and in fact a sense of our own personal autonomy seems crucial for us. Indeed, one might argue that it is the very touchstone of mental health and that the concepts of neurosis and psychosis are simply medical ways of describing its impairment or absence. Freud, after all, introduced the idea of the 'id' to signify that some force we feel to be alien, an 'it', is menacing us or has us in its grip, and the various forms of neurosis, and even psychosis, could all be seen as referring to different experiences of not feeling fully in control. This feeling of impaired autonomy, of the fight to hold on to some sense of agency and, if possible, extend it, is clearly illustrated in the following examples. The first is of a young woman I call "Fleur".

Fleur was nineteen when I first encountered her—a slim, if not rather slight, young woman of medium height, with soft, regular features and short, blond hair. Those who did not know her would ask if she was a girl or a boy, which always troubled her, but through all the years we met she invariably wore dark, loose-fitting clothes, and for reasons that

---

7   James Miller, *The Passion of Michel Foucault* (London: Harper Collins, 1993).

only later became apparent, had always, since she was a child, refused to put on a dress.

Fleur was studying English literature and was, by all accounts, a highly gifted poet. She had been brought up in Suffolk, where her father had worked as a photographer, and she was clearly missing her home and struggling with being separated from her family for the first time. There was an older brother, whom she loved deeply, and her mother, a nurse, with whom she had a much more conflicted relationship. Her mother, she complained, was fat, and her continual fear was that she would become like her. Though she would not have used the words, she experienced her as both dismissive and invasive, as a parent who would make light of her anxieties or leave her feeling she was not a separate person, but she clung to her for the warmth and reassurance she frequently needed.

Fleur's father had died of a brain tumour when she was about twelve. His health problems had dominated her childhood, and the day when his doctors had told them he had only a few months to live remained a vivid memory, but the cancer had then mysteriously receded, and only recurred when she was about to enter her teens. After the death of her father, letters revealed that he had had numerous affairs with other women, and for a period her mother would talk of him with contempt. That subsequently changed and Fleur, rather bewilderingly, found herself expected to share her mother's emerging idealisation of him. She became her mother's main support, even a sort of substitute husband, and she was concerned about her being alone now that she had left home and her brother was engaged on voluntary service in Africa.

She had referred herself to the health service where I was working, and had apparently had brief periods of therapy before, though it was not clear if they had been helpful. Quietly she told me she that she suffered from depression and that she was anorexic. It appeared that she took liquids, but ate very little, and that she cut or harmed herself in other ways, and often had thoughts of suicide. At that time, she also felt unsure of her sexuality: she had had relationships with both men and women, but increasingly found the idea of physical contact with men repellent and had begun to think of herself as bisexual or lesbian.

Soon after this first meeting, Fleur asked me what plans I had for her. Very much aware of her apprehension about being taken over, but also that I knew very little about her, I replied quite honestly that I did not have any, but that I could set aside a regular time for her if she found it helpful to come and talk. After a silence in which she appeared to be thinking this over, I found myself pressed on my attitude to anorexia. Even at this early stage, Fleur's extreme sensitivity to any comment on her looks or her body was very evident, and she was reluctant to go to doctors in case they wanted to weigh her. Any remark, complimentary or critical, would usually be followed by Fleur cutting herself. "Did I intend to set her goals to increase her weight?" she asked. I said that I did not. She rounded on me angrily: "Oh, so it doesn't matter if I starve myself to death."

"It matters a great deal", I replied, "I'm not in the business of helping people kill themselves, but I think you will decide for yourself about eating if we can get to the root of the distress that underlies your difficulty with it." This seemed to reassure her, and we began to meet regularly.

It is very difficult to distil so much complex and subtle material into such a short narrative, but this early period was marked by distrust and hostility towards me, often quite openly expressed. It would be evident even as we entered the room in that, on the threshold, I would politely gesture her to go ahead only to find myself having to grab the door to stop it slamming in my face. Sometimes after five minutes or so of silence, she would begin the session with a remark such as, "I hate you". The thought of becoming dependent on me felt extremely threatening to her, and indeed, as her dependence grew so did her hostility, although it could also give way to concern for my welfare.

It was about this time that Fleur began to bring pictures or leave them in the letterbox. They were sombre in colour and very lurid, and often took the form of a collage. They might be covered with captions such as "Kill babies" or headlines about atrocities against women and children that she had cut out of newspapers. Sometimes they included lines from her own poems. We would spread them out on the floor and I would feel that I ought to be able to understand them. In fact, I could rarely make anything of them, but that did not seem to matter: it clearly helped her to talk about them, and she continued to bring or send them, and to come regularly and on time.

One morning, I unrolled a picture she had left in my pigeonhole and saw a man dangling from a noose with the legend: "Consider yourself dead: I'm going to kill you". When we met later that day she spent the first few minutes in silence, then said: "What did you think of my picture?" My gut reaction was that I should be quite honest with her as she found it hard to gauge the effects she had on others, sometimes believing that her thoughts could kill them or had killed them, and sometimes feeling that she was insubstantial and that her actions had no impact on others at all. So I replied: "Well, most people would be upset to know that someone wanted to kill them, but I think it's most important that you should be able to voice these feelings if these sessions are to be of any value to you". This seemed to lessen her anxiety and we continued, though not much was said.

When we met again a few days later, Fleur sat down and carefully took another picture out of a large hold-all and laid it out on the floor. It was a collage, but this time of razor blades, knives, pieces of broken glass and even an axe, all stuck on to cardboard with sellotape: she had handed over to me all the implements she had been using to harm herself.

It was tempting to think we had turned a corner, but some weeks later Fleur entered my room and as usual placed her bag on the floor just in front of her. There was silence for several minutes before she reached down into it and pulled out a small gun, pointed it at me and told me she was hearing voices telling her to kill me. Later it turned out that the gun was a toy, but I did not know that at the time, and it certainly looked very real. Nor did I know if it was loaded or not, so I asked her to place the gun on the floor and push it over to me. She did as I had asked, and as she did so I added that she could say whatever she liked to me in our meetings, but that I did not allow people to bring weapons of any kind into the room and that in future she must leave her bag outside. Gradually she explained to me that she had been feeling desperate, had tried to contact her doctor, a nurse, her tutor, then me, but none of us had been available. On her way to see me, she had felt strong impulses to throw herself under a car or a bus. These suicidal impulses were alternating with homicidal ones, and again she reported hearing voices urging her to kill me and that she wasn't sure that she could stop herself. The threats seemed to be a way of telling me she felt no one was taking her seriously, but it was also clear that she was finding it difficult to use the session, and I wondered aloud if she might feel safer in an environment where there would be doctors and nurses around day and night. Her reaction appeared to be one of relief so I suggested that it might be best for us to end the session and go together to see one of the doctors. I made an emergency appointment for her while she was still in the room and then, because the surgery was in another building some distance away, accompanied her through the rain to the surgery door. "Give me the gun", I heard her G.P. say as she closed the door. A short while later I learned that arrangements had been made for her to go into hospital for a while: the first of a number of voluntary admissions.

In all this, we see a young woman trying desperately to gain control of her life and her body in the face of a confused tangle of conflicting emotions in her internal world. Any feeling of being free to live her own life was almost fatally choked by this "head fuck", as she frequently called it. Contradictory impulses about dependence tormented her: she needed a benign experience of it, an experience in which she would feel neither dismissed nor derided, neither abused nor invaded, but she was terrified of it and of the surrender of control she felt it entailed.

I believed that it was important for us to stay in contact, a view that appeared to be confirmed when I received a card from her a day or so later saying: "Don't die while I'm away". Shortly afterwards, I spoke to her consultant and explained my concern. Fleur needed me to stand by her and she needed to know that I was still alive, but her consultant was reluctant to agree to our meeting, and rather ponderously declared that he would diagnose Fleur's relationship with me as "hostile dependent". I wondered if he might prescribe a pill for it. Uneasily he agreed that I could visit, which I did, and a week or so later he gave permission for Fleur to come to me to continue our sessions—on one condition: that I reported back the content to a member of his team. I could understand their fears, for the hospital was medically responsible for her, but they seemed not to be taking Fleur's fears seriously: her childhood had been traumatised by invasion and very probably sexual violation, yet they were proposing a course of action in which all her most intimate thoughts and feelings would be shared with all the staff on the ward.

Fleur had told her key worker that her therapy was important to her and that she had become dependent on me, to which her key worker had apparently replied that a woman of her age ought not to need to be dependent. The comment left both of us feeling rather mystified, as though dependence were a moral failing, rather than a reflection of her precarious, if not dangerous, mental state. She decided to ignore the remark, so we continued to meet. Her condition improved, whether because of our sessions or because of the care she received at the hospital or both, is impossible to say, and after two or three weeks she was discharged.

Fleur had now become more trusting of me and, on one moving occasion, she brought a photograph of herself as a small child with her father and asked me to look after it for her. Her artwork ceased as mysteriously as it had begun, and she tried to talk about thoughts and feelings and memories that she had never been able to speak to anyone about before. Her mother had a brother, a priest, who lived nearby and was happy to look after the two children when their mother needed to visit her husband in hospital on her own. Fleur grew to hate being left in his care because she would find pictures of naked women and items of women's clothing in his study. Sometimes she stayed overnight and was put to sleep in his bed. She remembered him holding her back against him and being aware that he was sexually aroused, but she could only speak of these memories with great difficulty, and there were moments when she could not continue the narrative at all, however hard she tried. Her distress was made worse by the fact that she could not recall very clearly what had happened. Yet, as she pointed out on several occasions, she would insist on wearing underclothes in bed, even in the hottest weather. She had tried to talk to her mother about her uncle, but her mother—who came from a devout Irish background—had poured scorn on the idea that her brother, a man of God, would abuse her, and seemed to regard her as perverse for even suggesting such a thing. Her uncle died rather suddenly about a year after her father, and her mother, as next of kin, cleared his personal effects. These included sado-masochistic pornography and female clothing. She enlisted Fleur's help in burning everything on a large bonfire in their garden.

Actual details of the uncle's behaviour towards Fleur were very difficult to establish; nevertheless, it was clear that she had been exposed to a sexual culture that she found deeply threatening. When psychiatrists had later told her mother that Fleur's symptoms could be interpreted as pointing to sexual abuse, however, her mother's response was denial and ridicule. Fleur's dilemma was that she feared that she had indeed experienced some kind of sexual molestation as a child, yet it was the last thing she wanted anyone to confirm. To question it undermined her perception of reality, yet that reality was too horrifying to contemplate. She was left feeling profoundly troubled, and her contempt for Christians was withering.

I was conscious, as the months passed, that the anorexia was losing its grip, but Fleur remained depressed, extremely fragile, and very vulnerable to any setbacks in her work or relationships. The opening line of T.S. Eliot's poem *Ash Wednesday* always comes to mind when I think of her: "Lady of silences, calm and distressed". I shall return to her story in the next chapter.

My second example is from the story of a young man I call "Andrew", who was struggling not with psychosis, but loss and the cumulative conflicts with which earlier loss had left him.

Andrew had approached the health centre where I was working some years ago in the middle of September. I introduced myself to a tall, slightly built, good-looking young man in the waiting room. He appeared nervous and dejected. A few minutes later, seated in my room, he responded readily to my invitation to tell me what had brought him. He said that he suffered from "the blues", and that he had become estranged from his family. His mother had died only three months earlier, and there was little contact with his brother and sister or indeed his father.

Andrew's mother had suffered from heart problems for some time past, but her condition appeared to be well under control when she suffered a massive heart attack. A doctor took his father on one side and warned him that the following few days would be critical as considerable damage had been done to the muscles of her heart: it was touch and go as to whether or not she would pull through. Andrew was studying at a university some considerable distance from his home. He was in the middle of his finals, and his parents agreed that he should not be told about his mother's illness. The fact that he had already had to take a year out from his studies with glandular fever must have contributed to their decision. After several days in intensive care, in the early hours of the morning, his mother's heart failed again and the medical team was unable to revive her. So Andrew emerged from his last examination expecting to celebrate, only to be faced with his grief-stricken family and informed that his mother had died two days earlier.

Andrew was unprepared for the news and utterly devastated by it. He felt bewildered and angry that his family had not been honest about his mother's condition and had kept the fact of her dying from him until he had completed his finals. Within a month, he learnt that he had done extremely well, but the achievement felt trivial and hollow compared with the loss of his mother. Although there had been a history of hostility between him and his father, he tried in the early days after the funeral to mend the relationship, suggesting that they should go away for a weekend together, but his father remained remote and cool, with little awareness of any need for reconciliation with his son. Andrew once again felt rejected and his hatred of his father grew. Over the summer, Andrew's mood deteriorated as he desperately tried to find someone to talk to, but his family seemed indifferent and he did not know where to turn. He even went to a priest, though he was not religious, and, in fact, was suspicious of religion because his mother had always warned him against it. Eventually, angry and feeling that no one cared, he took an overdose, but he was found before he lost consciousness. An ambulance was called and he was admitted to hospital as a voluntary patient. It was a frightening experience, but it helped that a cousin with whom he got on well visited and took him off to the local pub and talked to him about sport, a passion they both shared. A day or so later, Andrew had an interview with a sensible psychiatrist who asked him a number of questions and then said to him: "If you were my son, I would advise you to discharge yourself and take up the place you have been offered to do postgraduate work, and then seek psychotherapeutic help." That was little more than a week before we first met.

In the sessions that followed, I learnt a lot more about Andrew's family. He was the youngest of three children, and had an older brother of about thirty, and an older sister who must have been twenty-seven or twenty-eight. The brother worked in a bank in a big city in the north of England. Though successful in his career, he had never, so far as Andrew knew, had a relationship with anyone, nor was he close to either parent. Andrew had never felt much warmth from him; their relationship he once described as "formulaic". His older sister, by contrast, had married and lived at some distance from his parents. She was close to his father and generally took his side in family disputes, but there was often tension between her and Andrew, and his brother and sister could unite in accusing Andrew of being selfish, feckless and spoilt. He believed that they were jealous because, as a child, he had been his mother's favourite, and he would complain that they withheld both material and emotional support from him by way of punishment. Andrew, in fact, seemed to be the family scapegoat, a word he found helpful because it corresponded with his perception of being demonised by them, and it enabled him to view their behaviour from a slightly different perspective. Although he never ceased to be distressed by it, the scapegoating would now leave him feeling angry.

It quickly became clear that he had a number of problems, and needed protracted therapy, but he was grieving deeply and, given that the health service was limited in what it could offer, his most pressing need was for help with mourning. Nothing could be more natural, but he needed to share his feelings with someone and it soon became clear why he was unable to turn to his closest relatives.

A rift had existed between Andrew and his father for as long as he could remember. He had always found him distant and denigrating. "You'll never amount to anything," he recalled his father saying in exasperation at something he had done or failed to do. Yet he had now got a first at one of the older universities. Andrew felt, however, that his father was not interested in his achievements, and remembered occasions when, as a child, he had tried to engage him in his activities only to find him reluctant to lift his head out of the book or newspaper he was reading. He felt that he was a nuisance and that his father did not want to be bothered with him. His father had wanted Andrew to follow him into the law, because he thought it would ensure his son a good living, but Andrew did not want to identify with his father, and felt pleased that his interests had led him in a different, even if less lucrative, direction.

It emerged that Andrew had slept in his parents' bed until he was eleven years old, not because of the common childhood fear of the dark or of being grabbed by a bogeyman, but because of a fantasy that his bedroom would detach itself from the rest of the house and float away if the door were closed, and he would lose his parents or they would lose him. His parents knew of these fears and would put him in their own bed, and his father would read the paper until he fell asleep. Then he would carry him off to his own bedroom and place him in his own bed. This seemed to be an act of some tenderness, but the tension between Andrew and his father made it difficult for him to appreciate that. Andrew's animosity towards his father was evident to his mother, who once told him, with a laugh, that he had an Oedipus complex. He had not understood what that meant, but Andrew and his mother would make trips together to beautiful places, and his siblings would look on with resentment and jealousy. He liked his mother's independence, and the fact that she had a job and a car of her own. When he was about eleven, however, all this changed. He sensed that his mother was trying to push him away, endeavouring at the same time to repair her relationship with her husband. Andrew felt hurt, angry and betrayed, and it was in these adolescent years that he began to harbour resentment towards her. As he became older, his mother would encourage him to sleep with his girlfriends, but his bitterness towards his parents remained. For a time he was anorexic, depriving himself, possibly, to punish his mother for depriving him, but that had passed. Later he responded to the distancing by distancing himself. When he was away at university, for instance, they would want him to come home at times such as Christmas and, in his own words, "play happy families", but he felt it would be utterly dishonest do so and a struggle would follow. Someone would be sent to remonstrate with him and bring him back, but his parents would then push him out again when it suited them to do so. The way the family handled his mother's death seemed like the culmination of this distancing process. He felt excluded, and he pressed his father on several occasions to tell him what his mother had said as she lay dying, but his father would only grudgingly offer him the consolation that his name was among the last words she had spoken.

Andrew's grief was overwhelming, but I sensed that his antagonism towards his mother and his attempts at retaliation had left him with paralysing guilt. I said it sounded as if he felt responsible for her death, at which he burst into tears. Gradually he explained that his mother had done everything in her power to look after her health, had taken great care over her diet, and she had become very interested in the role of stress in the aetiology of cardiovascular problems. She had read and was very impressed by the work of a cardiologist who argued that stress is about feeling trapped in a situation that makes one feel constantly angry and threatened so that adrenaline is perpetually pouring into the heart until, in exhaustion, it breaks down. Andrew was convinced that he had caused all the tension in the family and that he, therefore, had killed his mother. After her death, he had written her a letter, which he threw into her grave at the funeral, and then, quite distraught, had to be restrained. I said very firmly that responsibility for his mother's death could not possibly be laid at his door: her health problems had a long history, some of which he had already recounted, but that in any case there were other conflicts in the family, not least between his parents because he had already told me that their marriage had been an uneasy one. We returned to this guilt repeatedly, and it soon emerged that his brother and sister openly accused him of bringing his mother's death about. He felt mad, bad and sad, he said bitterly, and it was quite a time before he could feel angry with them for these baseless and cruel accusations.

For all that Andrew appeared to have been caught in acute oedipal conflicts, he did not seem to fear, at least consciously, his father's anger towards him. Rather, he feared his own anger towards his father, to the extent that he could not bear to be left alone in a room with him because he was terrified that he would attack him physically. This did not translate, however, into any general hostility towards male authority figures unless he found them authoritarian or denigrating. Then he could be defiant and challenging. If he sensed that they liked and supported and encouraged him, however, he could admire and feel great warmth for them, and he said on several occasions that he owed his academic success to one particular teacher who had been very friendly towards him and inspired him with his own enthusiasm for the subject. He also had a talent for friendship with others of his age, and it was very moving to become aware of the extent of their concern, support and affection for him at critical moments or simply at times when he felt low.

As the weeks went by, I learned more about the origins of the tensions in the triangular relationship between Andrew, his mother and his father. He had been seriously ill when he was about eighteen months old and had been rushed into hospital for an emergency operation to relieve a blockage in his abdomen. He did not know how long he spent in hospital; it may have been no more than a few days, but his mother had not been able to remain with him. So at an age when he was very much attached to her, and at a time when he really needed her, he had felt abandoned, alone and frightened, but unable, because he did not have enough language or a well enough developed sense of time, to understand that she would return. This seemed to throw considerable light on his troubled childhood, and I suggested that his fear that his bedroom would float away from the house and that he would be lost might have been a recapitulation of the experience of succumbing to an anaesthetic. There was no way either of us could know, but it helped him to make sense of it, and in particular of the fact that he was quite a clinging child who found it hard to let his father have an independent relationship with his mother, that he had to come between them, and probably found it unusually painful to manage any jealousy their relationship aroused.

Andrew had a number of problems, as I acknowledged earlier: anxiety, depression, a proneness to psychosomatic illness, difficulties with his family, and now, above all, bereavement. Although it was difficult to set these aside, the focus of our meetings was, as I have already mentioned, on grief. One of the main symptoms of it, perhaps the most graphic illustration of life slipping out of his control, was that he had become unable to travel: he had become severely agoraphobic. He had been in hospital in London, but if he tried to get on a train or a coach to leave, he would have a panic attack. I thought the problem would disappear in due course, but a friend unintentionally precipitated a crisis out of the kindest of motives: not liking the idea of leaving him alone in London over Christmas, he invited Andrew to his parents' home in Geneva, where his father worked for an international organisation. They had a spacious villa and Andrew could stay for a couple of weeks, go skiing or simply relax, eat, go for walks and get on with his reading. Andrew very much wanted to accept the invitation, but he was terrified of having a panic attack on the plane. We talked about it for several weeks, and the friend was very understanding about his fears. I neither urged him to go nor discouraged him as I felt it was essential for him to decide for himself, though trying to make a decision was agonising. I thought he needed to feel in charge and that he could change his mind right up to the last moment, the moment before departure, and we agreed that if he was able to board the plane he would ring me and tell me that he had arrived safely. It was a pleasant surprise to receive a telephone call from

Switzerland to learn that he had in fact managed it. We seemed to have passed an important milestone.

In both these examples, as indeed in the others I discuss later, Fleur and Andrew would have seen themselves as being free agents, although that freedom was constrained by depression, anxiety, agoraphobia and so on. With Fleur, for example, there were even moments when she seemed to be notably "wilful", as on the occasion when she had slashed her arm and rested her elbow on the arm of her chair defiantly displaying it to me. Yet, she often conveyed the feeling of helplessness in the power of forces she barely understood. Was she, or was she not, responsible for her actions?

Two hundred years or so before Freud's birth, Benedict Spinoza wrestled with this same dilemma. Free will, he declared, is an illusion, yet it seems we need to believe in it. Perhaps the critical issue for us, therefore, is to understand the conditions in which we feel we are free. What are those conditions? They lie, he contends, in understanding our nature as part of Nature, and living our lives accordingly. The language Spinoza uses is deeply religious: God is not separate from Nature, but immanent in it. Nature is God, in all its wild profusion or "modes". Human kind is one of those modes, and freedom is the feeling we have when we act in accordance with our "necessity"—a term we might interpret to mean something like self-fulfilment. Necessity, therefore, is not the opposite of freedom: the opposite is constraint or compulsion or being forced to be what we are not. For example, the research evidence increasingly seems to show that sexual identity is rooted in an interaction between genetic and environmental factors. One could adapt Spinoza's reasoning to argue that freedom lies in acknowledging that, even though writing two centuries before Gregor Mendel, he obviously could not have conceived of the issue in these terms. Two examples, of a young man and a young woman, may illustrate how an adaptation of Spinoza's arguments about the feeling of freedom could be useful in understanding the experiences of those struggling with conflicts about sexual identity. Let's start with "Raffaello".

Raffaello came to see me at the suggestion of a friend who happened to be a psychiatric nurse. She had referred people to me before and wondered if I would be willing to have an exploratory talk with him. I learnt little about him from our telephone conversation, and I had not encouraged her to say very much because I prefer to hear someone's story from their own lips. I gathered, however, that the young man in question worked in a botanic garden, though I did not know in what capacity. He sometimes confided in her apparently, and she was concerned about him and had urged him to seek professional help. He had reacted with relief and she had given him my telephone number.

I answered the door to a young man in his middle or late twenties with an open, good-natured face and short dark hair. He was of above average height and casually dressed in freshly laundered blue jeans and a khaki shirt that looked as if it might once have seen army service. From the name he had given me when he telephoned, I assumed that he was Italian or of Italian descent, but his English was faultless and he spoke with scarcely a trace of an accent. His name, in fact, was Raffaello, although everyone called him Raff, which he always taught them, rather playfully, to pronounce in the Italian way as "Ruff", though rough he was anything but.

When he had had a moment to settle, I invited him to try to tell me what had brought him. "Two things", he replied. The first was that the partner with whom he had been living for several years had just ended their relationship. This had come totally out of the blue, and had left him feeling devastated and bewildered. He felt it must be his fault, though ever since he had been wondering how. It had happened two or three weeks before he contacted me and he could think of little else. Some of his colleagues at work knew about it and had been very supportive, but he was loth to burden his friends by talking about it. The second was that he wanted to go home. He came from a village in Umbria, not far from Orvieto. His father was getting old and needed someone to take over the family farm. His brothers were not interested, and his sister had her own career as a primary school teacher. She had recently been diagnosed as mildly bi-polar, so her future, in any case, was very uncertain. He had left Italy because it was difficult to find work, and he had followed a friend to England to learn English. Although he enjoyed living in London and there was no pressure on him to return, the prospect of going back and running the family farm seriously tempted him. The problem was that he was gay, and his family would constantly be urging him to marry and have children. Though he liked the company of women, he had never felt any physical attraction to the opposite sex and had never had a girlfriend. He could not pretend, and in any case that would not be fair on any woman with whom he became involved. He thought he could tell his father, but it would be harder to tell his mother. When I queried this, he thought for a moment and then said it was because his mother was a rather anxious person and she would assume it was her fault: she would feel guilty, and he did not want that. His father might find it easier to accept because he, Raffaello, had always done a lot for the family. He had regularly sent them money and helped in any other way he could; he often did overtime so that he could send them more, but he could not be open about his sexuality, and people would not let him alone. It might be different in the big cities, he added, in Rome, perhaps or Milan, but not where he had been brought up. "The inhabitants of my village", he said "are always boasting to those who live in the next village, 'Our church is bigger than yours'. That's their mentality". The priests still teach that masturbation is a sin. How could they accept him living with another man?

"I wonder if you feel at all anxious about talking to me about these issues?" I said, adding: "That I, perhaps, might not accept your sexuality?" His response was that he had found it very hard to make the appointment and had thought about it for a long time before making the call. He assumed that I was a doctor and his nurse friend had told him that it was difficult to be open about such matters in the medical world. He felt quite concerned about my attitude and whether or not I would put pressure on him to change.

I said that most of the therapists I knew would consider that very misguided, but that it might be important for us to talk about his fears. He paused for a moment, then said that one of these was that I would analyse his sexuality. I said that I did not work in that way; that we could think about it if he wished, but there were only theories, and it was up to him. I was not sure if he was relieved or puzzled or perhaps a little of both, but he went on to explain that a gay friend, who knew he was contemplating therapy, had urged him to seek out a gay therapist. He had not followed his advice, partly because he did not know how to go about it, but he did not like the thought of being treated as a freak or a curiosity or someone who was sick. The friend who had given him my name had told him that certain prestigious training institutes would not consider homosexual candidates for training, though they would not admit that openly, and one such body had actually written to training therapists to tell them that they should not recommend homosexual or even bisexual candidates. The letter had been withdrawn after protests, and it was good to know that many people were angry about it, but there were clearly people in positions of power who held such views.

I said that I did not share these ideas, and that they left me feeling ashamed of my own profession. Furthermore, I did not believe that homosexuality was pathological since it cannot be pathological to love someone, whether of the same or opposite sex; and that we all go through times or find ourselves in circumstances when we love someone of the same gender, and for some people this may be expressed physically and become the predominant pattern of relationship. One could argue that repression is pathological, whether homosexual or heterosexual, and that one needed to think about the consequences, but it surely cannot be pathological to love.

We went back to the breakdown of his relationship and his thoughts about what had gone wrong. I could not decide whether I had allayed his anxieties sufficiently or said too much, but he was clearly desperate to talk about it all and clinging on to some hope, however tenuous, that he and his former partner might find some way of getting back together. The question of going home, however, was a very difficult one. Wanting to return to a country that was not tolerant of deviations from the prevailing sexual norm, and in some cases threatened imprisonment or even death, was a problem I had encountered before, and it always left me with a sense of helplessness. Beneath his polite and gentle exterior, however, I felt there was something about Raffaello that was hard to know. What did "home" mean to him? He had taken his courage in his hands and contacted me, and I suspected that much more lay behind these issues than was immediately apparent, so I suggested—and he readily accepted—that we should meet regularly once a week.

Over the next few months, I learnt a great deal more about him. He was the eldest of four children, and had spent his childhood, on and off, on the farm that his father had inherited. The land was stony and infertile, however, and making a living was really hard. When he was one, his mother had had another baby, but, tragically, his mother had died a day or so later from complications following the birth. An aunt volunteered to look after his baby sister, while Raff himself was sent to live with his maternal grandmother. She was poor, but warm and loving. She had been a widow for several years, but three of her grown-up, or nearly grown-up, children still lived with her, and, as a small child in a family of adults, Raff was adored. After a year or so, his father had re-married, and when Raff was six or seven, his father and stepmother decided to take him back. He had memories of going into the house and being fascinated by the electric light, which you could put on with a switch, for in his grandmother's house there were only oil lamps, but he also recalled feeling very unhappy and sitting around crying because his parents were almost strangers and he now had siblings he did not know. I was puzzled that he did not attribute his sadness to missing his grandmother and his aunts and uncle, but I made no comment at the time. Some months later, for reasons that never became apparent, his parents sent him to live with his father's mother, but he did not like her because she would tell him that his parents ought to be looking after him. Tragedy brought this period to an end in that he was knocked down by a car and sustained injuries that kept him in hospital for many months. He remembered a long convalescence on the shores of a large, nearby lake, and playing by the water with the other children. Almost two years later, he asked his father if he could return to the farm and live there with the family, which now included his younger sister. His parents agreed.

At school he had been rather "dreamy", as he put it, and often found it difficult to concentrate. Frustrated by this, one of his teachers had taken every opportunity to beat him. School became a nightmare, but when he complained to his father, he received no support. On the contrary, his father said he would tell the teacher to beat him more if he did not pay attention. "That must have left you feeling pretty desperate," I observed, but he remained silent, as though struggling for words. After a short pause, he added that he remembered an occasion when there was a litter of baby rabbits and two of them were particularly pretty. His brothers knew his father was about to kill them and they asked him to spare the two pretty ones. His father refused, and added that he would kill them first. And he did. "You must have felt that was cruel," I said. "Oh no," he protested, "That's just my father."

I suppose the kindest interpretation of his father's behaviour would be that his father, who had fought in the war and faced starvation, was trying to teach his sons to be tough, but this was a number of years after the war and there were not the same exigencies.

As an adolescent, Raffaello had attended church regularly, and was actually rather devout. When he left school, he spent some months in Thailand with other young people from his diocese helping in a church initiative to build an orphanage. On his return, he followed some courses, but he needed a job and work was very hard to find. Then a friend found him an opening in a restaurant in Paris. There he met another young man and for a time they lived together. He felt he ought to tell the priest about this in confession before mass. The priest said he could not give him absolution unless he promised to break off the relationship and abstain from anything of the sort in the future. The Church's teaching had changed little since 1476, when Leonardo da Vinci was accused of relations with "an ill-famed youth", which then, if proved, was a burning offence. Fortunately for Leonardo, the accusation had been made anonymously and evidence was not forthcoming, but, as he wrote on the reverse side of the sheet where he records the incident: "If there is no love, what then"?[8] Raffaello could not give up his relationship. He ceased to go to mass because he could not go to confession: "I'm too naughty," he said with a laugh, "and the priest would never give me absolution". It was another loss, though he remained some sort of a believer.

I was aware in all this that Raffaello had said very little about his step-mother, but I was even more struck by the theme of repeated loss. I commented on this and said that it seemed that he would get very attached to people and then lose them. His life was a story of worlds in which he felt he had a place, and there were key figures at the centre of those worlds to whom he would become attached, but he would lose them and find himself bereft of any sense of belonging. This clearly meant something to him; he looked sad and became silent for a minute or so. He said he felt unsure as to whether he belonged to any group anywhere. He was gay, but he did not feel particularly comfortable in the gay community. He did not like the gay "scene" and the "running around", as he called it, by which I understood him to mean having multiple partners. I reminded him that a lot of gay men and women did not like "the scene". He added that he also did not like the pressure on

---

8   Leonardo da Vinci, *Notebooks* (Oxford: Oxford University Press, 1980), 288.

people to declare themselves gay or straight or bisexual when the reality might be more complicated. Matt, his former partner, would always describe himself as bisexual, and he had had relationships with women before he and Raff met. Perhaps he'd decided he wanted a relationship with a woman again; to start a family and lead a heterosexual life. Hurt though he was he felt he could accept that, if it would make Matt happier.

Matt, I learnt, was a biologist who worked for a large pharmaceutical company. He would argue that homosexuality is un-biological because it is the life task of animals to reproduce. Homosexuals cannot do that, so gay relationships are futile.

There was a pause. I broke the silence by pointing out that I was not a biologist, but that the survival of the human race does not depend solely on our passing on our genes. We can only survive as a species if we can regulate our numbers according to the food available and manage the violent impulses that threaten our ability to live together. Animals might have nasty individual fights, but we humans, with our weapons of mass destruction, can simply wipe ourselves out. I also pointed out that homosexual behaviour is observed in many other species. Amongst Bonobos monkeys, for example, sex—including homosexual activity—seems to be used to resolve tensions and enhance social bonding. And these monkeys are, apparently, genetically our closest relatives.

Raff said he understood that, and added that you could not spend your childhood on a farm without becoming aware that homosexual activity was common amongst other species. Matt, however, was German (his family came from the Black Forest) and would tell him that fifty years before he would have been sent to a concentration camp if he had been suspected of being gay, and that he, Raff, would have suffered the same fate if they had been living together. Matt's parents did not accept his sexuality; in fact they wanted him to see a psychiatrist. He had refused, and they had now reached an uneasy truce on the subject. I commented that these details about Matt's background might point to the roots of Matt's inner struggles with his sexuality, but that he, Raff, had some rather negative feelings about himself. His reply was that, if you were raised as a Catholic, it was difficult to shed the guilt about homosexuality, but as he rather graphically put it, there was no other picture playing in his head.

Raffaello's repeated experience of loss led me to wonder how much fear of it had contributed to the breakdown of his relationship. He was not aware of keeping a part of himself back, but Matt had complained that he was not "in things", even though they were physically close. Perhaps, I suggested, it was a way protecting himself against the sort of loss that he had experienced several times in childhood.

He hesitated for a few minutes and then said that he had been wondering recently if that was why he was homosexual: he'd lost his mother when he was one, and then the grandmother he had loved. "You might have been left with the feeling that you cannot rely on women: they abandon you", I said. He nodded and looked thoughtful. After a short silence, he said that he also felt that his step-mother had never really loved him. She would hug and cuddle his brothers, her own children, and he would feel very jealous. When he asked why she didn't hug or cuddle him, she would say that, as the eldest, he didn't need it so much. Sometimes he felt that being gay was paying her back. But he did not experience any attraction to women. He became thoughtful and neither of us spoke for several minutes. Then he gave a sweet, reproving smile and said that we were not supposed to be analysing his sexuality.

I pointed out that I was not analysing his sexuality, that I was merely following his own train of thought. "In any case," I added, "as I've said before, there are only theories as to how our sexuality is determined. Some take the view that genetic factors play the leading role, others that psychological factors are more germane, but the likelihood is that there is an interaction between the two, and it may well be more one thing in one case and other factors in another. Gays seem to prefer to ascribe their sexuality to their genes, but genetic factors do not operate on their own, and I've never been able to see why psychological explanations should be regarded with suspicion or considered less cogent than physical ones. It doesn't follow from the fact that you feel you're paying your mother back by being gay that that is why you are gay: you could be gay for genetic reasons and simply feel it serves her right; or a genetic predisposition could have become established because of your childhood experiences. That would explain why you don't want her to feel guilty about it. It's all conjecture, but it seems tyrannical not to be allowed to play with these ideas, if that's what you want to do".

We talked over these issues for many months and we similarly revisited repeatedly the issue of his returning home, but initially it was the brutal rupture of his relationship with Matt and his feelings of hurt, humiliation and anger that filled our sessions. One day he came in and announced that he had received a letter from his former partner. It began in a conciliatory and concerned tone, but rapidly degenerated into the familiar self-justification and recrimination. He read it once or twice and then tore it up. He had finally lost patience with Matt and realised that Matt was not going to have a change of heart. His acceptance of that was made easier by a growing interest in someone else: a young man called Paul, who came from Ghent. Paul was an architect, and was spending a year or so in England to improve his English and gain experience in an English practice. Brought up in a deeply Catholic culture, with a Dutch mother and a Flemish father, Paul understood its values, but he, like his parents, was agnostic and somewhat anti-clerical. His family were in fact liberal intelligentsia with political sympathies considerably to the left; his relatives were architects, teachers and doctors who, during the war had risked their lives and hidden Jews, and were now deeply troubled by the resurgence of neo-fascist ideas in the Flemish speaking parts of Belgium. Paul's parents knew he was gay, but after some initial concern about the hostility and prejudice he might have to face, were warmly supportive. Raff and Paul shared a love of the arts, and although Paul had his struggles around the issue of sexuality he did not insinuate the sort of poisonous feelings about it that Matt did. Paul's time in England was limited and he needed to move on. Amongst other things he had applied for a grant for a research project in Leuven, and some months later he learned that his application had been successful. It was too good an opportunity to miss, but he did not want to leave Raff, and Raff by now was willing to give serious thought to giving up his job and going with him. Practically it would be possible because Leuven was only a short train journey from Brussels, where he could probably find work. He could always keep body and soul together, he said, as a gardener. Eventually he decided to give in his notice and join Paul, which meant, of course, that the issue of returning to Italy was shelved for the foreseeable future. And it also meant that our meetings would be coming to an end.

Before he left, Raff asked me if he could write to me. I believed it was important for him to feel he could stay in touch, but I did not really expect to hear from him again. I was both surprised and delighted, therefore, to receive a letter from him two or three years later, quite out of the blue. The letter was from the Netherlands, from Leiden, where, he explained, he was now living. The move to the Low Countries, he wrote, had been a good one, but his father had suffered a serious stroke only a year or so later and could no longer manage the farm. He had spent some weeks with his family helping them to sort things out, but he had finally decided against taking over from his father and it was agreed that his father should retire and rent out the land to a neighbour. He was still living with Paul. They had their ups and downs, but they were good friends. He felt Paul loved him, and Paul's family went out of their way to make him feel he was a part of it. In fact it was his relationship with Paul that had helped him realise that the idea of returning to the home of his childhood was something of a fantasy, and he could now let that go. He and Paul had moved to Leiden because Paul had taken a job there, which included some teaching at the university, and he, Raff, had found work which used his knowledge and rich experience. He looked back fondly on his time in London, but he could not forget the anguish in which it had ended. It was many months, however, since he had felt that low. He believed the work we had done together had helped him greatly, although he could not always say how. He thanked me for my commitment to him and hoped we could stay in touch. The letter was signed "with warm affection".

Raffaello felt that his sexuality was a key part of his identity: it was not something alien or a compulsion that had hold of him. Whether its roots lay in genetics or psychological factors seemed only of passing interest to him. He felt free if he could give expression to it, and constrained only in so far as there were pressures on him from family or society to pretend to be what he was not. The issues that had brought him were to do with loss and belonging. By contrast, "Frances", the young woman in my second example, felt invaded by and frightened of aspects of her sexuality, and driven to dangerous lengths to try to disown and deny them.

Frances drove a van collecting and delivering drugs for a large London teaching hospital. Some months before I encountered her, she had had an assessment with a clinical psychologist in another part of the same hospital. I was working there for a few hours a week as an "honorary therapist", as they called us, and we could offer people sixteen sessions. The assessment had concluded that this could help her and her name had been added to the waiting list.

The psychologist was someone I greatly respected. He was very insightful, thoughtful, and modest, and I was glad to have the position because I felt I could learn a lot from him. I particularly liked the notes he left behind because he would record much of what a patient said in their own words. He had written that he found Frances depressed and anxious. There were specific problems she did not know how to deal with, and these seemed to do with intimate relationships: they scared her so much she tried to avoid them. In her late adolescence, she had begun to worry about her sexual orientation, but she did not feel that this had in any way become resolved; if anything, in fact, it had got worse. She had met a woman called Bridget and fallen in love more than she had ever been in love before, but she did not like Bridget's personality because Bridget used her power to make her feel "bad". She felt she was going mad and sought psychiatric help. When she told Bridget she wanted to end their relationship, Bridget had threatened to kill herself. To escape, Frances had fled the northern city where she was then living and found the van-driving job in London. Bridget continued to pursue her, however, and Frances felt she was being stalked. The psychologist told her that he thought her sexuality was genetic and urged her to accept it, but she was very troubled by the idea that she might be lesbian. She wanted to live a "normal" life and have children with a man she loved. She did in fact have a boyfriend, and he, according to the notes, was someone she had met through the church they both attended. They had got to know each other on a trip to the religious community at Taizé, in France. Both of them seemed to be of high intelligence, and Frances was taking an access course with hopes of studying for a degree in theology in the near future, though not, it seemed, from any desire to become a priest.

I read on. Her boyfriend was called Simon, but he had been involved for a long time with another woman. He did not feel that the other woman loved him, and they spent weeks apart because her job involved a considerable amount of travelling. Simon had led Frances to believe that he wanted to extricate himself from this unsatisfying situation and settle down with her. Frances worried, however, that it was all self-deception. She had not told him of her uncertainty about her sexuality because she feared she would lose him if she did.

Some details of her family followed. Her father, who was Moroccan, ran a restaurant, and her mother, who had been born and brought up in London, worked as a cleaner. They had lived on a council estate near King's Cross, but her parents had separated acrimoniously when Frances was ten or so, and then divorced. One day her father was simply not there anymore. But the divorce had not brought her parents peace: they continued to have bitter fights, particularly over money and his failure to support his children financially after he had moved out, married again, and started another family. Frances tried to keep in contact with him, but felt caught up with and used by her parents in their quarrels. Her mother would send her to remind her former husband that he owed them money and he would react intemperately, even though he seemed to be doing quite well. Frances began to dread these meetings, and, as the relationship deteriorated, she distanced herself and they became rather rare. She loved her mother, however, and clung to her. When Frances was seven, in fact, she had been referred to a child psychiatrist because of a school phobia. She found it very difficult to go to school because she feared that her mother would die if she was separated from her or, if they were actually separated, she would be obsessed with thoughts that she might no longer be alive. The phobia developed when her older brother left the school they had attended to go to another one. The brother was several years her senior and Frances was highly attached to him, but there were times when she just hated him. He had struggled at school, but was now enjoying some success running his own small business with a friend as a tree surgeon.

People usually had to wait at least nine or ten months for therapy, but Frances telephoned the department again in great distress after only four months to ask if it might be possible for her to see someone urgently, and after a brief discussion it was agreed that I should offer her an appointment.

I said that I had read the notes from her initial interview, but it was clear that she was deeply upset about something and I wondered if she could tell me what had happened. She was sitting with her head in her hands, her attractive face and large brown eyes half hidden by shoulder-length black hair. After a minute or so of silence she raised her head and tried to speak, but no words emerged. A longer period of silence followed, punctuated by the whispered beginnings of sentences, which quickly petered out. After a while I said, "you seem to be trying to tell me about something unspeakable", and without looking at me she slowly nodded her head. More minutes passed, during which various speculations went through my mind. Had she been raped, or had something terrible happened to someone she loved? Had she run over someone in her van? Had some tragedy befallen her mother or brother? There were few, if any, clues. Eventually, after further despairing efforts to find her voice I managed to catch something barely audible about a call from a hospital. "You've had a call from a hospital", I repeated quietly, and again she nodded and hung her head. "From this hospital?" I asked, but she simply shook her head. After a further painful period of silence I allowed myself to ask her if she had had bad news about a relative or someone she loved. She slowly shook her head. Silence ensued once more, broken only by her futile attempts to formulate sentences, which then tailed off. In one of these I thought I caught something about Greece, and I started to wonder if some disaster had befallen her while she was on holiday. When I put this to her she made no reply, but buried her head in her hands in utter despair. She remained like this for quite a while, occasionally making futile attempts to find words. Most of the session passed like this, and I was very worried about her. I noticed that my attention had been riveted on her throughout and I had barely registered how quickly our time had gone by. As we had to end, I asked her if she had any friends or relatives who could help her, even by just staying with her. She was able to tell me that she shared a flat with two women she trusted. I decided to give her my home telephone number, and I urged her to ring me if she needed to be in touch. I was not happy that it would be another week before I could see her again, but I reminded her that we had fifteen more sessions and we arranged another meeting.

Frances and I met again in under week, in fact, and again she sat holding her head in her hands in silence, searching for, wrestling with, words. I asked her if there was any way in which I could help her tell her story. Would she find it easier to write it down? Or to try to draw what had happened? Her response was once more simply to shake her head. Eventually I said that I had gleaned two things from our first meeting: that something deeply troubling appeared to have happened to her in Greece, and that she seemed to have had some extremely frightening news from, or been very distressed by, an experience in a hospital. I was not sure if either inference was really justified, but I hoped that she might be able to correct me if I told her what I had surmised. She tried, but again could not speak. After short pause, I added that I wondered if the fact that she continually hid her face meant that she felt deep shame about whatever it was she was struggling to tell me. She looked at me and slowly nodded. I suggested that it might be possible to get nearer the problem if we could talk around it, and this seemed to help. I was eventually able to establish in this way that she had indeed spent a holiday in Greece and that she had met someone there just before the affair with Simon had begun. Gradually, over several sessions the whole story came out. The man she met in Greece was a South African, who was living in London and working as a barman. He was on holiday, staying in the same hotel, and over a week or so they had become friendly. One evening she went down to the beach just as dusk was falling, and she encountered him there. The evening was balmy and romantic and in the half light they lay together and made love. As she was leaving a day or so later they exchanged addresses and telephone numbers, but then she heard no more from him until he called her a day or so before our first meeting. He had given her name as a contact because investigations at a hospital had shown that he was suffering from a sexually transmitted disease. Frances was stunned. Then he told her that in fact he had AIDS. The clinic in question wanted to talk to her as soon as possible, and she was aware that they had been trying to get in touch with her, but she felt too panic-stricken to respond to their messages. The fact that a health worker at the hospital wanted to see her only confirmed her worst fears, but she was too terrified to make an appointment or even speak to them.

I wondered if he was in fact suffering from AIDS, or had tested HIV positive, but this was at a time when a positive result was invariably a death sentence, so it was not surprising that she was paralysed with fear. I asked her if he had worn any kind of protection, but I found it hard to make out her answer. I pointed out that he might not have been infected when they were together in Greece, but that she urgently needed to talk with the experts at the clinic. Having supervised health workers who were dealing with the AIDS epidemic, I was aware that doctors were beginning to experiment with giving those who had been exposed to infection a massive cocktail of drugs, which, as I understood it, could kill the virus if it could be delivered early enough. At least by now I knew why she was so distressed, and she was able to go over the painful details, however hesitantly, in the weeks that followed. It emerged that the experience on the beach was her first sexual encounter, and that she had gone along with it in part to prove to herself that she was not gay.

The need for Frances to engage with the health workers was imperative, but I worried that she would feel harassed if I pressed her too persistently, so we began to talk around her anxieties about her sexual identity. Though she had had very intense relationships with other women, she was not, in fact drawn to their bodies. "I find men's chests more attractive", she explained, "they're warmer; women's breasts are cold". I thought this was interesting, but I didn't really understand it. Then she continued: "I would love a more female man, one who doesn't mind crying, but who would be supportive... that's why I want to be with Simon".

Simon was two or three years older, a geography teacher in a large comprehensive school. Frances enjoyed his company, and she would cook for him. They also liked the same sorts of films and music, and she relished the physical side of their relationship. Could she really believe him when he said that he wanted to leave the other woman and live with her and have children? Frances did not connect her difficulty in believing Simon wanted to be with her to her experience of being abandoned by her father: as I mentioned, her most immediate anxiety was about her sexuality, complicated now by fears about her health and the almost unbearable thought that she might have passed the infection on. From her account of the physical side of their relationship this seemed unlikely, but it underlined the need for medical advice. Simon was away at that juncture and would not be back for several weeks; I hoped, therefore, that Frances would respond to the clinic's request to set up an appointment without delay. In the meantime, she spoke about her wider anxieties about her attraction to both genders. Should she tell Simon about her sexuality or not? And if she did, would he lose interest in her? I said that I did not know whether or not she should tell him, but there was little reason to think he would react badly. They had a mutual friend who was gay, and Frances had often talked with Simon about the relationship between genetics and sexual orientation. She uneasily recounted details of these conversations as the weeks went by, and anxiously related findings from studies that I already knew about through seminars I had attended. They had informed the sessions I had had with Raffaello, and I would listen again and reflect with her along these now familiar lines. Simon argued that there could not be a "gay gene" because it would not reproduce; nevertheless, the evidence pointed, he maintained, to the operation of genetic factors: an interaction, perhaps, between genes. It was complex, Simon would claim, and not as yet well understood. He knew about research that had demonstrated that fruit flies could be made gay by very simple interference with their genes, and indeed homosexual activity, far from being "unnatural" in the sense of being unknown in nature, could be observed in most known species. The idea that one creature had simply made a mistake about another's gender, as some people imagined, seemed inherently improbable. Current thinking appeared to be that several genes were involved in the determination of sexual identity, and that environmental factors in some way affected them. They might, for example, bring about a weakened uptake of testosterone in males and oestrogen in females, but these were areas that required further research. I asked her if the environmental forces she mentioned included psychological ones, but she did not know, though she preferred to think that same sex attraction was psychological in origin. All the talk about genetics worried her. Her assumption appeared to be that she could be "cured" of it if its roots could be traced to upbringing, though the clinical psychologist who had originally assessed her was an analyst and did not believe it could be changed or indeed that it was pathological. For sure, he knew, and I knew, of patients whose sexual identity had altered significantly in the course of therapy, and an individual became homosexual or heterosexual or more homosexual or heterosexual in the process, even though a re-orientation of their sexuality was not something they had originally sought: it just happened.

I was intrigued as to how these conversations between Frances and Simon had arisen, since it seemed never to have occurred to her that his interest in these issues pointed to the possibility that he had similar problems. Frances simply declared that he had originally studied geography and genetics and was now working part time for a Master's degree in which gender was one of the modules. But that, of course, begged a question: why he was drawn to these issues the first place? What was their attraction for him?

Simon had once been on some kind of geographical expedition to the South Pacific, and Frances listened with a mixture of fascination and apprehension to his accounts of some of the traditions and customs he encountered. He had described the *mahu*, young men who are homosexual and completely accepted as such by their communities. Gaugin had come across them and had written about them, he said, and something of the impression they had left on him survives in his painting. I could not make out whether there were female equivalents, but from time immemorial the Maori societies to which they belonged seemed to be much less bothered by sexual difference and gender variations than our own. They respected the *mahu* and valued them, and indeed there were parts in communal rituals that only they could perform. Captain Cook had included stories of his encounters with them in his journals, but Christian missionaries, both Catholic and Protestant, had been deeply shocked and had tried, unsuccessfully, to stamp them out. I noted that many societies had ways of integrating those whose sexuality differed from the norm, although in this part of the world we tended to be familiar only with the Romans and Greeks. The ancients did not know whether the spectrum of sexuality was genetic or psychological in origin or a mixture of both, and indeed could not have thought in those terms. In our own culture, by contrast, genetics and psychology form part of the framework through which we habitually try to make sense of our world; our feelings, however, remain conditioned by centuries of religious teaching and the influence of that teaching is evident in the very questions we ask. We have moved, patchily, from moral condemnation and criminalisation to medicalisation, but have a continuing struggle with acceptance, still less with the enjoyment of difference.

For Frances, the source of her fear of part of her make-up lay in her family culture. Her father had very rigid views as to how men and women should behave, which had been a major source of conflict between him and her mother when Frances was small, as her mother was a very "modern" woman. The family had struggled financially at that time, and Frances's father felt shamed and humiliated by his wife's insistence on going out to work. He had resorted to violence against her on several occasions, and Frances, her brother and mother shared memories of hiding from him in a refuge. Frances, like her mother, deplored her father's ideas, and would wonder why her parents had ever married, but she had absorbed these patriarchal values since she was a baby, values that deemed her attraction to other women as transgressive. Her mother did little to counteract this notion: if anything, she would make it worse because Frances was aware of clear signs of disapproval if her mother sensed that her daughter was becoming too close to another woman. Her internal world was very torn, which was particularly sad because her bisexuality, whether genetic or psychological in origin (or a bit of both), clearly would not in itself prevent her living the kind of life for which she longed. But "The mind is its own place," wrote John Milton in *Paradise Lost*, "and in itself / Can make a Heaven of Hell, a Hell of Heaven."

Frances did eventually summon up the courage to go to the clinic, and tests were carried out. After a week of agonising anxiety, she received a call from a health worker telling her that they had proved negative. Her relief was indescribable. The South African must have become infected very soon after that evening on the beach in Greece: Frances had had an incredibly lucky escape.

In the few sessions that remained to us it became clear that the relationship with Simon was cooling, and I sensed that she had begun to reconcile herself to the fact that he was not going to commit himself to her in the way she had wanted. I was not surprised, therefore, when she announced one day that she had thrown up her job, and had arranged to go and stay for a while with a relative in the U.S.A. Her mother had taken her there shortly after the divorce, so the place and the people were not unfamiliar. She had saved enough, moreover, to be able to live there for a short while and hoped that she might ultimately be allowed to work.

Frances left the country soon after we ended and I heard no more from her until I contacted her about this chapter. I learnt that her early experience in North America had been quite challenging: she had found work and secured a work permit, but had resigned after a few months as the only way out of a nasty situation that had arisen between her and her employer. I did not know the details, but I was struck by her resourcefulness and resilience and I hoped that our sessions, and the opportunity they offered for her to talk about desire that she felt threatened by and fearful of, had contributed to that. She refused to be compromised or defeated by the setback, and embarked on courses that would lead, as she had always hoped, to a degree. She had made a new life for herself, and appeared to have built a circle of friends. There was also mention of a new relationship, but she did not volunteer, and I felt it would have been indelicate to ask, whether she was living with a woman or a man.

Frances's assumption that homosexuality is "curable" if it has psychological roots is highly questionable. David Malan, in his authoritative book *Individual Psychology and the Science of Psychodynamics* (1979) lists "a confirmed homosexual asking to be made heterosexual" as one of several "excluding factors" in the selection of patients for full-scale psychoanalysis carried out by trainees.[9] We might infer from this that the more experienced might not rule it out. It is interesting that Malan does not use the word "cured", because it raises questions about what that might mean. It appears to be associated with a fantasy that there are individuals, many of them highly gifted, who happen to have this "quirk", which could, in principle, be psychologically cut out. But our creativity is nourished by our sexuality through a fine and intricate filigree of roots; condemning it or trying to eradicate it is rather like deciding to get rid of one of the colours of the rainbow: it would massively impoverish our world in all sorts of unforeseeable ways.

I have quoted at some length from the stories of Fleur, Andrew, Raffaello and Frances because I have always found it frustrating, on reading similar extracts in other authors, when there is insufficient background material to allow one to get a real sense of the person they are writing about.

These narratives also flesh out Spinoza's advocacy of the psychology of ethics in ways that are highly relevant to the twenty-first century. Whether he would regard this as an imaginative adaptation of his thinking or an impudent abuse of it, if we could resurrect him for an hour or so, I do not know. His commitment to securing a respected place for reason in ethics is admirable and entirely understandable, but the austere rationality of his propositions and psychological insight do not make a happy marriage. I suspect that many will find the former decidedly alienating, but his nature mysticism and his advocacy of a psychology of ethics both alluring and liberating. I am not a theologian, but the argument that freedom lies in giving up the belief that we are separate from the animate and inanimate world we inhabit, together

---

9   David Malan, *Individual Psychotherapy and the Science of Psychodynamics* (London: Butterworths, 1979), 225.

with accepting ourselves as part of nature in all its awe-inspiring diversity, reminds me of the Christian doctrine of grace. For all the religious imagery, however, Spinoza was attacked, not surprisingly, both in his lifetime and after his death, as an atheist. Whether or not that is fair, however, is another debate.

Spinoza's arguments invite a host of questions. For the moment, however, their value resides in the opportunity he offers us to side-step further philosophical wrangling, because the position he adopts turns the issue of human freedom into an empirical one and a matter, therefore, of psychology and observation. Writing half a century ago, the Oxford philosopher, Stuart Hampshire, says:

> Both Spinoza and Freud represent moral problems as essentially
> clinical problems, which can only be confused by the use of epithets
> of praise and blame, and by emotional attitudes of approval and
> disapproval. There can in principle be only one way of achieving sanity
> and happiness; the way is to come to understand the causes of our own
> states of mind.[10]

Spinoza is relevant, though, for a broader reason, a reason that is key to understanding the deeper psychological processes underlying the paradox of murderousness in the name of a reforming ideology, morality or religion. For the image of God that he jettisons, a God who stands apart from his creation to judge how well or badly it carries out his intentions, provides, Spinoza believed, a critical underpinning for theocratic oppression—an oppression from which he had suffered personally in the high drama of his expulsion for heresy by the synagogue in Amsterdam in his early twenties. As one of Spinoza's recent biographers has written:

> In Spinoza's adamant rejection of the anthropomorphic conception
> of God we may glimpse a very deep link between his metaphysics
> and his politics. According to the political analysis first laid out in the
> *Tractatus*, the orthodox idea of God is one of the mainstays of tyranny.
> The theologians, Spinoza suggests, promote the belief in a fearsome,
> judgemental, and punishing God in order to extract obeisance from the
> superstitious masses. A people living under Spinoza's God, on the other
> hand, could easily dispense with theocratic oppression. The most they
> might require is a few scientists and philosophers.[11]

10 Stuart Hampshire, *Spinoza* (London: Penguin Books, 1953), 142.
11 Matthew Stewart, *The Courtier and the Heretic: Leibniz, Spinoza, and the Fate of God in the Modern World* (London: Yale University Press, 2005), 162.

2. Instincts or Relationship: An Historic Divide

If "Nature" is the "green eminence" that guides the thinking of Benedict Spinoza and Sigmund Freud, what is this "Nature" to which they both refer? Writing after Charles Darwin, Freud's view of it differs from Spinoza's, but the latter's "Nature" is now only of historical interest, so at this point I shall bid Spinoza a grateful farewell and turn to Freud's more modern image, particularly the image he came to hold in the last two decades of his life.

What, then, was the image of nature, of human nature, that Freud came to embrace as he reflected on, revised, and summarised his findings in the darkening and increasingly menacing years before he died? It was an image constructed around all-powerful instincts, and, as we know, a 'death instinct', a concept that he tells us he introduced in an effort to make sense of the slaughter and savagery he had witnessed in the First World War. It is difficult, however, to see what its explanatory value might be. It seems reasonable to imagine that a 'death instinct' would play a part in any account of the dynamics of murder, especially of mass murder. Yet, in practice, Kleinians, who alone in British psychoanalytic circles have continued to be loyal the idea, and have contributed so much to our understanding of human barbarism, make ritual reference to it in theory, but have recourse to other factors in any given case. For example, Arthur Hyatt Williams, a disciple of Melanie Klein and an internationally acknowledged authority on the dynamics of murder, devised the concept of a "death constellation".[1] The death instinct features in this constellation, but, so far as one can see, only

---

1   Arthur Hyatt Williams, *Cruelty, Violence and Murder: Understanding the Criminal Mind* (London: Karnac Books, 1998).

          https://doi.org/10.11647/OBP.0416.02

formally, because it also includes a residue of hate that derives from our relationship with parental figures in childhood, and it is on this that Hyatt Williams concentrates. The hate is somehow encapsulated or 'split off', and becomes, as Jungians might call it, a 'complex'. Parental figures inevitably fail us, but it is a human need to believe that they are benign and loving. Whether we are aware of it or not, splitting is a way of contriving that—a compromise solution that allows us to dispose of the negative feelings. Any resolution we may have found may be threatened, however, by misfortunes such as a bereavement (or an impending bereavement), the prospect of divorce or abandonment, or a deeply disturbing piece of information about our past, present or future. In this event, argues Hyatt Williams, the balance of the life and death instincts may be upset, and a disparaging remark or sign of disrespect may spark some vicious acting out. To the onlooker, the provocation might seem insignificant—a policeman being bossy, perhaps, or a stroppy bus conductress—but the victim (who will often not be the individual around whom the homicidal fantasies initially arose) steps into the violent world of the other, and becomes the scapegoat precisely because he or she is a stranger or different, and lacks the protection that familiarity and bonds of affection usually afford.

The concept of a 'death instinct' as an organic drive that regularly requires gratification seems redundant here, but its inclusion in formal theorising masks the basic point that Kleinian psychology seems to be making: that the problem we face from the moment we are born is the age-old ethical conflict of love and hate, and that for all of us, this is the fundamental problem in life. Let's consider some examples again. First, we might go back the story of Fleur.

Fleur, as I described in the last chapter, could be both homicidal and suicidal, but any notion that the death instinct could help either of us understand and manage these impulses is simply mystifying. Like every other therapist I have ever known, I would try to get at what had prompted these murderous feelings towards herself or others on the never-ending occasions she reported struggling with them. I have already mentioned some of them, but others, such as the time when I visited her in another hospital under a different consultant, stand out. She had been sectioned following an attempt to hang herself that had only just failed. As I had feared, the sectioning only made matters worse: she felt taken over, as by her mother, and deprived of human rights. Key workers offered her time to talk, but then shared whatever she confided with their colleagues. Fleur again felt violated. She became more desperate and her efforts to kill herself redoubled. She also made several attempts to escape. After one such episode, she was held down in a small, windowless room and given a depot injection in her bottom. She felt deeply humiliated and murderously angry, especially because it stirred up memories of being molested by her uncle. On one occasion a nurse held her against a wall and pushed her breasts into her, adding mockingly: "That's what you want, isn't it?" For a long time Fleur talked of taking violent revenge on the nurse if she encountered her in the street. Another nurse told Fleur that she would never get a degree. The hospital experience had turned into a nightmare: in extremis, unable to protect or look after herself, she had allowed others to do so, only to feel violated, invaded and abused. Then, just as the future seemed at its blackest, a junior doctor realised what was happening and, deeply shocked at what he saw as an abuse of power, courageously took the risk of discharging her.

Cognitive behavioural therapy was offered to her as an outpatient for her compulsion to self-harm, and for a month or so Fleur availed herself of it. However, as she gained relief from cutting or burning or scalding herself, so her commitment to the therapy was less than wholehearted, and it was not long before she gave it up altogether. In the meantime, we had begun to meet three times a week with the aim of helping her return to her studies. Most of the sessions were taken up with the trauma of her experiences in hospital, and her anger about it smouldered on for years. I thought that one way she could give expression to this anger was by succeeding academically and making those who had mocked her eat their words. In the early autumn, she was actually able to return to her course and complete a second year. By the time she had entered the third year, her sadistic attacks on herself had largely ceased, and there were several other small signs of progress. "I hate my body", was a complaint Fleur had repeatedly made from the outset, but now it had become possible for us to talk about it. She hated her breasts, her vagina, and her womb, she explained, and had fantasies of cutting her breasts off or slashing her tummy, but she did not want to become a man: her dearest wish was to be androgynous.

The meanings of these attacks on herself, whether actual or contemplated, were multi-layered and often paradoxical. Most obviously, Fleur was goaded by anger and despair: anger at some comment or action of her mother's which left her feeling taken over, invaded or dismissed; and despair at not being able to express this anger because it would wound her mother. So the sadism was turned against herself: an attack on a body she felt was, and was not, her mother's. Self-injury was a gesture that stopped short of an attempt at suicide, but it was a game of Russian roulette, since we both knew that she could easily sever an artery and bleed to death.

Yet, there were occasions when Fleur was in touch with murderous feelings towards her mother. In a session immediately before they were due to go away together for a short holiday, Fleur told me she planned to kill her. "You don't believe me, do you?" she challenged, as she returned to the theme again and again. Eventually, I replied that I could really understand how murderous she felt and how desperately hard it was for her to control her impulses, but that she was also very frightened of them because her problem was that she also loved her mother. Moreover, quite apart from the legal consequences, she would not be able to live with her guilt if she harmed her mother in any way. I was left with the anxiety that Fleur's homicidal impulses might prove too much for her, so I was deeply relieved when she returned a week later and I learnt that her mother was still alive.

Anxiety was not the only feeling Fleur's behaviour evoked in me: I also, curiously, felt claustrophobic whenever she told me she had harmed herself, and this led me to wonder if she herself felt trapped and that this ratcheted up her anger and despair. What then was the trap? It seemed to me that the trap was that she turned to her mother at moments of acute distress, but her relationship with her mother was often the very source of that distress. It was a pattern that was unwittingly replicated by the hospital: she needed to find another way of soothing herself when she got into these states. We discussed the problem and it clearly meant something to her. Months later, she announced with a smile that she had found a novel way of soothing herself: she would think of my cat snoring in front of the fire!

Fleur succeeded academically beyond all expectations and went on to study for higher degrees. For one of them, her teachers told her that she had written the best thesis in the history of the department. Her academic work was largely a conflict-free area and one of the things that helped her to stay alive. Medication played its part, but the drugs did not prevent her attempting to cut or kill herself, partly because they curtailed her ability to lead a normal life. One week she came in and told me she had slashed her arm badly a few days before and had had to go to the accident and emergency department of a nearby hospital to have it sewn up. "Why do you think you did it, Fleur?" I asked. She fell silent for a few moments, then replied tersely: "To show them that they can't control me completely with their medication." At one point, Fleur's consultant, needing some feedback on the effects of the new medication that had been prescribed a year or so earlier, asked her what she thought she had benefitted from most over the same period. Fleur, after some hesitation, had replied: "I've gained a great deal of insight". If that was indeed the case, and if insight had played a significant part in her staying alive, ideas about an innate death drive could not have been more irrelevant: what mattered was that we were committed to tracking down the roots of her hatred and destructiveness in her day-to-day relationships in an atmosphere of growing trust. The absence of relationship was also a key element in it all, because Fleur often harmed herself in the early hours of the morning when there was no one she could turn to and she was totally alone.

The redundancy of the death instinct is also clearly exemplified in the story of Andrew, to take it up again briefly. He had been making progress, but the progress was not even, and there were periods when I worried about the depths of his despair and his renewed self-destructiveness. I remember on one occasion ringing his doctor, with his permission, because he had been voicing suicidal thoughts over several sessions. I wondered if we should not think of admission to hospital again as a voluntary patient, but his doctor, who was very psychologically minded, said he felt that was not the answer. Part of the problem was his conviction that his depression drove people away, and as it began to feel safe to tell me that and I was not driven away, he was able to talk about his phobia of knives. He was frightened by the sight of them in certain situations, that is, when his girlfriend was around. As we talked about the phobia, it seemed to me that it arose at times when separation was imminent. For example, on one occasion

they were staying in a farmhouse in Devon at the end of a holiday, about
to leave and part, for Andrew would be returning to his research whilst
his girlfriend lived and worked in another city. He had told her of his
fears, but seeing a knife on the table, he froze. Her response was to
laugh at him: nothing he had said frightened her. "Oh Andrew", she
had exclaimed, "you would never hurt a fly". Separation was associated
with anxieties about abandonment; it aroused anger and panic. Whether
I had got it quite right was, I think, less important than that his fear was
being taken seriously and that we could work on it. He was relieved to
think that the phobia might have a meaning, one that made sense in
the context of his personal history, and in a later session he reported
a dream in which he had been sleeping with his girlfriend and found
a large bomb between them. Terrified that it was about to go off, he
woke up. Again the interpretation that he was deeply angry with his
mother, that he was very afraid of the destructive power inside him, that
this was transferred on to his girlfriend, and heightened anxiety about
desertion tended to evoke it, offered him a way of understanding himself
and much needed soothing: he wasn't just 'bad'. But, to have suggested
that any of this made sense in terms of the death instinct, would have
left him feeling that his therapist had lost the plot to science fiction. The
reality, unfortunately, was that his girlfriend did find his depression
difficult, and she knew about his hostility to his father and was troubled
by it. Sadly, and reluctantly, after some months, she decided to end
their relationship. Andrew was angry and deeply upset: "She was all I
ever wanted", he said. It seemed a devastating blow because they had
been together for several years. I was worried that he might take it as
confirming his worst fears about himself, yet he survived because his
ever-supportive friends helped him through—perhaps also because he
had found a certain capacity within himself to mourn.

Klein herself had argued that our earliest and, in that sense, most
primitive way of attempting to manage the problem of love and hate
is by projection: that we unconsciously attribute our greed, our envy
and our hatred to other people. She called it the 'paranoid position',
because it leaves us with the conviction that these are the feelings they
are harbouring towards us; and she calls it a 'position' because we can
move in and out of it to deal with the pressure of forces from within
or without. Ronald Fairbairn, in correspondence with her, pointed out

that such a manoeuvre presupposes a splitting of ourselves and our world into all good and all bad. Klein agreed, therefore, to call this way of seeing our relationships the 'paranoid-schizoid position'. In its extreme form, it lies at the root of paranoid schizophrenia, but all of us unconsciously resort to it to a greater or lesser degree.

If the fundamental problem we all struggle with throughout life, however, is that of disposing of the hate that develops because of the failures of those we love and depend on, the implication is that it is not primarily pleasure and the discharge of instinctual tension that we seek, but relationship, or, to use John Bowlby's language, attachment. Fairbairn quotes, by way of illustration, the protest of one of his patients: "You're always talking about my wanting this and that desire satisfied; but what I really want is a father."[2]

Relationship, he claims, is our deepest need: to suggest that instinctual gratification comes first is to put the cart before the horse. In fact, it should properly be regarded as pathological; as a defensive, despairing position we only turn to when relationships have let us down.

Fairbairn's point is not a moral one: it derives from observation—from the observation that we often suppress our desires if we sense that they might offend or hurt someone we love or if we are committed to the pursuit of some 'higher' purpose such as the defence of the community to which we belong or aspire to belong. The celibacy of priests and monks and nuns throughout the world is an obvious example, as is the willingness of soldiers to face death for a nation or cause. Whether such sacrifices are right or wrong or indeed wise is another issue, and one to which I will return later; yet the fact that so many of us are willing to make them suggests that Freud's assumption that basic reproductive and aggressive drives are all-powerful is wide of the mark. Indeed, Fairbairn contended that it had been rendered obsolete by the biology of his day, which, he argued, saw instinct in higher mammals as weak.

Why might relationship matter? The answer to that question varies, as we all know, according to the stage of life we have in mind. Fairbairn, thinking about early childhood, writes of the critical importance for the child of feeling loved for his or her own sake, whilst Donald Winnicott describes in beguiling detail the interactions between mothers and

---

2   W.R.D. Fairbairn, *Psychoanalytic Studies of the Personality* (London: Routledge and Kegan Paul, 1952), 137.

babies around which this is secured in practice in the weeks and months immediately following birth. For both, this early meeting of physical and emotional needs is crucial to the establishment of what Erik Erikson calls 'basic trust'. If we cannot develop sufficient trust in those upon whom we depend, we attempt to manage the problem by the process of splitting: the schizoid process. There is a reaching out or 'seeking', whose origins are genetic and rooted in the maturational process, but parental figures need to match that seeking with a sensitive response. If that does not follow, our immature minds tend to interpret the failure as rejection, though it may simply be that one or both parents are depressed. The sense of rejection engenders feelings of humiliation, hate and anger, and that in turn creates a conflict that we attempt to manage by dissociating and isolating the bad experiences, rather as antibodies rush to surround and contain the threat of invading germs. It is a protective process that affects the way we see the world so that we find ourselves dividing it up into parts that are totally good or totally evil. In Freud's last short book, *An Outline of Psychoanalysis*, which was published in 1940 just after his death, he had begun to think that the 'ego' itself might become split. Fairbairn took this idea a stage further, contending that we dissociate parts of ourselves around good and bad images of parental figures so that we can identify with the good image and feel that our world is benign. We then repudiate the bad image, and see the malignancy as localised and lying elsewhere, in our bodies perhaps, or in some demon figure or enemy. The splitting is driven by our need to preserve relationships, and the patterns we set up in the process tend to be more or less permanent, though they may no longer be relevant to the circumstances we face in later life. In Freud they are policed, as it were, by the 'superego', a concept that is very helpful in conveying what Fairbairn means because the superego may be far from a faithful copy of the actual father, who may be gentle and kind, but an image that contains the negative feelings we cannot, and perhaps dare not, own. These 'internal objects', as they are called in the jargon, not only gather hate around them, but are sensed as returning that hate in all its malevolent force. The history of Christianity contains some vivid examples of splitting in the opposing images of Christ and Satan, or the Virgin Mary and the witch, for Satan and the witch are not, as it were, just passive, lifeless shadows: they are demonic figures full of evil intent. Their origins may lie in our internal worlds, but we habitually project them on to individuals and groups in the world around us and see in them a wish to harm us that then justifies our persecuting them. Fairbairn believed that it is this paranoid-schizoid demonisation and the dehumanisation that accompanies it that accounts for the phenomena Sigmund Freud attempted to explain with the death instinct.

3. Of Dark Materials and their Weaving

The value of Ronald Fairbairn's views was well demonstrated in the attempts made during and after the Second World War to understand the psychological allure of fascist ideologies and the psychopathological sources of the Holocaust. The leading figure of this work in Britain was Henry Dicks. Born in Pernau in Estonia of an English father and a mother of German Protestant descent, Dicks was bi-lingual in English and German as well as being fluent in Russian, since he had attended the English grammar school in Saint Petersburg for several years. Dicks' grand-daughter, in fact, has recently discovered his account of the experience of being in the city during the Revolution.[1] Dicks explicitly and extensively used Fairbairn's ideas in thinking about the psychodynamics of fascist ideology and the pathology of those who ran the death camps.

Apart from a brief period as the first Nuffield Professor of Psychiatry at Leeds, Dicks spent his career in clinical psychiatry, and was for a number of years the deputy director of the Tavistock Clinic. During the War, however, he intermittently held psychiatric responsibility for Rudolf Hess, Hitler's deputy, when Hess, following his flight to Scotland, began to arouse fears that he was on the edge of a psychotic breakdown. Hess, who was apparently on a peace mission, became both a prisoner and a patient, and Dicks contributed an account of his meetings with him to a book, *The Case of Rudolf Hess* (1947), edited by Jonathan Rees, then director of the Tavistock Clinic and the person with whom overall clinical responsibility lay.[2] It seems to have been around

---

1   Mentioned in Daniel Pick, *The Pursuit of the Nazi Mind*, 25.
2   Henry V. Dicks in *The Case of Rudolf Hess: A Problem in Diagnosis and Forensic Psychiatry*, ed. J.R. Rees (London: Heinemann, 1947).

    https://doi.org/10.11647/OBP.0416.03

this time, too, that the War Office asked Dicks to interview a number
of Nazi prisoners of war as though they had been referred to him for
a psychiatric assessment. These assessments would then be used to
develop a profile of the committed Nazi or, as Dicks calls it, the "high F"
character. He wrote up his findings in a 1950 paper, "Personality Traits
and National Socialist Ideology".[3]

None of the well-known histories of the Third Reich makes any
reference to Dicks, and no historian seems to have searched for (still less
through) his papers; at least, that is, until very recently when Daniel
Pick—an historian and a psychoanalyst—finally managed to track
down his archives. This lack of interest seems quite bewildering. Is it
because historians have seen psychoanalysts as people who make wild
conjectures and show little appreciation of the complexity of events
and the evidence? Yet, Dicks robustly repudiated any suggestion that
the rise and fall of the Third Reich could be explained in psychological
terms, and one would have thought that the memories and reflections
of someone who talked and sometimes ate with Hess daily would be of
the greatest historical interest. The only exception to this sorry tale of
neglect was Norman Cohn, whose work I referred to in the Introduction
and whose Centre sponsored Dicks in a major piece of research.

Amongst historians and sociologists, there seems also to be a belief
that psychoanalytic thinking on socio-political issues focuses on the
individual at the expense of the cultural context. That is often the case,
but it is not a criticism that can fairly be applied to Fairbairn or those
indebted to his thinking. Fairbairn, by all accounts, would have been
horrified at any suggestion that he was founding a school, but there
were figures like Guntrip and Sutherland who were very influenced by
his ideas, and it seems reasonable to infer from their accounts of him
and from Fairbairn's own theoretical papers that the answer he would
have given to the question: "What is the Nature to which both Spinoza
and Freud refer?" is that that nature, human nature, is the outcome of a
constant and very complicated interaction between needs that are inborn
and an environment that may or may not meet them. This is the model
that Dicks adopts, as he tells us throughout his work. Accordingly, it
made sense to see the psychological appeal of Adolf Hitler as deriving

---

3   Henry V. Dicks, "Personality Traits and National Socialist Ideology: A War-Time
     Study of German Prisoners of War", *Human Relations* 3, 1950, 111–54.

from the conflicts created by a patriarchal, authoritarian society. It offered a way of resolving them, and to understand that we need to look at the tensions with which the young were faced in their formative years.

Perhaps the most vivid portrait of this can be found in Chapter 9 of Erik Erikson's well-known *Childhood and Society* (1965): "When the father comes home from work, even the walls seem to pull themselves together," he writes in a colourful image.[4] The mother might well be the central figure in the home, but the father, the breadwinner and protector of the family, was also the distant, if not remote, disciplinarian who laid down the law and meted out punishment. In the domestic world of mother and children his presence was felt as that of an intruder, who "looked with disfavour", as Erikson puts it, on the ties of affection between the mother and the young ones she nurtured. She would be expected to be at the father's service, and from both wife and children he required unquestioning obedience. Family life was a hierarchy based on domination and submission. This model of male-female relations was one that the younger members of the family imbibed from the day they were born; a model that implicitly, if not explicitly, denigrated women. Duty was the supreme virtue: the mother's duty being "church, kitchen and kids", whilst that of the father was to bring up his sons in his own image.[5]

Dicks argued that such a pattern of parental roles would plunge the child into an emotional turmoil through which the individual would try to find a way by splitting and projection. The boy who became a committed Nazi, faced with the stormiest of those conflicts—the jealousy, rivalry, love, hate and fear of the three-person oedipal situation—had resolved them by identifying with a harsh, authoritarian father figure, disowning any thoughts, feelings, impulses or desires that might not be compatible with that identification in the conviction that they lay elsewhere. Jews, Russians, Marxists, Gypsies, homosexuals and other 'undesirables' became the focus of pitiless persecution because they were the figures on to whom these rejected, feared and hated parts of the self could easily be projected. The resulting perception of them as weak, greedy, dirty, secretly plotting, and potentially contagious provided ample justification for action to eradicate them. Both Dicks

4   Erik H. Erikson, *Childhood and Society* (London: Penguin, 1965), 322.
5   Ibid.

and Erikson point out, however, that the pattern of relationship with authority figures was often a rebellious one, especially in adolescence, only to yield later to a front of unquestioning obedience.[6] The dutiful mask that might then be donned was one behind which hatred could be hidden, and blame, for any crimes committed, dumped on those who had ordered them.

Attitudes to women were characteristically both idealising and denigrating. For the child brought up in such a patriarchal world, the protecting mother would usually be the focus of love; but she might also be seen as someone whose loyalties were divided, and, therefore, an untrustworthy ally against the father if the boy transgressed. In this uneasy ambivalence, mapped on to women in general, lay the roots of insecurities in relating to them: they were put on a pedestal, but at the same time debased. If that was the view of the feminine, masculinity, by contrast, was felt to be about the Spartan qualities of toughness and hardness: the willingness to hand out violence or endure it, so sadism might be seen as a mark of virility, or, if it were turned masochistically against the self, there could be bonding over bullying and "being beaten into a man." Tenderness was felt to be taboo; yet amongst the young, authoritarian, "high F" characters Dicks interviewed, he was struck by "sentimental", "barely desexualised" references to other young men, and was led, in consequence, to describe unconscious or repressed homosexuality as a significant feature in their make-up. Dicks attributes this to the widespread absence of the father during the 1914-18 War, and the consequent emergence of "an abnormally father-longing and father-hating generation".[7] Religious affiliations generally reflected these patterns in that the most nihilistic Nazis were commonly atheists, but there was also the "vague deistic mumbo-jumbo" of the "*Gottgläubig*", which was very closely associated with fanatical Nazism. Those who described themselves as such were able at one and the same time to reject the Jewish-Christian pacifist tradition as "effeminate" and Marxist materialism as "godless". The Sermon on the Mount, for example, might be dismissed as "un-German" and "unbiological". For some committed Christians, however, these despised, "maternal" values constituted a

---

6   Ibid. 326.
7   Henry V. Dicks, *Licensed Mass Murder* (London: Heinemann, 1972), 46.

central element in their faith and formed the backbone of their resistance to Nazi efforts to indoctrinate them.

Signs of neurotic anxiety were roughly double amongst the zealots as amongst the less convinced. Complaints of dysentery or abdominal pains could be understood as typical conversion symptoms concealing both anxiety and pleas for sympathy that would otherwise have been seen as weak and unmanly, and a cause, therefore, for shame.

Aggression, on the other hand, could be more openly displayed since it was much more consistent with the cultural stereotype of virility. The pretext would often be a projection: that the victims were not innocent and defenceless, but devious and unscrupulous enemies who had provoked their long-suffering attackers by abusing their simplicity, unsuspecting good nature and softness.

This is just the briefest summary of Dicks' views. It does not do justice to the detail and depth of his analysis, which was based on first-hand experience, and owes much, as he acknowledges, to German sources, including the writings of Erikson, Wilhelm Reich and Erich Fromm, who were all brought up in the same psychosocial environment and knew its toxic qualities from the inside. "The damage", Dicks writes, "is above all to little boys' normal tender attachment to their mothers."[8]

The above quotation comes from *Licensed Mass Murderer* (1972), which Dicks published in 1972. I drew attention earlier to the absence of any reference to Dicks' work by historians, but, as I also pointed out earlier, Norman Cohn, on behalf of the Columbus Centre, sponsored the research on which Dicks reports. The request, which was made in the 1960s, was for an in-depth psychological study of a sample of former concentration camp guards now serving prison sentences for "crimes against humanity". Eight of those approached agreed to be interviewed, but some of them had fearsome reputations and Dicks records asking for an armed guard. Understanding their psychopathology was greatly helped by the experience of Arthur Hyatt Williams with convicted killers in Britain. For the layperson, these former guards were men without feeling, a byword for brutality and pitiless, murderous hate. To view them as deeply schizoid on the Fairbairnian model, however, allowed Dicks to grasp that the hatred was "split off", that it came from

---

8   Ibid. 35.

parts of themselves that could, for much of their lives, remain inert, but could also, in certain circumstances, be worked on and acted out. That acting out could be a temporary phenomenon, which seemed to explain something that people in both Britain and Germany had observed: that at other times the same individual could be docile, harmless and co-operative, perhaps even amiable. Dicks realised that his armed guard had not been necessary. Gita Sereny describes a similar experience in her book on Franz Stangl, the former commandant of Treblinka. She recalls her first visit to him: "I lunched that day in the canteen and talked to several members of the prison staff. It was evident at once that they liked Stangl. 'If only they were all like Stangl', they said, 'our lives would be a bed of roses.'"[9] Stangl had been convicted of co-responsibility for the murder of 900,000 people.

Licensed Mass Murder contrasts the psychology of the run-of-the mill Nazi with that of the individuals Sereny and Dicks describe, whose inhumanity originated, the latter came to believe, in a deep-seated reservoir of hatred for the mother. That hatred might be unconscious, but Dicks' subjects differed from those studied by Hyatt Williams in the scale of their crimes and in the fact that their cruelty and homicidal tendencies had been deliberately cultivated and developed through training—rather as we now talk of "radicalisation". Such training would offer them a sense of belonging or affiliation, and, through it, a heady sense of power; however, this sense of power could co-exist with feelings of powerlessness and a perception of themselves as just a cog in a machine. Withdrawal became harder by the moment as the trainee became increasingly complicit in the crimes of the group, and any hesitation or "weakness" threatened shame and punishment. Rudolf Hoess, who ultimately became the commandant of Auschwitz, describes the dilemma in his autobiography. He felt he was not hard enough and had doubts about continuing, but he could not bring himself to admit his qualms to his superiors. Dicks dismisses this as self-exculpation, an attempt to conceal the split between the overseer of the camp and the loving husband and father who lived next door. "But greater than any of these fears for his reputation", Dicks observes, "is the dread of his tender emotions for his family and his secret doubts being published to

---

9   Gita Sereny, *Into That Darkness* (London: Pimlico, 1995), 24.

the world. He would still rather have been regarded as a good SS man and even a blood-thirsty beast, than a cissy".[10]

Dicks' views offer a detailed illustration of another way of thinking about "human nature" that derives from Freud, but is in practice more persuasive. Yet, in certain areas, he leaves some confusion. This is particularly evident when he is talking about homosexuality. Notoriously, some active party members in its early days were openly homosexual, but they were purged because Nazism, like other fascist movements, was of course overwhelmingly heterosexual and militantly homophobic. The historian Richard Evans, for example, describes how in 1933 one of their first acts of "moral cleansing" was to ransack the Institute for Sexual Science and publicly burn all its books in Berlin's Opera Square. On learning that Magnus Hirschfeld, its homosexual director, was out of the country recovering from an illness, the storm-troopers said: "Then hopefully he'll snuff it without us; then we won't need to string him up or beat him to death."[11] The sheer scale of the suffering of the Jews tends, perhaps understandably, to obscure the fact that a quarter of a million Gypsies were murdered together with a similar number of those the Nazis considered sexual degenerates and other 'undesirables'. Yet Dicks creates the impression towards the end of *Marital Tensions* (1967) that homosexuality was the source of Nazi values. In contrast, for instance, to the passage I quoted earlier about the destruction of the tie to the mother, Dicks writes of the "hidden, mother-tied homosexuality behind the so-admired masculine virtues with their ramifications in every sphere where men need to co-operate rationally, but mostly compete jealously and paranoidly."[12] Is it the homosexuality that is the problem, or indeed any variation from the gender stereotype, or rather a culture's intolerance of it, which then makes it a matter of shame, and something to be concealed, with the accompanying fear that others will find out? And if we are thinking about co-operation, which is rarely purely rational, is it not likely to be furthered rather than inhibited by friendly, or as Dicks calls it, "homosexual" feeling?

I interviewed Dicks a couple of years before he died to try to clear up some of these puzzles, although I was not primarily interested in

10   Henry V. Dicks, op. cit. 112–113.
11   Richard J. Evans, *The Coming of the Third Reich* (London: Allen Lane, 2003).
12   Henry V. Dicks, *Marital Tensions* (London: Karnac, 1993), 332.

his views on Nazism in general or, indeed, on Hess in particular. Dicks was a person of great courtesy, as others have noted, and I explained to him at the outset that my concern was with the social and political implications of psychoanalysis and wondered what someone with his singular experience, who had clearly devoted much thought to the question, might have to say on the subject. He said that every kind of socio-political implication had been drawn from the psychology. After talking about that for a bit I said that I was unclear about some of the things he had written: for example, was it his view that homosexuality and Nazism were intricately linked? He pointed out that the Third Reich had had draconian laws against it, and that the homosexuality to which he refers in his books and articles was repressed. In a well-known film of a Nuremberg rally attended by both Hitler and Hess, for instance, the latter appears almost to be in love with his hero, though he was both a husband and a father and shared the Nazi detestation of 'degeneracy'. After a pause for thought, Dicks added that there was a fundamental, structural, divide between the typical Nazi and those whose attraction to their own gender was not repressed: their identifications were different. The typical Nazi identified with an internalised, tyrannical father figure, whereas men who were conscious of their homosexual orientation tended to identify with their mothers, and for that reason were usually kindlier individuals.

For those not familiar with these distinctions, the theoretical background stems, of course, from Freud's view that we are all basically bisexual, that this mostly gives way to attraction to the opposite sex in puberty, whilst same-sex attraction is sublimated into friendship. For some, however, bisexuality persists, whilst for others, cross-sex attraction does not emerge. That comes at a cost to the individual, especially from the hostility of those whose attraction to their own sex is not sublimated but repressed, because that manifests itself in toxic masculinity and homophobia, which, as James Gilligan has argued (see Chapter 5) is a key component of the psychodynamics of violence.

Towards the end of the hour, I went on to ask Dicks how something like the "Black Miracle of Nazism", as Erikson calls it, could be prevented from happening again. A copy of his book, *Marital Tensions*, which I referred to earlier, lay on a small table and he invited me to read the last page. He pointed to a passage that linked two of his main

areas of interest, his work on marital relationships and his work for
the War Office, with a quotation from one of the young Nazis he had
interviewed. I do not imagine he knew much about feminism, but he
then he turned to me and said: "Anything that undermines the image
of the harsh, authoritarian father-figure as a model with which boys
should identify".

As I pointed out, Dicks drew on psychological ideas from Melanie
Klein, Fairbairn, Donald Winnicott, and others, often labelled collectively
as the "British School". They thought of themselves as Freudian, but
they shared an interest in the earliest relationship between the child
and the mother, and shifted the emphasis in psychoanalytic thinking to
the study of the mother-child relationship. The French analyst Jacques
Lacan, who visited Britain just after the war, believed the British School
neglected the father, but it is very clear from my brief account of Dicks'
work that Dicks saw the role of the father as of the greatest importance.
His findings detail the damage done by remote and authoritarian
paternal figures; he could not have been clearer that children need a
father who will respond warmly and sensitively to their attempts to
develop a relationship with him. One of the benefits of this is that, if
there are difficulties between the child and the mother, paternal figures
may play a therapeutic role; though they may also make matters worse.
For example, Suzanne Blundell, a child psychotherapist, writing about
fatherless sons, argues that in the lack of a father they miss someone who
could help them modify their violent and aggressive impulses, and that
they need to seek role models elsewhere, in an older sibling, perhaps, or
an uncle.[13] For Dicks, Hitler was a malevolent healer, a medicine-man for
the schizoid, who intuitively avoided the father role and acted instead
as an older brother, leading a defiant campaign against the "arterio-
sclerotic" old men who stood in the way of Germany's dynamic destiny,
licensing murder so long as it was done in his name.

Dicks, as I have said, was sponsored by the Columbus Centre,
where there was a shared belief that the phenomenon of Nazism was
not unique. European history, to take just one well-studied area, was
littered with similar examples, such as Stalinism in the former Soviet

---

13   Suzanne Blundell, "Fatherless Sons" in *The Importance of Fathers: A Psychoanalytic
     Re-evaluation,* ed. Judith Trowell and Alicia Etchegoyan (Hove: Brunner-Routledge,
     2002), 175.

Union. Moreover, Cohn believed that it is still with us, conspicuously, for example, amongst those who talk of fighting evil empires and the forces of Satan, or who urge their followers to kill the unbeliever, or who welcome a nuclear holocaust because it would usher in the 'Last Days', when the evil-doers would be destroyed and the righteous snatched up to receive their reward in heaven. The psychological features bear an unmistakeable resemblance to those described by Dicks: a splitting of the world into all good and all bad, into 'us' and 'them'; a belief that 'we' are the exclusive possessors of the truth, and that everyone else is not only in error but intent on harm; the demonisation and dehumanisation of those with whom they disagree, who are different or do not belong; the ambivalence towards women; the enforcement of rigidly defined gender roles; the intolerance of sexuality that differs from the prescribed norm; a value system in which duty and obedience are the highest virtues; and an apocalyptic mission to clean up the world in the name of religion or morality.

In the Introduction I outlined the origins of the Columbus Centre: that the initiative to establish it had come from the honourable David Astor, for a number of years editor of the *Observer*, and that he and other generous benefactors provided its funding; that Astor invited Cohn, then professor of French and German at Durham University, to take charge of it because Cohn's book, *The Pursuit of the Millennium* (1957), was directly relevant to its mission. The task its founders set, Cohn tells us, was "to investigate how persecutions and exterminations come about; how the impulse to persecute or exterminate is generated, how it spreads, and under what conditions it is likely to express itself in action".[14]

The Pursuit of the Millennium was a study of the mystical anarchism that flourished in Northern and Central Europe between the eleventh and the sixteenth centuries. The world view that animated the various different examples Cohn describes was that a final, apocalyptic battle was about to break out between the forces of good and the forces of evil, and that the outcome of that Armageddon-like conflict would be the triumph of the good and the establishment of a just and harmonious society, inhabited solely by the remaining true believers. Such ideas appealed to the poorest of the poor, to the peasant with little or no land,

---

14   Norman Cohn, editorial foreword to H.V. Dicks, *Licensed Mass Murder*, ix.

to individuals living on the margins of society. The leaders, by contrast, would probably have come from less desperate social circumstances. They might, for example, have been former priests. We can only speculate about the sources of their messianic message, but to the destitute, the abused, and the powerless, their ideas offered hope, and the heady promise of deliverance from their sufferings. They also justified revenge on those they blamed for them—the Jews, perhaps, or the clergy or the rich. As Cohn points out, it is a theme familiar to us from the biblical stories of the longing of ancient Israel for a messiah or saviour figure, a princely descendent of the royal house of David, who would drive out the Roman oppressors, purge and purify his people, and secure for ever the rule of the righteous.

Europe's Inner Demons (1993) was conceived in discussions about precursors of the Holocaust and the general consensus that the closest parallel was the great witch hunt. Cohn's classic study of the latter links up with, and traces further, the themes of the earlier book. First, however, he describes some forerunners: the persecution of Christians under Diocletian; the Church's campaign against heretics in the twelfth century; and the destruction of the Knights Templar. Where the lethal drive in *The Pursuit of the Millennium* originated in the lowlier reaches of society, responsibility for these other persecutions lay with the establishment, with emperors and kings, popes, prelates, and other individuals in positions of great power. Common to all, however, was the same contemptuous dehumanisation of their victims, and the same certainty that God and truth were on their side. The phenomenon has never been more vividly portrayed than by Albert Camus in *The Plague* (1960), which is usually understood as an allegory of fascism. Fear grips the inhabitants of an imaginary North African city as they begin to grasp the nature of the threat that faces them, but there are different reactions: "where some saw abstraction, others saw the truth", writes Camus. The response of the Church was to decree a week of prayer, the climax of which would be the sombre drama of high mass in the cathedral. The chosen preacher was Father Paneloux, a prominent Jesuit, and as the rain poured down outside, he launched with a "powerful, rather emotional delivery" into his sermon: "Calamity has come upon you my brethren, and, my brethren, you deserved it." The message is both reassuring and ominous:

> The just man need have no fear, but the evil-doer has good cause to
> tremble. For plague is the flail of God and the world is His threshing-
> floor, and implacably He will thresh out His harvest until the wheat is
> separated from the chaff.[15]

Cohn and Dicks became more and more convinced through their
historical and psychological research that Nazism in Germany and
Stalinism in the USSR were essentially twentieth-century versions
of a recurring historical phenomenon. In the one case, there was the
"parricidal right", as Dicks calls it, with the Jews taking pride of place
in its demonology; and in the other, the "parricidal left", with a list of
hate figures that was headed by the bourgeoisie. These differences are
superficial, argues Dicks, but the paranoid-schizoid processes in which
they originate, patently the same.

The danger that Dicks and Cohn court, unfortunately, is that of
psychological reductionism, though they start out with every intention
of avoiding it, because the idea that there is no real difference between
Das Kapital and *Mein Kampf* is impossible to defend. Historians might
well argue, for example, that Karl Marx was mistaken about certain
things or that he made too much of them, but the depth and rigour of his
analysis is widely respected, as is his importance in drawing attention to
the economic forces underlying social structures and historical events.
Ideologies, political philosophies, religions and ethical systems can be
studied in a variety of ways: we might look at their origins in a particular
context, for instance, or their place in the history of ideas, how they relate
to and compare with one another, to whom they might appeal and so
on. We might admire Greek ethics for its insight into shame, but deplore
Aristotle's failure to condemn slavery; we might agree or disagree with
Freud's view that the Christian command to love our neighbour lowers
the value of love and requires the psychologically impossible, and
people might or might not dissent from Friedrich Nietzsche's claim that
Christian morality is a slave morality that originated amongst slaves.
What we cannot do is simply reduce these notions to psychological
concepts, not least because those concepts can themselves be analysed
in similar ways. We need, furthermore, to be very careful of confusing
them with the actions of those who claim to be their followers. If, for
example, we were to draw conclusions about Christianity solely on the

---

15   Albert Camus, *The Plague* (London: Penguin Books, 1960), 80–81.

basis of the crimes of those who claim to be Christian, it would not be hard to argue that there is no real difference between Christianity and fascism. Most people would instinctively feel this to be absurd, if not blatantly offensive—not least because the killing and cruelty that have so often been carried out in the name of Christianity are an obscene violation of the Christian message. We need to make a clear distinction between the behaviour of those who hijack a creed to claim religious or moral sanction for their barbarity, and the creed itself, between the beliefs and values it enshrines and the transference to it of those who abuse it for their own vengeful or paranoid purposes. Some creeds, however, may be more vulnerable to this kind of misuse than others, and I earlier suggested reasons for this. The creeds themselves may differ from one another in important ways, but the psychology of those who exploit them for their own ends may be virtually the same.

4. Pascal's Paradox

"Men never do evil so fully and so cheerfully as when they do so for conscience's sake".[1] Blaise Pascal wrote these words in a century that had witnessed the Thirty Years War and the decimation of the population of Central Europe by starvation and every conceivable kind of barbarity in the name of religion. How can we understand this terrible paradox? Can psychodynamic psychology shed any light on it?

Lord John Alderdice, a psychiatrist and former Speaker of the Northern Ireland Assembly, touches on the question in his paper "Understanding Terrorism: The Inner World and the Wider World".[2] Alderdice writes from his experience of the 'Troubles' in the Province and his close personal and professional involvement in the peace process. Doing evil in the name of conscience and terrorism are not quite the same thing, but there is significant overlap:

> Terrorism is not a structure, an organisation or even a belief system. It is a tactic. It may be used by the left or the right or by more populist or national extremists. It involves the premeditated use of violence to create a climate of fear, but it is aimed at a wider target than the immediate victims of the violence. The victims may have symbolic significance, but the real target is not the victim. The target is the responsible authority. The purpose of the terrorist act is to provoke.[3]

For tyrants, it may also be used to intimidate and maintain control. If we think, by contrast, of the sickening persecution of the Yazidis, the difference becomes clear: they were the real target, the victims of genocide, but not to remedy an injustice: they were persecuted because

---

1   Blaise Pascal, *Pensées*, ed. Léon Braunschvicg (Paris: Editions Cluny, 1934).
2   Lord John Alderdice, "Understanding Terrorism: The Inner World and the Wider World". *British Journal of Psychotherapy 21*(4), 2005.
3   Ibid. 584.

          https://doi.org/10.11647/OBP.0416.04

they were seen as evil, as worshippers of Satan. Purification was the aim of the perpetrators: they saw what they were doing in trying to wipe them out as an act of moral cleansing. The psychology is about projection.

There are differences, but there are also similarities: both the terrorist and the religious or ideological zealot believe that their cause is a moral one for which they are prepared to sacrifice their lives, and in both cases their murderous acts stem from powerful emotions, especially from the experience of humiliation and disrespect. The mistake we often make is to imagine that these emotions can easily be laid aside, but if there is any learning to be had from psychodynamic psychology it is that our emotions are much more powerful than our reason. As Alderdice says:

> The appeal to the rational is of limited use. People who propose
> peace plans in such circumstances seem to be living with the unstated
> assumption that if the "right plan" could be invented everyone would
> suddenly grasp it with relief and implement it. Of course this is an
> illusion. It is not the content of a solution that is critical but the process
> of achieving it. We know in our clinical work that merely telling the
> patient where the problem lies or giving them an analytic text to read,
> is rarely a healing intervention. It is taking the patient through the
> analytic process, which is transformational.[4]

In other words, for those whose hatred derives from feeling that they and their community have been disparaged, made to feel worthless, treated like trash, respect is only restored—if it can be restored—by endless, patient, non-judgemental listening and the slow re-creation of trust.

Alderdice stresses the power of feeling behind the acts of these two groups of people and contrasts it with the relative impotence of rational argument. He does not, however, explore the psychodynamics of Pascal's observation, and for that we need to turn elsewhere. Ronald Fairbairn, echoing John Milton, touches on it in his suggestion that the third great tragedy to which the schizoid are prone is a reversal of values: they make a pact with the Devil in which they say "evil be thou my good" and "good be thou my evil", one of the sources for which may be despair.[5] "And therefore, since I cannot prove a lover... I am determined to prove

---

4   Ibid. 586.
5   W.R.D. Fairbairn, op. cit. 27.

a villain, / And hate the idle pleasures of these days" says Richard in the famous soliloquy with which William Shakespeare's *Richard III* opens. Shakespeare makes Richard's decision conscious, whereas Fairbairn argues that the reversal of values is rarely a conscious choice, but he does not develop the point. For a fuller examination of the problem we need to turn to Roger Money-Kyrle.

Money-Kyrle originally trained as a philosopher, studying in Vienna when it was the centre of logical positivism. On his return to Britain, he re-trained as an analyst, and collaborated for a time during and just after the war with Henry Dicks. Money-Kyrle, who was particularly interested in ethics and politics, offers an illuminating way of thinking about what is essentially an ethical puzzle. His theoretical position was more un-reconstructed Melanie Klein than that of Dicks, but it allows him to distinguish between two types of conscience: the "persecutory" and the "humanistic".

The persecutory or "paranoid" conscience keeps us in line by rules, and the threat of punishment if we disobey those rules. The rules are laid down by some authority outside us; in childhood, of course, the father, but later by other figures in authority: by the law, and ultimately by God, the vengeful God (in the Christian view) of the Old Testament; but we internalise them. Being good is about obedience, and obedience is the highest virtue. Its deepest roots, however, lie in the very earliest bond with the mother and the paranoid-schizoid position, in the need to split the maternal image or aspects of it into all good and all bad to manage the primitive ambivalence I outlined in Chapter 2. Seen through the lens of the persecutory conscience, our world looks black and white, divided into friends and enemies, the former human and the latter sub-human. We and our kind are good, we do our duty, and those who do not fully agree with us can only be against us. Relationships are governed by paranoid guilt, a notable feature of which is the evasion of responsibility. We are only too familiar with it from the claim "I was only obeying orders". It seems like a contemptible excuse, but for those who place obedience at the summit of their value system it is the only valid justification for their actions.

The humanistic conscience is very different, marked as it is by a reluctance to split the world into entirely malign or benign and the ability to see even enemies as human: we become aware that there may be good and bad on both sides. The tendency to demonise loses its grip, there is more doubt, less certainty of one's own rightness, and a perception of the world that can allow for shades of grey. We are more open to the influence of evidence, and more willing to be guided by it. The humanistic conscience is based on empathy and identification rather than projection. It is associated with a reluctance to hurt others and, if one has caused harm, a readiness to accept responsibility for what we have done, to make amends, make reparation or atone. The key virtue associated with it is compassion.

Money-Kyrle's distinction between the two types of conscience is a distinction in principle. In practice, we all have both and they may well conflict. Conflict, he argues, may very easily be observed at the oedipal stage, where a boy may face a lot of persecutory guilt if he disobeys an autocratic father. To obey such a father, however, may feel like deserting a defenceless mother, a move which is then felt to be wrong because it arouses "depressive" guilt, or guilt about abandoning or harming someone who is loved. When persecutory feelings predominate we react by propitiation, but if we are more troubled by the fear or the fact that we have harmed someone, we respond by trying to make reparation. Money-Kyrle separates out two clusters of traits or syndromes for the sake of contrast and clarity. They form poles or extremes at either end of a continuum, and social forces may cause us to move in one direction or the other. We may, for example, begin more at the schizoid-paranoid end if our experience in childhood has been damaging; but if our environment improves, we may move closer to humanism, toward Klein's "depressive position" or as Donald Winnicott preferred to call it, "the stage of concern". Equally, an individual who feels threatened by disturbing impulses or fantasies may turn to an authoritarian moral code as an aid to repressing them. Money-Kyrle describes these changes in our ethical outlook on the world as changes that may come about through deep analysis, but we all experience them every day. In a context of trust where we do not feel threatened, we are less inclined to demonise and dehumanise, but we may change our "position", in the Kleinian sense, from moment to moment. And all of us do.

This is a rather simplified exposition of Money-Kyrle's attempt to conceptualise both his experience with patients and his work with

Dicks on the authoritarian personality. In the original, it is unnecessarily complicated by being set within the framework of Sigmund Freud's final instinct theory, which includes the death instinct. Envy is viewed by Kleinians as the main way in which the death instinct expresses itself and, like the instinct itself, is regarded as innate. If we imagine it has organic origins, however, there is probably little we can do about it, but if it derives from a sense of injustice we can try to put the injustice right. Kleinians make a difference between envy and jealousy, arguing that we feel jealousy in three-person situations; for example, where we love someone and they love or are loved by someone else. Envy, by contrast applies to two-person contexts in which someone has some quality like intelligence or beauty or youth or the ability to play an instrument really well. Sometimes it can be eased and transformed into appreciation by, say, encouraging the person who envies to use it to enhance their own performance, but if it cannot be harnessed in this way it can take the form of sabotage or assume some other characteristically destructive guise such as smearing or denigration. There is a German saying, I am told, that every lamp-post attracts dogs who will lift a hind leg against it.

Envy may be conscious or unconscious, and we can envy others enjoying the freedom we have resolved to forego. In the film *Philomena* (2013), the story of a mother searching for the illegitimate son a convent had forced her to give up for adoption, the source of the sadism of the mother superior responsible for the cruelty to Philomena and her child is clearly the mother superior's own vow of celibacy. Some of the other women in the convent trying to lead a religious life may have been able to sublimate their maternal feelings in caring for mothers and babies, but the sadistic mother superior could not and makes "evil" her "good".

Henry Dicks quoted an interesting example in the interview I mentioned in the last chapter. He recounted the comments of a loyal young sailor in Adolf Hitler's navy, whom he interviewed in 1943. The sailor claimed that his parents had brought him up too softly, describing how on a visit across the Rhine to Strasburg he had seen "all these slouching young fellows with long hair, with their arms round girls, idling their Sunday away. I felt a pang as I recalled our Führer's motto for us German lads: 'Tough as leather, hard as Krupp steel, fleet as a greyhound!' How weak of me to envy those French boys! Yes—I was weak, I must curb my animal spirits." The individual decided to join the navy "where I would have this weak will beaten, where I would be hammered into a man".[6]

Psychological insight can be the source of envy, as can any 'good' such as democracy, respect or status or stability. It is often forgotten that in the Gospel of Mark, the author says that Pilate knew that the chief priests had delivered Jesus to him "for envy". In *Man's Picture of His World* (1961), Money-Kyrle argues that history can be seen as a cyclical process in which there is a perpetual struggle between envy and persecutory and humanistic guilt.

Money-Kyrle's distinction has an ancient lineage in ethics, and other psychodynamic schools or writers reach for something similar, though their language might be their own. For example, Winnicott, writing about "Morals and Education" in 1963 says:

> Compliance brings immediate rewards and adults only too easily mistake compliance for growth. The maturational processes can be by-passed by a series of identifications, so that what shows clinically is a false, acting self, a copy of someone perhaps; and what could be called a true or essential self becomes hidden, and becomes deprived of living experience. This leads many people who seem to be doing well eventually to end their lives which have become false and unreal; unreal success is morality at its lowest ebb as compared with which a sexual misdemeanour hardly counts.[7]

Elsewhere, Winnicott argues:

> A sign of health in the mind is the ability of one individual to enter imaginatively and yet accurately into the thoughts and feelings and hopes and fears of another person; also to allow the other person to do the same to us.[8]

Children, in fact, do not lack a conscience—on the contrary, they are often fiercely moralistic towards themselves and others, and need parental figures to help them judge themselves and others less harshly. The examples I gave earlier show that this is equally true of young adults. People who work with this age group will be very familiar with their tendency to blame themselves mercilessly for tragedies for which

---

6   Henry V. Dicks, *Marital Tensions* (London: Karnac, 1993), 332.
7   D.W. Winnicott, *The Maturational Processes and the Facilitating Environment* (London: Hogarth Press, 1965).
8   D.W. Winnicott, *Home is Where We Start From* (London: Penguin, 1990), 117.

they could not possibly have been responsible: the death of a family member, for example, or the break-up of the parental marriage, or the suicide of one of their parents. Fairbairn, struck by this, observed that often patients seem to be looking for something like "the forgiveness of sins" or "the casting out of devils".[9] The following story of a young woman I call "Clare" illustrates this problem.

Clare's father had been a doctor in Bristol, but had died of a rare lymphoma when she was seven or eight. Cancer had been diagnosed before Clare was born, but her father had fought it relentlessly and had enjoyed several years of remission until it was discovered that seventy to eighty per cent of his bone marrow was affected. Clare remembered the last time she saw him: he gave her a dress, and his final words to her were: "Look after your mother". For several years after his death, Clare used to imagine her father was actually still alive and that he was working in Russia, for he had always had strong left-wing sympathies. She believed that one day he would come back or that he would send for his wife and children to join him.

This was a very difficult time for Clare, and her memory of it was patchy and unreliable. Much of it she may have repressed. She thought her mother had struggled to look after her family, but failed, and that they had been found starving. Her relatives were worried about them, and she and her brother and sister may have been taken into care. But it was all a muddle. She had clear recall, however, of being attacked by her mother in the middle of the night, and, somewhere around that time, of going to live with her maternal grandparents in their rambling stone house in a small town on the edge of Dartmoor. The house was old and beautiful, but rather dilapidated because they rarely spent any money on it. Even so it held out the hope of security and stability and there

---

9   W.R.D. Fairbairn, "Psychotherapy and the Clergy" in *From Instinct to Self: Selected Papers of W.R.D. Fairbairn. Vol. 11. Applications and Early Contributions*, ed. Eleanor Birtles Fairbairn and David Scharff (New York: Jason Aronson Inc., 1994), 364. Fairbairn writes: "...it is something very like *salvation*, rather than medical cure, that the average patient is seeking when he embarks on a course of psychotherapy. From a religious, or at any rate Christian point of view, what a man seeks *salvation* from is sin, estrangement from God, spiritual death, and that fear which is cast out by perfect love. Correspondingly, from a psychotherapeutic point of view, what ... the patient seeks salvation *from* is anxiety, guilt, his own aggression and the bad, persecuting parental figures which haunt his inner world as the result his experiences in childhood..."

was talk of Clare's mother and her three children moving permanently into a nearby cottage her grandparents owned. For some reason this did not happen, and their daughter's condition continued to be a source of anguish for Clare's grandmother and grandfather; Clare could remember occasions when it would reduce both of them to tears. She felt her grandmother had been fond of her, and she would encourage her to sit and talk. She taught her to cook, and, as her grandmother's health deteriorated, Clare took over more of the household chores. Then, when Clare was sixteen, her grandmother died. After the funeral, her aunts decided it was time for her mother and the children to return to their own home and fend for themselves. If and when that failed, they reasoned, she and the children would be rescued by the social services. Clare, however, refused to go: she did not want to live with her mother, and was also at a rather critical stage in her education. Fortunately, her grandfather stepped in and asked her to keep house for him. She felt relieved at not having to live with her mother, but also guilty that she had been spared, especially when, at her grandfather's insistence, she spent time with her mother during the school holidays and witnessed the squalor in which they were all living. Her sister never forgave her for abandoning her.

Clare's grandfather ran a livery stable and a riding school. The widespread view of him was that he was a hard and taciturn man, but she knew that he had been deeply scarred by his experiences in the First World War. He was like the boy from the West Country village in *War Horse*: mad about horses and capable of deep feelings, but he did not know how to express them. Over the years, Clare and he had become very close, and she knew that he loved her, but she needed to talk and he could not help her. He would take her on long, largely silent walks through the country lanes, which strengthened the bond between them, a bond that Clare sensed lay in their unspoken anguish about, and hatred of, her mother's illness, of the mad woman she had become.

Not long after we had begun meeting, Clare reported a dream in which she was taking me on a tour of the house that had been her home before her father died. It felt very strange and haunted. Then she woke up and found the room eerily lit up by moonlight. In reality, the house had become like Miss Havisham's in *Great Expectations*, kept exactly as it was at the time of her father's death, full of memories and mementoes, but her brother had painted his bedroom black. The feeling in the dream was one of horror.

Clare and her brother had been close when they were children. He was three or four years older and she had felt loved and protected by him; but grieving deeply for his father and daily distressed by his mother's madness, he had become increasingly withdrawn. He had quitted school as soon as he could, and had left home. He tried to hold down a job, but a relationship had broken up, and he had sunk deeper into depression. Then he disappeared. Clare thought he was living on the streets, but actually, at that time, did not know if he was alive or dead. She clung to the hope of finding her brother, but alternated between that and a sort of distracted despair.

It was in these early days that Clare told me of a television programme that had upset her. It was about a man who had committed a crime and was serving a prison sentence, but every time the date of his release drew near, he did something that would ensure that he would stay in prison for a further term. She did not know why the programme had troubled her or why she had wanted to tell me about it, but the theme was guilt and punishment, and I wondered to what extent she was warning me of the fight she would put up if anyone tried to set her free.

Clare had always felt that her mother showed her little affection. Her brother and sister were often naughty and would be punished, but she, Clare, had been a good child, though her mother would claim that she was every bit as bad as the others, if not worse, because she was devious and dishonest. Clare's birthdays were ignored and, if she won a prize at school, her mother would not attend the prize giving. In fact, she won many prizes, but her mother would insist that her brother and sister were equally as clever; it was just that the teachers were too stupid to see it. Not surprisingly, Clare feared more than anything else becoming mad like her mother, and she worried that the doctor who had referred her to me had seen signs of psychosis in her, especially as he had said that she needed to see someone several times a week. There were no such signs, however, and she was palpably relieved when I reassured her of that. I also explained that the doctor had viewed her as having in effect lost both parents as a child, a double abandonment, and having come, therefore, from a background of considerable emotional deprivation.

Clare also worried that therapy was a punishment, but she had no idea for what.

Although there was little information about Clare's father, I always had the impression that the two were close, and that she had felt loved and protected by him against her mother's failings. Such memories as she had of him were positive and life affirming. She remembered, for example, that he had rescued her when she had stumbled into quicksand on a family holiday, and she recalled the occasion when he had stopped the donkey who had bolted with her on its back when her parents had bought her a donkey ride. And then there was the moment during the school nativity play when, suspended in mid-air as the angel Gabriel, she forgot her lines, only for them to come back to her when she saw her father's face in the audience. She had uncles whose violence she feared, but her relationship with her father and grandfather had left her with a scintilla of hope, if not confidence, in the opposite sex. She could relate to men in general, and she could relate to me. Women were more of a problem, especially if they were older and in a position of power over her. Some years later, Clare wondered aloud how she would have fared if her therapist had been female, and then, with a smile, answering her own question she wryly observed: "I wouldn't have lasted".

Clare's relationships with key male figures in her early life may have been benign, but she talked with quiet anger about a succession of later involvements that could only be described as abusive—to the deep distress of her grandfather. The experience that had preceded her first period of therapy was with a man ten or so years older than her. He was educated and intelligent, but devious and full of guile. He was initially a friend, but the friendship turned into a highly erotic infatuation. The thought of an unwanted pregnancy had always terrified her, yet it seemed to offer "a solution of sorts". Although she had always been scrupulous in taking precautions, Clare found herself pregnant. Significantly, this was shortly after she had been through the trauma of being obliged to have her mother sectioned. Clare went to her doctor and asked for an abortion. Her doctor was horrified, but sensing, perhaps, her ambivalence about becoming a mother, gave her two days to decide. She felt rather as if faced with an ultimatum, but opted for a termination. On the day it was carried out, the father of the baby deserted her and refused to have anything more to do with her. Alone and struggling with feelings of guilt and abandonment, Clare turned to a male friend from Eastern Europe who was gay. He wanted to work and settle in England, but could not get a work permit, so she married him. She felt suicidal, and after a few weeks they divorced. It was then that she had her first period of therapy: it helped her, she said, with her feelings about these events, and led her to realise that she was in no state to look after a baby, who would be totally dependent on her. Perhaps that is what her doctor had surmised.

The first period of therapy may have helped her to allow herself to be drawn into a better relationship with a young New Zealander called Scott, who had come to Britain to study for a higher degree in international relations. Scott was a person of integrity and much more straightforward. "I fell in love with him", Clare said, "when I realised how different he was to my previous lovers". They argued a lot but he looked after her; she felt that he had really cared for her, and had indeed been in love with her. They had talked seriously about her going back with him when he had finished his studies, but she was frightened that their relationship might not work out in the long run and that she could find herself alone and far from home without the support or comfort of friends. Sadly, they both became aware that the relationship between them could not continue and Scott visited her to tell her that it was at an end.

In her youthful romantic dreams, Clare had imagined finding a sort of idealised version of her father; Scott, however, could be authoritarian, more like her grandfather—a trait that became more pronounced as the day of his departure drew near. She must finish the degree course on which she had embarked, he insisted, get a good job, and stay away from her desolating family. Perhaps Scott became more controlling, I suggested, because he felt anxious: anxious about her, and anxious about himself. Clare's reply was that she did tend to go to pieces when faced with desertion. She did not usually have suicidal thoughts, but would sabotage herself and wreck her life in some way or other. Unconsciously, and maybe even consciously, she would contrive a mess.

It was the ending of this relationship and the sense of despair and desolation that followed that had led Clare to look for therapy again. She felt ugly, though the truth was that men found her attractive. When she felt secure and there was some warmth in her life she would blossom, but at bleaker moments the blackness of her mood would be written all over her face.

The pattern of Clare's relationships, as she was fully aware, was one of compliance: if one partner wanted her to be thinner, she would try to slim; if another wanted her to be fatter, she would endeavour to put on weight. She needed their affection, yet she feared that if they got close they would see the ugliness inside her and the ugliness of her family and walk away. "Perhaps", I suggested, "the problem is shame." She paused for a moment, and then said very sadly: "I simply want someone to love me".

Clare also wanted a baby, although she was not at that point in a state to take care of one; nevertheless, she was single and her biological clock was telling her that she was leaving it late. She was still grieving for Scott and the loss of the life and the family she might have had, and it was many months before she could let anyone near her again.

From the outset, Clare's complaint was that she needed more in her life, and indeed her existence came over as pretty bleak, an unremitting battle with poverty and loneliness and persistent feelings of rejection and humiliation. She persevered, however, in trying to improve her lot by studying in her spare time to enhance her qualifications. Someone observed that she appeared to be addicted to courses, but it made sense for her to try to make herself more employable. When we first met, Clare had just abandoned a higher degree course in the same field as Scott. It was as though she was trying to hold on to him by identifying with him. But she embarked on other courses over the years we met and similarly pulled out at the last moment. It was always maddeningly difficult to try to disentangle what was going on, but it was as though she could not allow herself to succeed. She would apply for a better job, only to fail at the interview. Was it simply that she came over as withdrawn and depressed or did she have a deep-seated urge, whether conscious or unconscious, to subvert her own efforts and deny herself the fruits of them? We revisited this subject again and again as the theme of her working hard at something and then failing to reap the rewards regularly resurfaced: she wanted more in her life, but found it almost impossible to allow herself to succeed. And then she would feel envious and jealous of "sister figures" who did succeed, especially when they were less well qualified and experienced. The image came to mind of a child who builds some elaborate castle out of toy bricks or Lego and then destroys it.

Sometime later Clare wrote me a letter in which she said she was painfully aware of how at times she had abused and thwarted my efforts to help her. She imagined, she added, that I must view her as Miranda feels about Caliban in *The Tempest*:

> Abhorred slave,
> Which any print of goodness will not take,
> Being capable of all ill! I pitied thee,
> Took pains to make thee speak, taught thee each hour
> One thing or other: when thou dids't not, savage,
> Know thine own meaning, but woulds't gabble like
> A thing most brutish, I endow'd thy purposes
> With words that made them known. But thy vile race,
> Though thou dids't learn, had that in't which good natures
> Could not abide to be with; therefore wast thou
> Deservedly confin'd into this rock,
> Who hads't deserved more than a prison.[10]

One of the areas in which there did seem to be some progress, however was that Clare did eventually meet a man, a professional musician she had come to know through her work in a music library. He was ten years older, but a good companion, and classical music, books and films were their shared passions. In all the time I had known her, Clare had never taken a holiday, but he enjoyed travel, and—in contrast to her frugal life style— found pleasure in food and wine. He had a good sense of humour, was not controlling and, as a bonus, Clare's friends and relatives liked him. Feeling she could no longer endure life on her own, she "grabbed him", as she put it, and invited him to live with her. For whatever reason, however, he did not want children and Clare foresaw tension arising between them over that in the future. In fact, she declared she would come to hate him if he remained resistant to the idea of having a family, and for many months she wondered about the wisdom of allowing the relationship to continue. It did continue, however, and they seemed to find some way of living together. Sadly, he had serious health problems and one night, after several emergency

---

10 William Shakespeare, *The Tempest* (London: Methuen, 1958), Act 1, Scene 11, lines 353–364.

hospital admissions, she found him dead on the landing near their bedroom. A couple of years before this, her brother had been found dead in the council flat the authorities had found him after a period when he may well have been living on the streets.

I tell a little of Clare's story because shame and guilt figure in it so graphically. Guilt about her consent to the abortion regularly resurfaced, with her mother's condition and her feelings about it being a deeper source of anguish. For much of her life, Clare did not know what her mother's diagnosis was: it was just "madness", and decades passed before she found out that psychiatrists were treating her for paranoid schizophrenia. Clare just experienced her as someone who would telephone and ramble on about conversations she had had with her dead husband and conspiracies to destroy her reputation in various parts of the country. Clare detested this talk and felt deeply ashamed of her mother's state. But she also felt guilty about her anger towards her and her hatred of her or, as she corrected me on one occasion, of her mother's illness. She felt guilty about being her grandfather's favourite and, in contrast to her siblings, being partially spared the fate of having to live with her mother during her adolescence. Above all, she felt guilty about surviving when her father had died, her mother had collapsed into psychosis, and her brother's life had been so severely crippled by these desolating events. As I have said, Clare rarely talked about suicidal thoughts or harmed herself in conventional ways. Nevertheless, I had the persisting sense that she struggled continually with impulses to punish me as a substitute for her parents by refusing to thrive, and that in the process she was paradoxically engaged in continually punishing herself. On one occasion, Clare referred to her "masochism"; initially I wondered at her use of the word because she did not appear be masochistic in the common, sexual sense. Freud, however, distinguished different types of masochism and amongst them a "moral" masochism characterised by the need, whether conscious or unconscious, to receive what at some deep level we feel are our just deserts. And that was what Clare felt was her due.

Perhaps a recap would be helpful: in the early part of this chapter I outlined psychoanalytic thinking as to how we can come to demonise and dehumanise others, and the contrast between the paranoid or persecutory and the more inclusive, humanistic conscience. There is, as

I argued, a continuum between the two, and we are all of us at various points along it: we may, and do, move towards one pole or the other according to circumstances, though the process is largely unconscious. Guilt may drive us in one direction or another, and in Clare's case, since she did not easily feel able to blame others, she inflicted her punitive impulses on herself. But shame, as I said, was also, though more covertly, a threat with which she constantly had to contend; and shame and fear of shame and their role in the demonisation and dehumanisation of others is the subject we need to turn to next.

5. Guilt and Shame

Shame and the fear of shame are feelings that have played a major role in ethics for the last two and a half thousand years, yet shame figures in only a very minor way, if at all, in the works of writers like Melanie Klein, Ronald Fairbairn and Donald Winnicott. This neglect is odd because it is the emotion supremely associated with splitting, with the 'false self' and with schizoid states, for so often the wish to be more authentic or honest is inhibited by fear of shame and its relatives: humiliation or ridicule. It is difficult to distinguish between guilt and shame, and some would deny that there is any difference between them, but the philosopher Bernard Williams, in a series of fascinating lectures published under the title "Shame and Necessity" (1994), defines the difference with unusual clarity. He argues that the literature of Classical Greece describes and explores the psychology of shame with a subtlety and insight that we have lost. Western civilisation, especially Christian civilisation, has tended to focus on guilt, but shame is the feeling we experience when something the culture deems private is exposed to public gaze. Typically, it is being seen naked in a situation in which we are not supposed to be naked. Attempting to distinguish between shame and guilt, Williams writes:

> The psychological model for each emotion involves an internalised figure. In the case of shame this is... a watcher or a witness. In the case of guilt, the figure is a *victim* or an *enforcer*.[1]

Williams continues:

> In contrast to guilt, there is no need with shame that the viewer should be angry or otherwise hostile. All that is necessary is that he should perceive that very situation or characteristic that the subject feels to be an inadequacy, failing or loss of power.[2]

---

1   Bernard Williams, *Shame and Necessity* (London: University of California Press, 1994), 219.
2   Ibid. 221.

    https://doi.org/10.11647/OBP.0416.05

Several years ago, I was contacted by a young woman whose story illustrates these themes very clearly. I call her "Lucy".

Lucy was an anaesthetist, who worked mostly with children. She had trained late after an earlier career as a singer. "Not the kind of music that would have appealed to my parents", she casually confided, but she had enjoyed it and been successful at it; there had been stints at nightclubs in Buenos Aires and Paris, and then a growing reputation in Britain. Although it had been glamorous, she had decided to make the change to medicine because she felt she wanted to do something more "meaningful", and after long years of study had ended up, in her own words, as a "gas lady".

After introducing herself in this rather engaging way, Lucy took a moment or two to collect her thoughts. Then she explained that she had had a period of depression two years earlier and that she had never come off the anti-depressants: it had been about not feeling good enough and fearing she was going to fail. She had had some sessions with a psychiatric nurse, a man, and had found the work they did together really helpful; now, however, she was worried that she was "going down" again.

Could she associate it with anything? I enquired. From her reply, I learned that she suffered from multiple sclerosis, a diagnosis that had been made some fifteen months before. She couldn't imagine herself ending up bedridden or in a wheelchair, but there was a good chance that just that would figure in her future. She wanted children, moreover, but wondered what kind of mother she would be able to be. At the moment she could work, and her employers knew about her illness, but beyond finding her a position outside the operating theatre, they tended to ignore it. One reason for that was her determination to prove that she was fine: keeping up the pretence, however, left her particularly exposed to the pressures she and her colleagues were under, and the frustrating sense that there was no time. A diagnosis of multiple sclerosis, I thought, was enough to depress anyone, but I sensed that other factors were involved.

I wondered if she didn't feel rather alone and frightened by the way her life had turned out.

Loneliness, it became clear, was a problem for her not least because the nature of the work she and her husband did meant that they rarely met, and she could not talk to him about her condition because it would upset him. He was an academic lawyer who specialised in civil rights issues. They had not long been married and had begun to argue a lot. "We can be so vicious to each other," she added, "and then we end up in silence and ignore each other". She also missed the friends she had left behind when they moved to London.

We passed on to talking about her family. Could she tell me a little about them? Did she feel supported by them? The family, she replied was "a bizarre set-up". I invited her to explain. Both parents had retired, it turned out. Her father had been a clergyman, actually the dean of a cathedral, but the church was a second career for him: he had originally taught mathematics, whilst her mother had been a nurse. They were both sympathetic to her physical problems, but any attempt to talk about feeling down, however desperate her situation, would fall on deaf ears. They couldn't hear her in such negative moments, and her father would hang up on her if she rang. When she had suffered her earlier bout of depression, her parents stopped speaking to her. "They can't talk about feeling," Lucy protested, "they never want to know". Yet, there was depression in the family. Her father's mother had killed herself when Lucy was four years old, and her father had had a breakdown when Lucy was a teenager. He had been workaholic, totally wrapped up in matters to do with the church, and she had never really known him, but subsequently, brought together for the first time by the crisis, they began to sit and talk. She worried that he might kill himself because he had already made two bids with tablets. Her concern about his safety had been such that she would at times secretly follow him around the small city where they lived.

Perhaps her parents had little patience with her when she was in a "blue period", I suggested, because they could not cope with another depressed member of the family. Or was it that they lacked the language to talk about feeling? Or perhaps a bit of both? Lucy's reply was that she had long felt dismayed by her family's inability to be honest with each other; the treatment her father had received following his breakdown might have provided an opportunity to address that, but it had done nothing to help him open up about the issues that troubled him. He had just been given medication and a single session with a psychiatrist. He would never go again, he declared since "he did not like that kind of thing".

There were siblings, with Lucy being the youngest of three sisters. One became pregnant when Lucy was eleven and gave birth "down the toilet", as she put it, by which I imagined she meant that she had a miscarriage. The other tried to take her own life when Lucy was twelve because she felt she was not good enough and was going to fail. I suggested that the unspoken fear in the family was of shame, and that it was shame that underlay the difficulty they had with being truthful with each other. I was not surprised to learn that there were secrets in the family and that her parents were fixated on achievement. Lucy had done her medical degree at one of the grander colleges in Oxford, and then her clinical training and her first job in the same city, but she had never warmed to the place. People were "self-obsessed and cliquey" and looked down on everyone, but when she tried to say as much to her parents they were dismissive. "Of course you like it," they would insist, "it's Oxford".

I felt that, before we ended this first session, we ought to be clearer about how she hoped therapy might help her: it was, after all, an organic condition that had led her to seek assistance, though clearly other issues were involved. Lucy had encountered or read of therapists who appeared to conceive of physical illness as a symptom of unresolved psychological conflicts, the implication being that if you got to the bottom of the conflicts the symptoms would go away. Any hint that something of that sort was being suggested made her angry. I said I did not subscribe to such ideas, and that they rather reminded me of the beliefs of some religious people that everything could be cured by trust in God and prayer. I had met several people from charismatic or conservative evangelical backgrounds who had suffered, or had relatives who had suffered, as a result of such convictions. Indeed, the bi-polar mother of a young man I happened to be seeing around the same time had killed herself because the church to which she belonged viewed any resort to or reliance on medication as manifesting a lack of faith.

My own position was that Lucy needed to manage her condition with her doctors; at the same time, she was bound to have, and indeed clearly did have, fears and feelings about the matter. Her doctors, I suggested, would be able to discuss some of those fears, and perhaps reassure her and help her understand what was happening to her body. Lucy's assumptions about her life had been shattered, however, and she was faced with a degenerating physical condition, loss and more loss, and what this all meant for herself, her marriage and her future. Her employers appeared to have acknowledged this implicitly in urging therapy and offering to pay for it. A regular time to talk might be a relief, I suggested, and perhaps help ease the tensions with her husband. Lucy and her husband might also benefit from some sessions together at some stage.

Over the next few months, the thought of a growing physical dependence on other people, and especially her husband, troubled Lucy more and more. She hated the idea of becoming a burden on him. She was a convinced feminist and a feisty defender of women's rights, but her horror of dependence derived less from any dislike of being beholden to a man than from repugnance at having to make demands on others and complicate their lives. Again, this was something Lucy and her husband had not been able to discuss, but he had his own hopes and aspirations, and she did not want to be a hindrance to them. In fact, they each had their dreams and ambitions and, as far as I could understand, had always done their best to help each other realise them. Lucy felt she would be a millstone round his neck and he would increasingly resent her. And what kind of companion could she be?

I imagine that Lucy's parents might have pointed out that they had married in church and had vowed to love each other "for better or worse, in sickness and in health"; Lucy's fear of increasing dependence, however, was intricately bound up with shame. She began one session by telling me that she had fallen in a public place. The doctor in her knew that, as muscles weakened and walking grew more hazardous, this was the kind of thing that would be likely happen, but she had been surprised at her emotional reaction to the incident and her overwhelming wish that the ground would open and swallow her up. I said that many people would have brushed the incident off with a joke, made a quip about drinking too much or cursed the local authorities for not repairing a damaged pavement, and I could only guess that people around her had been concerned and sympathetic. For Lucy, however, it betokened a weakening grip over her body that could only grow worse in the years to come. On another occasion, the loss of control was different: she wet herself when she was at home. She kept both mishaps to herself, but felt humiliated, dismayed and frightened by these signs of increasing physical fragility, and more anxious than ever at the possibility of making herself look pathetic in public.

Periodic reviews with her doctors confirmed that her condition was deteriorating, although slowly, and the emergence of complications had a lowering effect on her mood. Over several weeks, Lucy began talking about putting an end to it all. By now, she seemed to have concluded that she could not have children because it would be unfair on them to have a crippled mother, and she dreaded more strongly becoming a nuisance to her husband as she was compelled to rely more and more on his care. Lucy's concern was for his future and the way in which her health problems were curtailing his chances of happiness. If she killed herself, she reasoned, he could find someone else: he would not find it hard, and he could enjoy a normal married life and a family. I pointed out that there could be a lot of help available to someone with her physical problems, and wondered if she could imagine how her husband would feel if the wife he loved had died by her own hand, however altruistic the intent. What sort of guilt and shame, however unjustified, might he be left to face? Lucy talked very calmly and rationally about her suicidal thoughts but the reality was that she was telling me about preparations to murder herself, and I wondered how angry she felt about her illness and the way in which it would foreshorten her career and rob her of the prospect of ever becoming a mother. She could not blame God because she did not believe in the kind of God that might be held responsible for what was happening to her body; if there was no one she could legitimately rage against, perhaps that only added to her despair. There was a history of suicide and attempted suicide in the family, as I mentioned earlier, and, as a doctor, Lucy had access to ways of bringing her life to an end. I asked her if she ever imagined how she would do so. Her reply was that she was an anaesthetist and knew what to do.

As if that were not alarming enough in itself, Lucy began to report around the same time that the hospital authorities were becoming restive about her continuing to see me and wanted her to stop. This in itself may have contributed to her deteriorating mental state as it played into her feeling of being a burden and added to her guilt and shame, but the very last thing we needed to do at that point was to terminate. The recommendation that Lucy should seek therapy had originally come from the consultant in charge of her case. I had spoken to him on the telephone on a number of occasions in connections with earlier referrals, and I knew he had had his own experience of therapy following the death of his wife in a car crash. He clearly valued it and he trusted me to see individuals he referred for as long as I thought necessary. However, the manager of the department, a former nurse, was in charge of the relevant funds and her attitude towards any form of therapy that was not physical was decidedly more sceptical. I knew that Lucy no longer had the means to pay for herself and in her present mood would not have considered herself worth spending money on, even if she had it. She had made money in the past from her singing career, but she had spent most of it on her medical training. The right thing to do, given that she was dwelling more and more on ideas of self-destruction, was to increase the frequency of the sessions, not reduce them or bring them to an end. I asked her permission to speak to her consultant and I explained the situation to him without going into details. I added a little angrily that I could not remain responsible for her if the hospital cut off funding. He responded very calmly that there was no problem about her continuing and asked me if there was any other way in which he could help. I learned a little later that he had telephoned her to reassure her that they would go on supporting her for as long as necessary.

Perhaps the practical expression of concern by him and my own concern was a turning point, because after this crisis Lucy's mood gradually began to improve and she started to envisage a shared future with her husband. Some months after these events, our meetings did draw to a close, but that was by Lucy's own choice: her husband was offered a post in a university some hundreds of miles away, which, after a lot of thought, they decided to accept.

Lucy's narrative provides examples of shame that most of us would recognise, but it also illustrates a further important point that Williams makes, which is that it is not being seen by anyone that we fear: it is being observed by someone whose values we share. Shame is related to belonging and meaning, and it is a way of regulating membership of a community. If our values are academic and we feel we belong, or aspire to belong, in academia, shame is associated with failing or not doing justice to one's self academically. This, as anyone who has worked in an elite university knows, is a common source of the kind of examination anxiety that students find crippling. A degree of anxiety is useful, but beyond a certain point the anxiety paralyses. I've always understood that beta-blockers were originally developed to help students at music colleges overcome nerves that threaten to wreck the final performances they needed to give to graduate. If one is not an academic or a musician or does not dream of being an academic or musician, failing or not doing very well in these spheres is something we simply brush off. Williams tells us that athletes who failed in the ancient Olympic games would slink off home unnoticed, but if one is not athletic, not making the Olympics or not winning a medal in them is highly unlikely to make us feel we dare not show our faces in public. Raffaello gave a particularly touching example in one of our sessions when he reported a conversation with his father about the family's herd of cows. Raffaello told his father he should sell them because they made so little money out of selling the milk. His father was shocked: "but only poor people don't have cows," he protested. For his father, in the community in which he had always lived, not having cows, would be a sign of poverty and a cause for shame. What, by contrast, would it have meant to the dean of a cathedral? The "bizarre set-up" that Lucy portrayed was a family culture that valued achievement, particularly academic achievement; one could infer from her account of it that feelings barely figured. The origins of shame in meaning and belonging may also explain why bankers do not feel shame about gross levels of remuneration in a society where thousands of homeless are sleeping rough on the streets or forced to have recourse to food banks. The rest of society may think their rewards are obscene, but for members of the financial community, shame only bothers them when they do not succeed in the bonus race or otherwise fail to keep up with those they consider their peers. What the wider society thinks is ignored or shrugged off.

There have been various attempts to address the neglect of shame in the past two or three decades, but the practitioner who has recently put it at the centre of his thinking on violence, and drawn attention to the part played by social systems in exposing people to it, is James Gilligan, head of studies in violence at Harvard University and for close on thirty years in charge of the mental health programme in the Massachusetts prison system. Like Henry Dicks, Gilligan argues that the origins of violence lie in the interaction of biological, psychological and social determinants. In my Introduction, I referred to Gilligan's account of his work with prisoners convicted of acts of great brutality. The answer they invariably gave to the question, "Why did you do it?" was: "He or she 'dis'ed' me"—slang for disrespected. Violence, they taught him, was a way of restoring respect. The dynamic has to be understood in the context of an authoritarian, patriarchal society. In such a society, the ability to inflict or endure acts of violence commands the highest honour. The hero figure is the warrior, and the warrior is the very model of what it is to be a man. Lacking any other way of dealing with the threat of shame or humiliation, the recognised route is to exaggerate the gender stereotype and to be violent. Not to do so is felt to be unmanly, and unmanly equals gay. Gilligan writes:

> The prisons were not only a pure culture of violence... but also a pure culture of patriarchy, machismo and homophobia. Since all these attitudes seemed to group themselves together and to reinforce each other, thus forming a syndrome, and since their defensive purpose seemed so transparent (namely, to reassure the individual that he is a real man, whose sexual adequacy as a man cannot be doubted), I could not help but conclude that perhaps homophobia also underlies the whole value system and cultural pattern that we call patriarchy. This includes the exaggerated polarisation of gender roles—the purpose of which is clearly to prove something that would need no proof if it were not doubted, namely, that 'men are men and women are women, and never the twain shall meet'. Prisons are, among other things, a microcosm of the society that produces them, but a microcosm in which some of the problems that exist in the society at large are so concentrated, distilled and exaggerated that we can see more clearly there some of the uglier, or at least more dangerous and destructive aspects of our society.[3]

Gilligan argues that those who are convicted of violent offences and end up in prisons have, in general, no other way of restoring their self-respect because, overwhelmingly, they come from poverty-stricken backgrounds, from the very lowest social and economic levels of society; they are often from minority groups, have little education, and many, indeed, are illiterate; they lack any skills they could take a pride in, or that others could respect, so when they are exposed to shame they have no compensatory internal reserves of self-esteem on which they

---

3   James Gilligan, *Preventing Violence* (London: Thames and Hudson, 2001), 65.

might draw, no resources that might enable them to parry denigration, disparagement or mockery; all that remains to them is to be violent and make others afraid of them.

In his discussion of the literature on shame, *Shame and Jealousy* (2002), the psychoanalyst Phil Mollon writes:

> The integrity and preservation of the core self is crucial to shame. Shame arises both from violation of the self, *and* from exposure of the self when this is not met with the expected or hoped for empathy. In a context of empathy, the self and its needs can safely be exposed and expressed—but without empathy the self feels threatened. The presence of shame signals a lack of empathy—either an actual lack or a fear of such a lack. Similarly, the cure for states of shame and humiliation is empathy—but in its absence, shame expands unchecked, becoming increasingly toxic. When in the grip of shame, the person has no empathy with him/herself—and, without the soothing words or touch of another, hatred of the self may grow without limit.[4]

Or, we must add, hatred of others.

Gilligan shows that more may be needed than a simple expression of empathy, and more indeed may be possible. He points out that education programmes have a powerful and proven effect in reducing recidivism, and writes about the value of groups that challenge cultural stereotypes as to how "real" males should behave. But above all, action is needed at the level of public policy. What does he have in mind?

If shame is the bacillus that causes violence, the vector is the kind of society that leaves people vulnerable to it; that is, societies where there is a significant degree of inequality in the form of poverty, racism, and discrimination on grounds of gender, sexuality or age. Central to all, however, is poverty. But it is not poverty as such that is associated with violence: in a society where everyone is poor—for example a religious community—poverty is not felt to be shameful. Rather, it is deprivation in relation to others, or poverty in a society where contrasts between rich and poor are pronounced. If violence is our concern, it is relative poverty that is its most reliable predictor.

Gilligan's argument is a powerful one, based as it is upon the statistical evidence, on his day-to-day clinical experience, and a theory that provides a coherent and convincing explanation of both.

---

4   Phil. Mollon, *Shame and Jealousy: The Hidden Turmoils* (London: Karnac, 2002), 20.

His experience has been mostly with male violence, whereas the sole example of violence I related was from a woman: Fleur. It was in fact only a threat of violence, but Gilligan contends that if women act in a way that is culturally uncharacteristic of their gender, it is because they have felt so abused that they have nothing more to lose.

We internalise these cultural expectations of gender behaviour to form our "ego ideal", as Sigmund Freud called it. Charles Rycroft, in his *Critical Dictionary of Psychoanalysis* (1968), defines it as "The self's conception of how he wishes to be. Sometimes," he adds, "used synonymously with the *super-ego,* but more often the distinction is made that behaviour which is in conflict with the super-ego evokes *guilt,* whilst that which conflicts with the ego ideal evokes *shame.*"

Gilligan's conclusions are remarkably similar to those of Dicks, and the prison inmates he studied held attitudes that were very reminiscent of the "high F" personalities the latter describes. Gilligan makes no reference, however, to Dicks' work, though he does point out that Hitler was elected to power on the basis of a campaign to "undo the shame of Versailles".[5] If there is any difference between Gilligan and Dicks, it lies in the fact that Dicks says little about shame and even less about inequality. That could be because the social backgrounds of the individuals on whom they based their findings were very different. Dicks's group was made up of members of the armed forces who ranged in rank from private to lieutenant colonel or their equivalents; they came from all walks of life, and from every step on the educational ladder from farm labourer to university lecturer. Gilligan's work, by contrast, was typically with offenders whose lives had been stunted by the extremes of poverty and deprivation. Together they lay bare the bones of the authoritarian personality and the ethical dispositions through which we see it displayed in practice. Our own society, like many others, has to struggle with it, to struggle, in effect, with two problems: how to nurture children so that they do not develop authoritarian values, and how to contain the authoritarian personalities we, like most communities, harbour. Gilligan and Dicks both have a number of suggestions to make about the preventive action we might take.

---

5   Op. cit. 53.

My earlier observation that Dicks was less struck by inequality needs to be qualified, because he was as critical as Gilligan of the damaging effects of gender inequality and makes his sympathy for feminist and other challenges to it very clear. It is material inequality and privation to which he seems less sensitive, whereas that figures so significantly in Gilligan's thinking. Given that there are individuals everywhere peddling some pathological ideology, whether religious or secular, and that there is always a threat from groups who may unite around them, the perennial problem is how to keep such individuals and their followers out of power. The danger becomes hardest to contain in times of crisis, social upheaval and disintegration because they have clear and simple answers that seem, however misguided, ill-informed or even crazy, to offer hope to those who feel left out, abandoned, overlooked, disparaged, exploited or ill-treated. They offer scapegoats for their very understandable anger, and divert their frightening feelings of helplessness, shame and humiliation into fantasies about re-gaining control of borders, for example, or making the country great again and being treated with respect.

We are similarly vulnerable to criminal organisations such as drug cartels, the mafia, and gangs engaged in activities like people trafficking and prostitution, but there seems to be a readier perception of the menace they pose and a wider acceptance of the need to combat and curb them. Why is there the difference? A familiar view blames dangerous ideas. That was one reaction to both the French and the Russian revolutions, and John Gray's characteristically thought-provoking book *Black Mass*, in which he traces the origins of apocalyptic fantasies and the utopian aspirations associated with them, appears to be in that tradition. An historian of ideas will, by the nature of his discipline, be interested in the intellectual sources of those ideas, but apocalyptic and utopian thinking has its origins in our psyches and it gathers followers because of its psychosocial appeal. The French and Russian revolutions did not come about simply because radical thinkers propagated notions as to how society might be reconstructed on utopian lines: the collapse to which they refer occurred in societies that had, for complex reasons, become catastrophically dysfunctional. Reform was urgently needed, but resisted by vested interests until there was breakdown.

In situations of this sort, the most paranoid find their opportunity and they can exploit it because they have a demonology that identifies and dehumanises enemy figures. It also offers the illusion of power to those who have felt powerless and the chance of revenge on those who have humiliated them. And, above all, it offers the hope of a better life for those who knew little or nothing but deprivation, destitution and despair. Those who seize power in these circumstances are likely to feel ever under threat, whether imaginary or real, and find themselves spiralling uncontrollably into a paranoid-schizoid bloodbath. Avoiding this sort of disaster, if it can be avoided, depends less on our building up some sort of ideological immunity than on recognising and rectifying injustices and abuses before they get out of hand. In Russia an imperative was to withdraw from the war. Where there is evidence that people feel diminishing control over their lives, governments need to take action to help people regain a sense of control; where there are signs of shame and humiliation, action is needed to rebuild dignity and respect; where there is anger that physical and emotional needs are ignored, trivialised or treated with contempt, steps should be taken to ensure that the disaffected and the excluded feel heeded. Disputing the notion that the appeal of utopianism can be undermined by showing that it is irrational, Gray writes: "To dissect the errors in Marxian theory that underpinned Lenin's *State and Revolution* may be useful, but the utopian mentality is not nurtured on falsifiable social theories. It feeds on myths, which cannot be refuted."[6] So indeed it does, but it feeds even more greedily on the anger and grievance, the shame and the guilt those myths enshrine.

The phrase "utopian mentality" is nevertheless unclear. Gray seems to be warning us, but what is he warning us against? If he is not referring in a rather pejorative way to much-needed humanitarian social reforms, is he concerned instead about an aberrant mindset, the psychodynamics of which, as I said in the Introduction, are the subject of this book? From his writings and, perhaps to a lesser extent, from those of Norman Cohn it would be easy to infer that utopian ideas originate in apocalyptic fantasies and that utopian movements become violent because apocalyptic movements always and inevitably entail violence. If those are indeed his claims, they were asserted some decades after the

---

6   John Gray, *Black Mass: Apocalyptic Religion and the Death of Utopia* (London: Allen Lane, 2007), 53.

demise if the Institute for Research in Collective Psychopathology. Its research drew heavily on history and psychology. Let's look, therefore, at some historical examples of utopian and apocalyptic movements in the light of those two disciplines and try, in the last part of this chapter, to tease out more clearly the relationship between violence, apocalyptic mythology and utopian visions as to how society might be re-made.

What is the historical evidence that apocalyptic movements are always and invariably violent? The answer is that sometimes they are, and sometimes they are not. Apocalyptic beliefs, for example, lay at the very heart of early Christianity, as Albert Schweitzer pointed out over a hundred years ago in his book *The Quest of the Historical Jesus* (1906). Early Christians were convinced that the end of the world might happen at any moment and that Jesus would come again in glory to preside over a Last Judgement of both the living and the dead. Early Christianity, however, was very firmly committed to non-violence in both its teaching and practice. The author of St. John's Gospel recounts the moment of Jesus's arrest when Peter draws his sword and cuts off the right ear of the High Priest's servant. Jesus tells Peter to put his sword away and heals the servant's severed ear (John 18, verses 10-11). A little later, at his trial before Pilate, the same Gospel records Jesus as telling Pilate: "My kingdom is not of this world: if my kingdom were of this world then would my servants fight that I should not be delivered" (John 18, verse 36). Belief in a Second Coming has lain at the very heart of the faith of Christians for millennia, and this is nowhere more vividly symbolised than in the siting of Michelangelo's fresco of the Last Judgement behind the high altar of the Sistine chapel. By the sixteenth century, when Pope Paul commissioned it, many centuries had passed since the infancy of Christianity, but the idea that "the last days" were and are imminent remains a key Christian belief, as Christians attest to this very day in reciting the Nicene creed, though some take its tenets literally and others allow them poetic licence.

This is not to deny that a number of apocalyptic movements have ended in death and destruction. The last days of Hitler's Third Reich were very much like a Wagnerian Götterdämmerung, though it was not remotely Christian in its inspiration. The Soviet Union, on the other hand, collapsed without a terrible bloodletting, though untold millions had been purged or died of starvation in its formative years and, as I pointed out in the Introduction, there are claims that some ten million fatalities followed in the wake of the capitalism which replaced it.

More recently, but on a much smaller scale, there has been the case of the Branch Davidians in the USA. Its apocalyptic convictions, which were quite explicit, stemmed from its origins in the Seventh Day Adventist Church. It came to a dramatic and horrifying end, though how the Davidians actually died is disputed. Rumours that they had abused their followers in a variety of ways and that they were stockpiling weapons aroused alarm in the authorities. An FBI team was sent to investigate but the Davidians responded to it with armed resistance. The result was a shoot-out, during which many members of the sect were killed. And many others died in the conflagration that accompanied it.

Apocalyptic thinking can be conceived as displaying two elements: one destructive and the other creative. Anger at injustice is clearly the force behind the destructive urge and in religious movements it is split off and projected onto a god figure: a clear example of the paranoid-schizoid dynamic I've described elsewhere in this book. But the creative urge may be expressed in utopian ideas, whose function it is to bind the burgeoning chaos. Utopian aspirations, however, do not always stem from apocalyptic thinking: they may have other roots; and utopian societies do not, by any means, always come to a bloody end. Erich Fromm's *The Sane Society* has been described as utopian, but it is not based on apocalyptic or millennial ideas: it derives from the author's experience of the rise of Nazism in the country of his birth, his belief that an entire society may be sick or suffer from "collective psychopathology", and his concern as a sociologist and a psychotherapist to describe the contribution a psychology derived from clinical experience might make to stopping any disasters of that sort from ever happening again. His heroes are figures like Albert Schweitzer, Roy Jenkins, Tony Crosland, R. H. Tawney and others—hardly a collection of hopelessly impractical idealists or violent, psychopathic revolutionaries. David Astor's motivation in pushing for the setting up of the Institute for Research in Collective Psychopathology was the hope that we might learn lessons that would help us forestall any future outbreaks of the "scourge". Fromm's books were not sponsored by the Institute, though with his experience and psychological expertise they might well have been. The Institute was not really given to offering prescriptions, assuming perhaps that those who were interested in its work would draw their own conclusions, but if it had been so minded would its suggestions have been dismissed as "utopian"? It was never just an academic exercise.

Roger Money-Kyrle had attempted something similar in works like *Man's Picture of His World* (1961) and *Psychoanalysis and Politics* (1951), though in contrast to Fromm's writings they have the feel of armchair musings on the 'good' or 'just' society, As with Fromm, they were reactions to and reflections on the spread of fascism in the nineteen-thirties and first-hand experience of the authoritarian personality—they do not, in that sense, lack a basis in clinical experience—but, unlike Fromm's reflections, they have a nebulous, academic feel about them, and this and the fact that they simply do not provide a practical programme of reform may be why they have been neglected.

There was, in contrast, nothing academic or dreamily impractical about a community like Robert Owen's New Lanark: it worked and it prospered, and Owen, though by all accounts not very interested in money, became a wealthy man. New Lanark had drawn its inhabitants from places such as the poorhouses of Glasgow and the Highland clearances. It offered them employment, comparatively decent pay and working conditions, including (ultimately) an eight-hour day, good housing, free education and child care. At a time when child labour was shamefully widespread, Owen would not allow children under ten years of age to work. He believed that character, good or bad, was formed by an individual's environment and that benign conditions would banish vice. There is no evidence that Owen's "utopian" ideas derived from anything other than humanitarian feeling, from empathic concern, and there are few references in his writings at the time to Jacobinism or the revolutionary events in France. Owen's socialism might more accurately be described as paternalistic, but the label "utopian" was attached to it by Marx to contrast it with his own kind of socialism, which he claimed was scientific. By that Marx meant that Owen's vision of a humanitarian society could only be brought about through class war. A vital difference between the two was that Owen's "socialism" rejected violence, and in doing so it lacked the destructive element that characterises apocalyptic convictions: what Cohn had called the "urge to purify the world through the annihilation of some category of human beings imagined as agents of corruption and incarnations of evil", was missing. People might refer to his ideas as "millennial", but he did not feel comfortable with this description of them—at least in his early years. Moral regeneration was certainly at the forefront of his thinking, but he simply believed, and convinced many that he had actually shown, that this could only be brought about by education and by treating the poor as human beings. He believed that ignorance stood in the way of this rather than any ill-intentioned group. In fact, his first direct appeal to the working people, his "Address to the Working Class" in 1819, was to dissuade the poor against class hostility towards the rich. It was the poor who were being demonised, and Owen was fighting against that and the Malthusian indifference to their fate that was a manifestation of it. He attacked all the religious sects he knew about because he believed they colluded in the demonisation by blaming the poor rather than their upbringing and the conditions in which they worked and lived. Anticipating later psychoanalytic findings, he held that character was formed in the first year, if not the first six months of life. Education, and particularly the education of the poor, was absolutely central to his thinking. G.D.H. Cole, one of his biographers, writes that he did develop apocalyptic and millennial ideas later when in fact he went slightly mad. In Cole's words he became a "prophetic bore" and took up with spiritualism. But earlier he had been highly influential in persuading government to involve itself in the management of industrialisation by legislating on child labour, by limiting hours and ameliorating working conditions, and ultimately by concerning itself with education. Throughout the nineteenth century, governments feared the outbreak of the kind of revolutionary violence that had afflicted France: if Britain was able to avoid that, then Owen's practical experience at New Lanark and his influence with powerful members of the establishment must surely have contributed to the fact that humanitarian social change, right up to the creation of the post-1945 welfare state, was peaceful.

Owen left New Lanark in 1826 because he had bought another community, "New Harmony", in the New World. At New Harmony, however, eschatology lay close to the hearts of the Harmonists who had been its original founders. Owen attempted to introduce practices that he had successfully tried out and tested at New Lanark, but the community did not flourish and after a couple of years he returned to Europe. Adin Ballou's "Hopedale", also in the USA, was more successful. As with

New Lanark, it offered humane conditions to its inhabitants, and lived up to its name in engendering hope. It strove, amongst other things, to address the inequality between men and women, and maintained a strong commitment to non-violence. In so far as the inspiration for these ventures was Christian, as it manifestly was, they were all informed by apocalyptic convictions, though those convictions were foregrounded more in some cases than others. When the end came for them however, it was peaceful. Quakers took the helm at New Lanark for some fifty years after Owen left; New Harmony fizzled out after a couple of years, and Hopedale simply re-integrated into the surrounding parish when two of the people who had financed it pulled out. But they and Adin Ballou remained friendly and the experiment had lasted for some sixteen years.

For anyone who works in the field of mental health, the conviction that the end of the world is imminent is concerning because it is invariably seen as a symptom of an impending psychotic breakdown. That was Carl Jung's reaction as he describes his own experience of being invaded by such ideas in his autobiography, *Memories, Dreams and Reflections* (1963). As a psychiatrist, he says, he knew what they signified, but he managed to cling on to his sanity because of the needs of his family and his patients. It helped, too, that he was able to draw on his fantasies creatively, to learn from conversations with his "anima" and other, imaginary, split-off parts of himself so that they became the inspiration for his theory of archetypes and the source of his "analytic psychology". He could also feel that his fears were justified by events in the outside world and the collapse of civilisation that was threatened by the outbreak of the First World War. Jung's story illustrates the difficulty of teasing out what is going on. The medical man in him might make a worrying diagnosis, but the world around him also faced a crisis of the first order. The two things could be true, and indeed were true, at the same time, and the one should not be dismissed in favour of the other. Psychiatric help might be needed for the individual, but political action was required to try to alleviate the growing international tension. I once, similarly, saw a man who was suffering from deep depression, but also angry and despairing about the looming cataclysm of climate change. The complacency of governments about the latter certainly contributed to his depression, but it had not originated in that and it would have been a great mistake to have reduced the one to the other and suggested that his concern about the environment was simply a symbol of his deep underlying melancholia. Actually his depression left him unable to throw himself into the struggle to raise awareness of the environmental threat: the hope was that his recovery from it might free him to join with others who shared his alarm at the signs of fast approaching disaster.

Borderline psychotic states are characterised by moments when the individual may feel, and indeed act on, homicidal impulses, and moments when their murderousness is turned against themselves, as we saw in the story of Fleur. The parallels with the patterns of cults like the Branch Davidians may shed some light on the psychology of the 'Pied Pipers' who play a leading role in them, but the motivations of the vast majority of those who become intoxicated by apocalyptic thinking may be very varied. It would be absurd to suggest that the millions of Christians who regularly recite the Nicene creed do so because their sanity is precarious: they may well attach little more weight to the meaning of the words they utter than they do to the tenets of a multiplication table. If this sounds cynical, cynicism is not intended. Many of us buy a newspaper because we share its overall values, but it may also contain sections that do not interest us, or articles with which we disagree. A person who walks up and down Oxford Street with a placard announcing that the end of the world is nigh may be a little dotty or he may have just stumbled on it as a way of making a bare pittance. Reference to individual psychopathology may have its uses but it doesn't explain very much: borderline psychotic imagery is often lurid, which fascinates some and repels others. Cohn suggests that we find apocalyptic ideas weird because they have a mediaeval feel about them, but for others that has little meaning because their appeal, he argues, is that of a sort of primitive folk remedy for their desperate social conditions. The implication of that is that there is a need for a genuine and realistic effort to ameliorate those conditions.

If apocalyptic convictions have not always lead to violence and 'utopian' visions are not always based on them, we need, finally, to ask: are they always irrational? In the past century we have faced two deadly serious apocalyptic threats: the first was of nuclear war, a danger that remains even if, with the collapse of the Soviet Union, it was generally believed to have receded—until recently, that is, when Vladimir Putin's pronouncements have re-awoken widespread fear. The second, of course, is climate change, with warnings of ever-increasing urgency from the scientific community of floods and gales and other extreme weather events that will wreak havoc, make large parts of the planet uninhabitable and cause massive socio-political problems as extensive areas of the world become too hot to live in and populations try to migrate to cooler climes. One possibility is that the two threats could react with each other as attempts to manage mass migration lead once again to the rise of authoritarian regimes and increasing international tensions. The overwhelming scientific evidence is that we face an existential crisis, yet there is a widespread lack of urgency, if not apathy, dismissiveness and denial. Why is this?

There may be a number of reasons: until recently, the threat, for many people, has felt remote; people do not have the facts, or the training to understand them if they do; powerful vested interests challenge those facts and lobby against attempts to curb their activities or encourage the development of energy sources that do less damage to the environment. Would a psychotherapeutic perspective have anything to offer?

The Climate Psychology Alliance is a movement of psychotherapists who try to understand the psychology of those who persistently and perhaps wilfully ignore the warnings. They are in denial, the Alliance claims, but it is a claim that just leads to a stalemate: the question is why? And can we do anything about it? Part of any answer to these questions may lie, if we may return to it again, in the model put forward by Money-Kyrle, in the two kinds of conscience he writes about and the two ways of seeing the world associated with them. It is characteristic of certain mental states that we pay little heed to the evidence unless it comes from people with whom we identify: 'facts' are not trusted unless the person providing them can signal that they are 'one of us'. Denial, moreover, is not just saying "no" to something or "I don't believe it." It is a manic defence, and as such, an attempt to manage anxiety. There is a hint of powerfulness about it which points at what lies behind it: that it is an attempt to protect ourselves against the threat of being overcome by feelings of powerlessness, of depression, of loss and despair. Denial is a common reaction to the loss of a loved one, it is part of the process of finding some way of accepting the loss; it may similarly be a way of coping with a piece of terrifying information such as a diagnosis of cancer, or, in the case of the climate crisis, a fast-approaching threat to our continued existence. To envisage denial of the danger as a manic defence suggests that we need to confront and alleviate the anxiety that underlies our resort to it, and challenge the argument that there is no alternative to the neo-liberal consensus that, for the past three or four decades, has held parties on both the left and right of the political spectrum in thrall. That consensus stripped the poor and disadvantaged of a once-trusted advocate (its own party) and has left a sense of abandonment, betrayal and cynicism. Cohn tells us that one of the factors that lay behind the lure of apocalyptic ideas in the Middle Ages was that those who were drawn to them had no other reliable means through which they could seek redress for their grievances. Skilled artisans, by contrast, often fared better because they were organised in guilds. It is not hard to understand, however, that those who felt defeated, isolated, and destitute, those who had lost the last vestiges of any human dignity, might well clutch at the hope of divine intervention. In the present situation we may dispense with fantasies of chariots of fire bursting through the heavens to come to our rescue and punish the evil doers: we need to convince people that there is an alternative, and that alternative, humanistic policies based on the best available evidence, is one to which psychotherapeutic thinking can make an invaluable contribution.

It may also be helpful to look at denial from the perspective of Gilligan's findings. How are they relevant? It is not hard to understand how people on the breadline fail to be alarmed by dire warnings about climate change because their struggle for basic survival is so immediate and desperate. They may well feel that "these things are not for the likes of us", even though they stand to suffer most from the disasters scientists foresee and fear. Their lives are stymied by a crippling sense of powerlessness. Those politicians and industrialists who ignore or deride the evidence appear, however, to be stuck in a different, more 'macho' mindset. From their public utterances one gets the impression of individuals who feel it is not manly to allow themselves to be troubled by concerns about the future of planet earth, and underlying that are the same sorts of anxieties as lie at the root of the violent behaviour of the prisoners Gilligan worked with. To act like a poor, frightened woman is not how 'real' men should behave: it would invite derision.

The attitude may be modified a little by the fact that the forebodings with which they are challenged come from scientists, and scientists in the patriarchal gender divide are seen as highly rational. Rationality is associated with maleness, so we might expect respect for what scientists are telling us, but it seems that fear of derision outweighs all other considerations. One might speculate that the reason why the other apocalyptic threat of the past century, that of nuclear war, was by contrast taken so seriously was that it seemed like a male stand-off with the two sides confronting each other and locking horns, like two stags. The slang expression "willy waving" suggests that many people know what it is all about. Some readers may react to this scornfully, pointing out that there was a danger of armed forces taking over all of Europe and it had to be resisted: we needed to prevent the Cold War becoming a hot war. Denis Healey was Defence Secretary for part of that time and he tells us in his autobiography that he shared that view, but later came, like others, to believe that he had been mistaken, that the Soviet Union had no ambitions to overrun all of Europe: it simply wanted a buffer zone between itself and Germany. When we remember how much the Soviet peoples had suffered during the Second World War that makes very good sense. Others would highlight the fact that the military-industrial complex in the West depended on the tension between East and West for its livelihood, as indeed did the many thousands of people to whom it gave employment. To suggest that anxieties about gender roles may have had a part to play in all this may seem like trivialising something extremely serious, 'man's work', but my point is that a threat may be perceived as a matter of life and death when it is congruent with the values of patriarchy and more patchily respected when, as in the case of climate change, it relates to them more ambiguously.

It is hard to know how to conclude these reflections on apocalyptic prophecies and some of the better-known utopian experiments because their history has been so diverse. The warnings of scientists about the damage we are doing to the environment need to be taken with the utmost seriousness, but some of the movements that have been fired by millennial fantasies in the past and in the present day have been malign and some benign, some have been homicidal and others harmless; some have inspired utopian initiatives but there have also been visions of more humane societies whose roots have lain elsewhere. The link between apocalyptic ideas and violence is problematic; they certainly contain anger, but it does not follow that that anger can only be vented in violent acts. All psychotherapists make a distinction between the recognition of anger as an emotion and how it might be expressed: recognition is regarded as healthy whereas violence is seen, except perhaps in cases of self-defence, as pathological. In a similar way, the early church may have believed that a Second Coming could happen at any moment, but its members were urged to put their relationship with God right, not to grab the opportunity to settle old scores or take it upon themselves to punish evil-doers. "Repent, for the kingdom of heaven is at hand" was the message that has echoed down the ages. Any blanket blackening of apocalyptic thinking ignores these facts. If, moreover, the conviction that the Last Days are imminent does not invariably lead to violence, apocalyptic fantasies cannot in themselves be the source of such violence. They may signify that an individual's state of mind is disturbed, but those who are borderline psychotic do not always become homicidal. No one has ever claimed that Jung, whom I mentioned earlier, ever went on a killing spree. The fantasies of the borderline psychotic may resonate with others because their sanity is similarly precarious, or because they live in a society where the prevailing religion portrays its god or its gods as inhabiting a world outside our world, a divinity or divine figures who will break through into our world and punish behaviour they have designated disrespectful and transgressive – in the case of Christianity the dishonouring of the Almighty's creation, as, for example, in the neglect or ill treatment of the poor and the powerless. It is worth repeating what Cohn tells us in the conclusion to *The Pursuit of the Millennium* (1957): that the pain that attracts people to millennial fantasies is the pain of not belonging, of rootlessness, marginalisation, destitution and abuse, and the feelings of shame, humiliation, hatred and murderous rage such misery evokes. The violence that may erupt derives from the patriarchal values that guide the way these feelings may be expressed: as Gilligan argues, these are the values that provide the licence and the encouragement to kill. Money-Kyrle's model and Gilligan's findings complement each other in that the individual whose ideal self is patriarchal sees the world in terms of black and white, in terms of obedience and disobedience, in terms in which any self-respecting man believes it to be his duty to become the enforcer of what Lacan calls the "loi du pere"—including the "laws" of gender it entails. The danger of any uncritical blackening of apocalyptic beliefs as the source of violence is that they focus on a lifeline of the desperate. They may be pathetically deluded, but the failure to grasp that they are "not waving, but drowning" and act accordingly, will bring about the very violence we fear.

A further problem is that violence may indeed be something we fear but we may at the same time have some 'secret' sympathy with it. I know from experience of working in an institution plagued for a period by violence how tempting unconscious, or half-conscious collusion can be, because, in a culture marked by explicit or implicit denigration, others act out the anger we cannot otherwise express. There is also resistance to moving more to a position of concern because it is hard to give up our demons, which may be why we prefer 'poverty porn' or holocaust 'porn' or crime 'porn' to efforts to do anything about the social evils that gave and continue to give rise to poverty, racism, and criminality. None of this merits either optimism or pessimism: we can only try and hope that, with a better understanding of the dynamics of shame and guilt, these evils can be more imaginatively and effectively addressed.

6. Only Connect

"What can psychodynamic psychology contribute to our understanding of the persecution of people on religious or moral grounds? Can we learn anything from it as to how we might prevent or at least contain, the barbarism it sanctions? Can the practice of psychotherapy offer us any insights into a different, more inclusive, sort of ethics? And, if so, can we glean any guidance on steps we might take to further it?" These are the questions I said in the Introduction I intended to explore, and in this penultimate chapter I gather together some of the threads I followed earlier and attempt some sort of answer. The final question, however, I shall leave to the conclusion. I will start by quoting from a letter I received a few years ago from the late Anthony Ryle, a former consultant at St. Thomas's Hospital in London and the originator of cognitive analytic therapy:

> It has long seemed to me that therapy usually ends up addressing
> ethical issues and is effective when it offers genuine respect to those
> who have been 'dis'ed'; many therapists provide this despite rather
> than because of their theories and many I feel fail because their theories
> and practices incorporate complacent negative social values or drown
> their essential respect in theoretical complexity.
> Egalitarian social beliefs and practices are the only defence against Cohn's
> plague, and therapists should proclaim and defend them. But often
> therapists follow rather than lead, offering spurious scientific support
> for harmful beliefs (e.g. in my lifetime in respect of homosexuality and
> gender inequalities).[1]

As I did not have a chance to discuss these observations with Ryle face-to-face, I am not sure how far his first sentence reflects a view one commonly finds amongst therapists that issues may arise from time to time that require and justify one taking a moral stand. This is

---

1   Letter from Anthony Ryle, 11 April 2009.

         https://doi.org/10.11647/OBP.0416.06

a difficult problem, but I recall seeing a young woman some years ago who had had an analysis and then, after several years, came to me for some further sessions. In response to her behaviour on one occasion, her analyst had referred to her "tarting around". When she queried the moralistic tone of his comment, his response was: "Well, isn't that what anyone would say?" Rather angrily she retorted: "But the whole point is that you're not anyone: you're an analyst and you're supposed to be helping me understand what I do". She felt alienated by the analyst's remarks, any therapeutic alliance between them was weakened, and she found it harder to trust him thereafter. Would her analyst have made a similar remark to a man?

Ryle's letter conveys his concern that the therapist's attitude to the patient should be one of respect. He does not refer to Roger Money-Kyrle's writings, perhaps because Money-Kyrle focusses much more on the changes that might come about in the internal world of the patient. I described these in Chapter 4. Ethical issues and shifts in the way we perceive and relate to other people, Money-Kyrle argues, are an integral part of any therapy, but he uses his clinical experience to look at its wider implications. He had shared the prevailing consensus after the First World War that moral ideals and dispositions were simply a matter of taste, but the rise of fascism in the thirties made it impossible for people to believe that the values of a Hitler or a Mussolini were as good as those of the liberal democracies. Where Plato had argued that the model for ethics and politics must be the ethics and politics of the wise, Money-Kyrle contends that the questions we should ask are: "How do our moral and political preferences change with increasing psychological insight? Do the preferences of different people remain divergent? Do they tend to converge? Or do they converge in some respects and remain divergent in others? If so, what is the type of morality and ideology towards which they converge?"[2]

Money-Kyrle puts the problem in this way because, as a student of Moritz Schlick in Vienna, he had been steeped in logical positivism and its invalidation of ethical discourse. When we find some atrocity such as

---

2   Roger Money-Kyrle, "Psychoanalysis and Ethics" in *New Directions in Psychoanalysis*, ed. Melanie Klein, Paula Heimann and Roger Money-Kyrle (London: Marshfield Reprints, Tavistock Publications, 1955), 424.

the bombing of a school or a hospital unspeakable, however, we need a language that expresses our horror and revulsion. The implication of a logical positivist way of thinking—that our feelings about such atrocities are simply statements about what we enjoy or do not enjoy—feels like a further atrocity. Troubled by the logic of the philosophical tradition in which he had been trained, Money-Kyrle found himself obliged to take up a position that is implicitly very immodest: that the analyst is the model of insight and therefore of morality. This is neither credible nor defensible, as several examples I cite later (in this and the next chapter) show. Nor is it necessary. Insight, moreover, is the picture that emerges when there has been some emotional, rather than some simply cognitive, connection; it is the description of an experience rather than something purely cerebral. Therapists merely need to describe what they observe, that is, that there is a tendency for a conscience based on love to replace one based on hate and fear. The following examples illustrate what may happen. First of all, let's return to the story of Fleur.

In the two excerpts from Fleur's story that I recounted in earlier chapters, readers may recall that she voiced a lot of hate towards me personally, on and off, for several years, the culmination of which was the incident in which she directly threatened me. The hate and the threats arose from fear: fear of being invaded and fear of abandonment. As I was concerned that she would feel any attempt at interpretation as an invasion, interpretation was for a long time a temptation I carefully avoided. This worked and, after a while, Fleur began to respond with interest to my tentative efforts to make links. I remember one occasion in particular, when I suggested that she identified, perhaps, with the aggressor, because it was too frightening for her to feel weak and helpless. I could see from her physical reaction that the thought had struck home and she herself reported in the following session that for a few days it had stopped her harming herself. But it did not last, she told me thoughtfully. It did, however, reflect her growing trust and openness to psychological ideas. Much later, as I related, Fleur became very affirming about the insight she felt she had gained. Apart from these touching signs of diminishing defensiveness, there was one occasion when she came in and declared that she had discovered a new way of committing suicide: by eating apricots.

"Because they contain cyanide?" I said.

"Yes," she replied.

"But you'd need to eat an awful lot of them."

"About two hundred weight," she replied wryly

"But you're anorexic," I reminded her. And we both laughed.

The humour seemed, amongst other things, to be a sign of increasing friendliness, though I was fully aware of the grimly serious underlying message, which after a week or so led to a further admission to hospital. The increase in trust it reflected meant that we could talk about her relationship with those who were medically responsible for her and that she would listen when I pointed out to her that her psychiatrists had their own anxieties. If she treated them as enemies and simply refused to take some drug they thought would help her, there was a danger that her refusal would be seen as coming from the psychotic part of herself. But if she could explain her reluctance to take something they had prescribed because of the side effects she suffered, her treatment could become a more collaborative affair and they would be likely to offer her something else. Fleur also became quite thoughtful about me in small ways, asking me one day when I had fitted her in over the midday break if I had managed to have some lunch. I began to feel I was being treated as a real person, and I attributed this to her sense that our sessions were a place where she could feel safe: safe both emotionally and physically because she was, after all, a woman who needed to talk about sexual abuse, sitting alone in a room with a man. But I also had not abandoned her; I had in fact fought to make it possible for us to continue meeting. Her psychiatrist had had a long-term plan for her to go into a therapeutic community and a place eventually became available. Although there was sadness on both sides when Fleur received a letter offering her the vacancy, she was now able to find the resources within herself to move on. Therapy had not been a "miracle cure", she observed, but she had survived. And so indeed had I.

For the second illustration, I want to return to Clare. Readers may remember that she did not know what psychiatrists were treating her mother for until she was a grown woman, but her mother had been in and out of hospital throughout her childhood and adolescence. Often her mother wanted to be rid of institutions and her relatives would have preferred her to be living in her own home. Often they seemed to assume that Clare could move in and look after her, and one major problem for Clare about being single was her fear that her aunts would put pressure on her to become her mother's carer. She resisted the idea, but constantly felt it as a threat hanging over her. I said on a number of occasions that there was no way she could do what her aunts had in mind: it would destroy her. Her mother needed professional care, and she, Clare, needed to be free to live her own life. Eventually, her mother became a resident in an institution that could provide the nursing she needed, and Clare would struggle to find the fare to visit her there, usually managing it every two or three weeks. She also rationed telephone conversations with her, but gave her mother a small monthly allowance because she had next to nothing from which to buy toiletries and other things she needed. These visits were not easy because Clare's mother could be abusive and would occasionally bite her, but Clare would take her out, buy her clothes, and sometimes take her to church. Although her mother would often talk nonsense, it seemed that Clare would try to say something to calm her and bring her some peace. I was left with the impression that Clare had found a gentleness and a tenderness towards her mother, now ninety, that contrasted markedly with the tone in which she had talked about her before. This was just a year or so before her mother's death, after the deaths of her brother and partner. Her brother had often spent time with his mother before he died, then Clare became the sole visitor and kept up her visits until her mother passed away, aware of how much that meant to her. After her death, Clare gradually began to succeed in various small ways as if she could now allow herself to realise some of her aspirations and potential. We talked about this from time to time and I wondered if in these final months she felt that there had been some sort of reconciliation, that she had been able to atone for all the hatred that had festered in her for so much of her life. Psychodynamic psychology has no concept of forgiveness but it sounded as if that might be the appropriate word for what Clare now felt. In forgiving her mother she was also, perhaps, forgiving herself. She had always been deeply distressed by any abuse that her mother had been subjected to, as, for example, when her mother was attacked on one occasion by two youths with baseball bats in an underpass, but equally by the poor quality of the food served up to her in the residential care home. Now, however, anger with her mother and hatred of her madness had given way to sadness that her mother's life had been one of such cruelly protracted suffering.

In the last paper Harry Guntrip wrote before he died, he records something similar. He had been a congregational minister until the age of forty-nine, but had also been drawn into emergency psychotherapy during the war by the professor of medicine at Leeds University. In 1946 Guntrip accepted a post offered to him by Henry Dicks in Leeds University's Department of Psychiatry. Faced with a choice between continuing his religious ministry and committing himself full-time to teaching and psychotherapeutic practice, he decided to devote himself to the latter, acting, amongst other things, as therapist to the Anglican Community of the Resurrection at Mirfield. He describes a childhood in which his mother, depressed and worn out emotionally by the care of younger siblings when she was little more than a child herself, was unable to give him the warm affection and engagement he needed. Initially unable to relate to him, as he experienced it, she later physically abused him in a way that can only be described as sadistic, sending him out to buy new canes to beat him with when the old ones broke. His father, by contrast, was gentle and supportive, and his mother would never lose her temper in his father's presence: his father's love in fact appears to have mitigated some of the lifelong harm the abusive relationship with his mother wreaked on his mental health.

Guntrip appears to suggest that his mother's ambivalence about being a mother lay behind a tragedy that befell the family when he was three and a half: the loss of a younger brother. He had no memory of his brother's death, and could only repeat what his mother had told him: that he begged her not to let his baby brother go. Throughout his life, however, he felt a compulsive drive to keep active, which alternated with mysterious collapses into exhaustion. He felt that this was somehow linked with the tragedy. He had a lengthy analysis with Ronald Fairbairn in Edinburgh and then in London with Donald Winnicott, but neither broke through the amnesia. Then, on the very night that he learnt of Winnicott's death, a series of dreams began in which he found himself, night after night, re-visiting all the houses of his earlier life until, after some six or seven months, he had a dream in which he saw his dead brother lying on his mother's lap. "What can psychoanalytic therapy really accomplish?" he asks. All the analytic work with Fairbairn seemed to have prepared the ground, both intellectually and emotionally, but it was Winnicott's insight into the sense of abandonment and the fear and bleakness felt by a child with a depressed mother that ultimately enabled his death to lift the repression. Guntrip felt that he benefitted greatly in different ways from the two leading figures from whom he sought help; they had, with their infinite patience and insight, made it possible for him to go back to and work through the damaging experiences of his early life. "You can't give anyone a different history," he says, "or a new set of basic memories. But one's 'centre of emotional gravity' inside shifts more and more into everyday life in the present, and the deep underlying past changes into an accepted 'sadness' as much for one's parents as for one's self".[3]

My final example, Stephen, is someone I have not written about in earlier chapters. He had begun his working life as a journalist, but now held a senior and very responsible post in the Press Office of a prestigious institution in London. He was in his mid-thirties, and well over six feet tall. With his shaven head and self-assured manner he was a powerful presence, but he was also friendly, good humoured and invariably engaging. He said that he had come because he was troubled by "an undisciplined kind of heterosexuality", and that for the last nine or ten years he had been leading a double life. He was happily married, with two small children, a boy and a girl; he was a good husband and father, but there were days when he would waste hours surfing the internet for pornography, and nights when he would find himself frequenting prostitutes. At that moment he was "in a repentant phase", and feeling ashamed of his behaviour, but he knew that this was part of a pattern, and that sooner or later "a compulsive attraction to the very seamy end of sexuality" would return. He had found a road alongside a common a mile or so away from where he worked where there were girls under lamp posts looking for business. Sometimes "things would happen", as he put it, but more often he just wandered around. He felt as if he had a split personality.

3   H.J.S. Guntrip, "What does Psychoanalytic Therapy Really Accomplish: My Experience of Analysis with Fairbairn and Winnicott", *International Review of Psychoanalysis 2*, 1975.

I asked him which side of himself he felt was real. "That's the kind of question psychiatrists ask", he replied. Then he thought for a moment and said "both". I wondered how he managed to conceal this "wild side" of his sexuality from his wife, but his work, he explained, offered him the perfect excuse. He commuted to London from a town in Essex, but he often had to stay late and he could always say that he didn't want to disturb the family in the small hours. A friend, an engineer, who was temporarily working in Saudi Arabia allowed him to stay in his flat whenever he needed; he was pleased to have someone keeping an eye on the place. Stephen's wife knew where he was, or thought she knew, and she trusted him. He was aware that his exploits were "stupid" and "dangerous" and "wrong", and he'd swear to himself afterwards that he wouldn't do it again, but he'd fallen once more in the past two or three weeks. "Curiously", he added, these night-time jaunts were not a "source of joy" or a "thrill". It was often "grinding", "going through the motions", travelling up and down the road and not enjoying it.

The morality of his double life deeply troubled him. He knew full well that the women he sought out were likely to have had a history of abuse, and he was perpetuating it. The drug dependence that drove them into prostitution was a form of self-medication, a way of trying to alleviate the pain in their lives, but he was adding to their degradation and colluding with it. He described his moral outlook as "very masculine", and then went on to explain that in most areas of his life he was very disciplined. As he put it, he had "a strong sense of should" and of "obligation". He was also very religious. When he felt troubled he would at times sit in the Lady Chapel of a nearby church, where he found the atmosphere and the stillness calming. He was taking instruction with the aim of becoming a Roman Catholic, and he'd recently been on a retreat and talked to the person conducting it about his problem. It was there that he had been advised to seek out someone who could offer him professional help.

He worried that his interest in pornography betrayed some deep misogyny, but he found that disturbing because it conflicted with the values he consciously espoused, and indeed those with which he had been brought up. His mother, for example, was not an avowed feminist, but the humanitarian foundation to which she had devoted so much of her life was fighting, amongst other things, against the exploitation and abuse of women.

I said it would help me to form a clearer picture of him if he could tell me a little about the family in which he grew up. He told me, with understandable pride, that his father was a sports personality of international renown, but he had been left disabled by a vicious mugging just before he, Stephen, was born. His father had made enough money, however, to provide for his family and his wife gave up her job to nurse him through it. When Stephen was about eighteen months old his mother went back to work as the family finances were becoming more precarious. His father stayed at home and busied himself with fundraising for sports facilities, coaching and committee work, and he was in considerable demand to open events and commentate on radio and television. His mother continued to work. She held a managerial position in the foundation he had mentioned and she had served for as long as he could remember as a lay magistrate. His parents, he said, shared a loathing for the mean and materialistic values they believed had poisoned the country since the eighties; both were "on the side of the angels", concerned by the plight of the poor, or women, or children, and would initiate or join with others to do something about it. "That's my parents", he added. They had been very driven, had reaped the rewards of their labours, and their marriage had been "idyllic".

Stephen had in effect been brought up by his father, not least because his father was the parent who was normally around the house. His childhood, he said, was "as near blissfully happy as it gets". He and his father had been physically and emotionally really close throughout these years. He had always been closer to his father than his mother and they were very much alike, but he missed him and worried that his mother might die before him, though she was physically stronger and would most likely outlive him. If his mother died first she had her friends and would cope, but his father, he thought, would be lost. He, in a way, was the more dependent of the two.

There were siblings: an older sister and a brother. Stephen was the youngest. His brother was happily married and a successful solicitor, but his sister was single and a continuing worry to her parents. Stephen's relationship with her was "scratchy"; she was "bossy" and "patronizing". She had never had a relationship with either a man or a woman. Perhaps she would prefer the latter. He didn't know and it didn't matter: she just needed to find someone.

He was convinced she had been badly affected by the traumatic assault on her father, but she would always bat away any suggestion that she might benefit from professional help. His parents, who were now retired, had lived for some years in an old farmhouse they owned in the hills behind the southern French port of Toulon, and his sister ran a not very successful picture framing business in the town, but I was never clear whether she lived with her parents or independently.

Returning to his own problems Stephen said he didn't think he was depressed. He had read a book about it and he felt it did not apply to him. His mood was more one of sadness. He knew that in part this was about the loss of his mother and father. Living in France they were now more physically distant, but he was also dismayed by his father's decline, and the sight of someone once so strong in body and mind now clearly becoming more frail.

Stephen had originally imagined that he might need about ten sessions, but I thought the issues that underlay his compulsion were deep seated and that he needed to give himself two or three years. He was concerned about being taken for a ride and asked me how we would know when to stop. I said that people often brought a symptom or symptoms, and that it might be clear to both sides that the therapy could end when the symptoms were no longer a problem. That could be the aim, but I sensed that he had very mixed feelings about being "cured", so I added that I believed that if we could engage with the conflicts he was trying to manage through his risky behaviour he would find a better way of coping with them and both of us might feel that the therapy had worked. I realised that this might seem rather vague so I proposed that we should meet for ten sessions and then have a review. He agreed to this, but added that he could not possibly commit to coming once a week. He also wanted to pay me himself in cash, partly because he did not want his wife or any possible funding body to know, but also, I think, because of his conviction that his compulsion was a moral issue for which he felt he should pay some kind of penance.

Sessions would usually begin with an account of whether he had "fallen" or not, and we would then explore the context in which this had happened. Early on he reported that he had spent a couple of hours looking at a pornographic video of a man urinating in a woman's mouth. I thought for a moment or so and then I said "perhaps it's a question of what you do with your hate". He reacted as though transfixed and for some minutes remained silent., but it was as if for the first time he could recognise that alongside his love of women there were also some significant negative feelings, and we needed to learn more about them.

When we next met, two weeks later, he spent much of the session talking about the comment I'd made. Eventually I said that wrestling with love and hate is, for most of us, the most difficult task in life. We all have to manage the hate we feel towards those we love, but for some the burden is harder than others because of their upbringing. He had become aware of the hate in him, but it was a mystery to him. He found it difficult to fathom because he remembered his childhood as idyllic. There was a silence. I broke it by saying that one of the things I had noticed when we first met was that he had said very little about his mother and I wondered if that might in some way be significant. He said that his relationship with her was good and always had been. Good, but distant. They spoke on the "phone" every two or three weeks, though there was "not much exchange of feeling at depth". He had never been as close to her as to his father, but he had a lot of admiration for her. She was very intelligent and able. Then, after a pause, he said he didn't want to find excuses for himself in family relationships. He disliked the tendency of social workers and psychiatrists to blame the parents of children who got into trouble. He knew perfectly well that there were inadequate or abusive parents, but it was too easy to accuse the mother or father when a child went astray.

I said that it wasn't a question of blaming the parents, but unless one believed in innate wickedness the behaviour of the children had to come from somewhere. The parents might have, or might have had their own problems, parents who, for example, had in turn failed them, or there might be other factors for which they could not possibly be held responsible such as physical or mental illness. He himself had conjectured that his sister's difficulties stemmed from his father's depression. Such things might not be the parents' fault, but a child could hardly remain unaffected by them. Therapy was not about making glib excuses for them, but acknowledging that a child is a human being, has feelings about the way other members of the family relate to them and how they experience their lives and their world, and if they can be given the opportunity to voice those feelings there is the possibility that they can learn to manage them constructively and move on.

Stephen said he felt a moral failure. He was a married man and had made a promise to be faithful, but he was being disloyal to his wife. Yet he found his "sexual indiscipline", as he called it, beyond his control. I mentioned Carl Jung's observation that we don't have complexes: they have us, rather as in mediaeval times people talked of possession; but it led one to wonder how much tensions in his marriage might play a part in it. "You've described your marriage as a happy one", I commented, "but you've said very little about it". "On the whole it's happy", he replied, "and good for both of us, but it's quite hard work. We were never a thunderbolt couple, but it's pretty sound". His wife was slightly older and they had married when he was in his late twenties. Occasionally he wondered if they had drifted into it. He sometimes thought he could have been quite happy as a monk. Recently he had felt some resentment at his wife's wish that he spend more time with her. There was a certain amount of tension between her needs and his own ambition and preoccupation with being a hero. He could appreciate that she wanted more of him, but he felt an almost demonic need to impress. His sexual indiscipline, however, had started before he got married and he had believed it would "just fade" when his first child was born. He found the demands of his children exhausting, and he did not feel he was a particularly good father. He also reported that his wife had been away for a few days and he had not felt tempted. He acknowledged that his relationship with his wife contributed to his compulsion, but I think we both had the feeling that it had deeper roots.

I privately thought that if the state of his marriage had been the source of his Jekyll and Hyde metamorphoses he would have had been more likely to have had an affair, but, as he pointed out to me on reading this through, you have an affair with someone you love: for the prostitutes he felt little but contempt. "Would he feel embarrassed to tell me what it was about them that turned him on?" I had once asked him. He was not embarrassed, he replied: he was attracted to the despair of women on drugs in short skirts. "Attracted to their desperate neediness", I said. "Yes", he replied, and then after a short pause I said that I wondered if he was in some way trying to be in touch with a desperately needy part of himself. "There is the adult Stephen, who is successful. and confident, and portrays his marriage as a happy one, but there may be a very different part of you that we only get glimpses of in this way—rather like a small child who does not have the language to tell you what he wants, but takes you there and points." Stephen responded thoughtfully that the sadness he had mentioned when we first met was linked with a haunting sense that there was something missing. But he didn't know what. After a pause he described a dream he had had several years before. In the dream he was lying in bed beside a tramp. He feared that the tramp might be hostile, but then realised he was simply needy.

Towards the end of this first period, Stephen said that he was feeling rather positive about our sessions and wanted to continue. His earlier fears about therapy had faded and he now realised that it might take longer than he had originally imagined. He also agreed to come once a week. He remained ambivalent, however, and would tell me that he had been too busy to think about our sessions or that his problems were trivial and that I must have more troubled people who really needed my help. But his problems were not trivial because he would have lost his job if he had been found out, and it might well have cost him his marriage and left his children without a father. I really worried, too, that he would not be able to cope with the shame. Another indication of his mixed feelings was that he would occasionally make pointed remarks about how much I cost, but seemed not to resent parting with money for prostitutes. I never found an opportunity to bring this out into the open, but as with others who shared his addiction I could not help comparing charges and services, and wryly reflecting that I seemed the cheaper option! I remembered, too, his fear of being taken for a ride, though he allowed this to happen to him two or three times when a woman would ask him for money and then make an excuse that she needed to get something, presumably a fix, promising to return in a few minutes. He knew that this was a trick but he would let himself be cheated because he felt guilty about having the money they needed.

I made a mental note of all these things, but I did not feel able to put them all together into powerful interpretations partly because the dynamics seemed very complex, but also because I sensed that that would not help him anyway as he would simply reject ideas for which he was not ready. Perhaps we both need to bear "unknowing", I suggested, a word he later told me he found helpful, not least because of its religious connotations. As time went on, however, and we continued to struggle with these issues, his compulsions weakened, and he reported two incidents that brought home to him the risks he was taking. The first was that he received a call from a prostitute in the middle of the night whilst he was in bed with his wife. He managed to reassure his wife that the woman had got the wrong number, but I had wondered before if "mishaps" like this reflected an urge to wreck his life. At the back of my mind was the paper by Winnicott in which he writes that some high-achieving people destroy their lives because their success feels false. An outside observer may be puzzled, but the individual concerned is seeking the hidden gain of feeling real. But Stephen did not experience one side of his divided self as false or unreal. As I recounted earlier, he was clear that both felt authentic.

On the second occasion he said that he had narrowly missed being caught when, in the small hours, a police car had drawn up alongside him as he was walking away from the red-light district. "What was he doing there?" they asked. He had had the presence of mind to say that he had been working very late, couldn't sleep, and had come out for a breath of fresh air. His explanation was accepted, in part, no doubt, because he was well spoken and it seemed very plausible, but it was a close shave and on more than one occasion he showed me headlines in the local press about arrests being made in the area he frequented.

I asked him, as one might ask someone who voices suicidal thoughts, how his parents might react if he were arrested. He said he didn't know how his mother would take it, but his father would acknowledge that people do some very strange things in pursuit of sex. He had heard him make similar observations before. It would cause them both considerable distress, but he knew that they would not disown him.

From the outset I had always felt that Stephen was an impressive young man and I had always wondered whether I was good enough. As I intimated earlier, this often took the form of fantasies that there must be practitioners who could make penetrating, incisive interpretations that would sort it all out. Then I would remind myself that he could make little use of insights that went over his head. Moreover, he did not complain that I wasn't helping him. Quite the opposite, in fact:

he told me that our meetings stirred up a great deal in him and he regularly tried to give himself space afterwards to reflect and digest. All of which led me to believe that the anxiety was actually something that he, Stephen, was constantly plagued by, and that I constantly picked up. I remarked on several occasions that, for all his outward success, I suspected that he was constantly troubled by doubts as to whether he was good enough, "up to it", "measuring up". He usually responded by agreeing that this was really a problem for him, but one day he came in and started the session, almost before he had sat down, by telling me that it had struck him with the force of a revelation that he had grown up in a family that included some extraordinary people and that he had never really appreciated how this had affected him. His father, as he had told me when we first met, was famous, his mother was a person of immense quiet competence in her own right, his American wife was the daughter of a senator, his uncle, who had been a very senior civil servant, was master of an Oxford college, and so on. It was important to understand, he added, that his parents had never put any pressure on him to shine; his mother was not remotely like a Chinese "tiger mother". His parents would simply ask their children about their dreams and aspirations and give them emotional and material support to pursue them. They would only worry if they saw them drifting, as his sister clearly was. He had begun to feel that the obsession with being impressive was a poison. Larkin's lines about parents "fucking you up" haunted him, and he had become concerned about the effect his own need to be a hero might have on his own young family.

I suggested that behind his driving ambition lay feelings of inner impoverishment, emptiness, despair and futility, and that his "sexual indiscipline" was a way of trying to manage them. In response he described an occasion before his marriage when his uncle had invited him to dinner at his Oxford college. The setting was grand, and the food and wine superb, but he was nauseated by the narcissistic parade of glittering prizes: this former student had become a judge; another was the president of an investment bank, another was a prominent politician, and yet another was being courted by all the senior members because he was worth millions and they were hoping for a substantial donation. Even the college chaplain seemed to be involved. He couldn't help contrasting their lavish self-indulgence with the poverty and desperation he witnessed in his secret life, where he often in fact felt more at home. As he rose in the hierarchy he felt an ever greater need to escape from it because it was all so meaningless and hollow. The lower depths and the darkness of the red-light district were the places to which he escaped, and when he did find himself there he often just walked around thinking.

A few weeks later Stephen announced that he would be taking a short break to visit his parents in France. His wife was going to Washington and taking their children with them. He would therefore be with his father and mother alone. When we met again soon after he had returned, he started by telling me that he had had an insight that felt as momentous as when he had been struck by the impressiveness of his family. Spending time with his mother had suddenly brought home to him how self-contained she was, how carefully she hid her vulnerability. Somehow you couldn't get near her; she seemed sealed off. A year or so earlier a younger brother of whom she was very fond and with whom she had had a close relationship had died of a brain tumour. It had happened quite suddenly, and everyone, including his mother, had felt it was a terrible tragedy, but she did not cry. She had simply stepped in and taken care of everyone. He knew that if he left his own children with her, he could have total trust in her looking after them and protecting them from harm; they would want for nothing, physically, but she was emotionally undemonstrative and always had been. You couldn't get near her. He contrasted her with his wife, and was rather amused to realise that he had married someone who was the very opposite. He had spoken to one or two relatives about his mother and they all expressed surprise that he had never been aware of that before; he simply hadn't seen what was clearly apparent to other people. I said that the way people are when you are a child is simply part of your world and it usually does not occur to you that there is anything odd about it, or that the way you relate to others may be linked with your experience of key figures in your early life. He said he now realised I had been right to connect his nocturnal adventures and his attraction to pornography with his mother, although he did not understand all the ins and outs of it.

His nocturnal forays, however, were becoming less frequent and at the same time he reported that his relationship with his wife was much improved. The physical side of it was good and there was a growing warmth between them. They were mutually supportive and he described himself as being "in love" with his children. Unlike his wife he was not besotted with babies, but as they grew into small children so did his enchantment with them. Then one evening he came in and said, almost before he had sat down, that he had had a momentous week: he had taken his laptop home and his wife, while briefly searching for a website, had stumbled across some of the pornographic sites he had visited. He had forgotten to wipe out the traces. She was very angry and upset. Stephen said he would not have expected her to react in any other way. He didn't try to justify or excuse himself, and it led to their really talking. For the past two or three days they had done little else. He thought that it had helped that he could reassure her that he was struggling with the problem in therapy, and it now meant that he no longer had to conceal his sessions with me.

I wondered if there was a part of him that wanted to be found out, especially given his carelessness in destroying the evidence, but he reacted, as before, with scepticism. His use of pornography was now out in the open, but he continued to keep quiet about his dealings with prostitutes for fear that, if his wife found out, it would create a storm that their relationship could not survive. His visits to the common were rarer now, but he would still occasionally find the temptation irresistible. As I mentioned earlier, he had become friendly with one or two of the women and would ring them up and arrange to meet them in their homes. On one occasion he had gone to the flat of a woman he knew around midnight. There was a small girl of around eight lying in the corner of the living room. She was clearly unwell and the sight of her completely changed how he felt about the whole encounter. He suddenly felt moved by her vulnerability: she needed her mother, and maybe a father, not this male stranger who was about to do nasty things in the bedroom to someone she loved and depended on. The mother, moreover, chain smoked, so it was hardly a healthy environment. The child needed a parent who would take care of her and protect her from harm. His concern was such that he found himself unable to continue, so he paid the mother and left.

Not long after this, Stephen announced that the institution he worked for in London was re-locating to the south west. This meant that he and his family would be moving and our sessions would have to come to an end. I was concerned, as he was, that this was earlier than would have been desirable, but there was nothing we could do about it. There were perhaps three occasions before we ended when he succumbed once again. Whether or not they were associated with our ending I could not tell, but on the last occasion he reported that he had made a date with a prostitute and had found himself on the doorstep in the pouring rain at two o'clock in the morning. A sense of the sheer stupidity of what he was doing overwhelmed him.

When we met for the last time he sat down and said that he did not know what my attitude was towards gifts, but he had brought me two presents. One was a book in which he had written some words of gratitude and appreciation. I was touched. The other was a compact disc of songs by Bruce Springsteen. "I know it's not your taste in music", he said, "but I thought you might like to listen to the song I mentioned early on. Do you remember?" It was a song both despairing and defiant about a man who has lost his money and his wife, a wife who now lives in style somewhere else. It hints at hurt and exclusion, at rejection and humiliation, at failure and loss, but he feigns indifference and claims that it no longer signifies because he has found solace elsewhere. "These things don't seem to matter much now. Tonight, I'll be on that hill with everything I got. Lives on the line where dreams are found and lost. I'll be there and I'll pay the cost for wanting things that can only be found in the darkness on the edge of town".

I met with Stephen at his request several years after he had moved and he told me that, although there was a red-light district not far from where he was now living and he had felt its temptations, he had not yielded to them. Two or three years later he came to see me again. He had moved once more, and was very happy in his new post. His children were now almost grown up, his relationship with his wife was very good, and he felt that his compulsion was no longer a problem. He was confident now that it was very much under his control.

I'm not sure if it would be appropriate to describe these as examples of love replacing hate; rather, perhaps, they reveal that as fear lessens, hatred is more easily left aside, and other feelings, perhaps above all compassion, surface, and there is reconciliation, and peace, however fragile. In Stephen's case, which I have only been able to outline in the barest detail, the morality of what he was doing had led him to follow advice and seek therapy, but initially he had thought of his problem as one that he should have been able to resolve by will-power. In his own words, as I related them, his morality was a "masculine" one, rooted in rules and obedience, discipline and indiscipline. A different kind of morality emerged as we talked over these issues week after week, one more centred in empathy, in the ability to identify with the feelings and needs of another, and as that grew so did his sense of personal autonomy; the split that had driven him, quite literally, to dark places, had lost its force and if we had been able to continue we might have better been able to track how that had come about, but he had markedly changed his life, and now felt much more in charge of it.

My examples are taken from work with individuals, but John Alderdice, as I related in Chapter 4, depicts a parallel process that, in favourable circumstances, may bring peace between hostile communities. In the case of both individuals and communities, a great deal of time, work and patience was needed to bring about these developments because the trauma they had suffered was both cumulative and deeply entrenched.

It is also sad to observe that a change to treating others more compassionately is not invariably the outcome of psychotherapy. In a recent volume, *Psychoanalysis in the Age of Totalitarianism* (2016), the chapter by the German psychoanalyst Knuth Muller describes the involvement of American analysts in some very sinister programmes during and after the Cold War, sponsored by the US Intelligence Community or, to refer to it by its initials, the "IC". Muller proudly acknowledges the part played by the US psychoanalytic community in the fight against fascism and Nazism during the Second World War, but then adds:

> At the same time, it is lamentable that some analysts seem to have lent their services so uncritically to the US military and intelligence community by using analytical material for intelligence purposes. The reputation and influence of analysis rose to unprecedented heights in the US between the late 1940s and early 1960s. In receiving continued financial aid from the IC for Cold War-related research on topics including SD, stress, sleep deprivation and psychoactive drugs, aspects

of their work—sometimes undertaken in utter disrespect for the
Hippocratic Oath and the Nuremberg code of 1947—contributed to the
development of modern psychological torture techniques, thus in some
ways supporting the totalitarian structures that they were originally
committed to counteracting.[4]

For Muller, as for most of us, such behaviour is ethically indefensible:
a despicable betrayal. But how could it come about? For Christians and
Buddhists the cultivation of compassion lies at the very heart of their
faith, yet in Christendom there was the Inquisition and the defence of
slavery, and Brian Daizen Victoria in *Zen at War* (1997) has described
the largely unquestioning complicity of Japanese Buddhists in Japanese
militarism.[5] One can only speculate that there are individuals who
can undergo a training yet remain untouched by it at any but the most
superficial and intellectual level. They may be further examples of
the phenomenon I mentioned in the Introduction, individuals who,
as characterised by Fairbairn, are in love with a system. It is hard to
comprehend.

Perhaps this is the point at which we might take stock. For two
thousand years, the Christian Church has taught that we shall go to Hell if
we disobey the Almighty's commandments. Dante's *Divine Comedy* is just
one great literary work that famously conveys this message, but countless
"Doom" paintings, frescos, mosaics and other representations of the
"Second Coming" in churches throughout the Christian world remain to
warn the faithful. After two world wars, however, not to mention more
recent cruel and bloody conflicts, there are many people who feel that
we have made quite a good job of creating Hell for ourselves on earth.
For those of us who have survived, there may be some lessons we could
learn from those experiences if we think it worth trying to understand
the psychosocial forces involved. Some scientists speculate that we might
do better if we were able, while we still have our wits about us, to wander
off into the universe and find another planet on which we could settle,
but the problem is that, like Lear, we can only take ourselves with us. We
need to become more insightful about our make-up.

---

4   Knuth Muller, "Psychoanalysis and American Intelligence since 1940: Unexpected
     Liaisons", in *Psychoanalysis in the Age of Totalitarianism*, ed. Matt Ffytche and Daniel
     Pick (Abingdon: Routledge, 2016) 159–60.
5   Brian Daizen Victoria, *Zen at War* (New York: Weatherill, 1997).

"O! let me not be mad," cries Lear, "not mad, sweet heaven; keep me in temper; I would not be mad!"[6] But are we mad? A few years ago a Belgian colleague described the society in which we live as borderline psychotic and asked me whether I agreed with him. Certainly there seems to be something in his observation, given the homicidal and suicidal violence with which we are confronted; the delusions and the paranoid-schizoid demonisation and dehumanisation of minorities, immigrants, "benefit scroungers" and others; the splitting and the double binds; and the widespread resort to self-medication in the form of alcoholism and other drugs. It is a common experience in psychotherapy to sit with someone who is borderline and wonder if they are mad; but madness is so much part of our everyday experience that we can easily feel helpless when we see it all around us, put it down to human nature, and sink into a pessimistic and stoical resignation. Yet, as I have shown, there is a history of analysts who, alongside those who specialise in forensic work, have both practically and theoretically tried to fathom this psychopathology. Dicks says quite explicitly that, apart from some notable exceptions like Rudolf Hess, his interviewees were not insane; rather, their authoritarian personality traits were an attempt to find a way of living with the values of a patriarchal, authoritarian culture.

What, then, might we learn about ethics from psychotherapy?

If the concern from which we start is human suffering, there are at least five areas in which psychotherapy has important contributions to make.

First and foremost, psychotherapy offers connections—and the possibility of connectedness. Critics often argue that practitioners teach their patients to see things according to their theories, that they learn nothing from their patients, and that any change in those patients, as Gellner contends, comes about through suggestion. I have tried to show that, on the contrary, it is the patients themselves who often make key connections or the connections may be suggested by the context. We are often so transfixed by the idea of the unconscious and of the analyst's supposedly privileged access to it, however, that we find it hard to

---

6   William Shakespeare, *King Lear* (London: The Arden Shakespeare, Routledge, 1991), Act 1, Scene V, lines 43–44.

imagine that such information would be available to anyone who can create an atmosphere of trust and has the patience to listen.

Secondly, much of our suffering, especially 'neurotic' suffering, derives from our reluctance to recognise ourselves as part of nature. For Sigmund Freud, that meant human biology, and in particular sexuality. Indeed, Freud's lifelong campaign to make people aware of the effects of our antipathy towards ourselves as sexual beings became the subject of dispute amongst those who originally followed him, just as the role of sexuality remains controversial between and within the various schools today. Some worry that it is in danger of being relegated, whilst others believe that it is only one amongst a number of forces that motivate us and that our emotional needs and the feelings associated with them are as much a part of our nature as the urge to reproduce. Whatever position one adopts (and feelings, in fact, figure as prominently in Freud's case histories as instincts do in his theoretical writings), the crucial point is that Freud's courage in speaking about things that could not normally be spoken about established the view that there are 'internal' forces that we neglect at our peril, even if, for one reason or another, we are uneasy with the details of Freud's portrayal of them—and even if the concepts of Freud and Jung are ultimately superseded by those of neuroscience.

Thirdly, emotional needs may not simply atrophy or cease to trouble us when they are not met, and impulses and desires cannot, therefore, be banned without consequences. They often become laden with hate and find expression in forms that harm us insidiously. Dependency needs that are unmet, for example, do not simply fade away: they usually persist into adult life where they may wreak havoc in relationships, or, if repressed and entangled with shame and anxiety, betray themselves in a censorious, persecutory response to the very legitimate dependency of others. In rare cases, they may erupt in some mind-searing tragedy, or, as the jargon has it, 'acting out'. The Jamie Bulger murder could be seen as an example of this in that a small, defenceless and trusting toddler triggered the fear, the hatred, and the contempt the two young perpetrators had come to feel for a projected, dependent part of themselves. Similarly, sexual impulses may not simply be prohibited with impunity: the danger, as with homosexual desire, is that they become the locus of splitting and projection and then persecution, the source of a paranoia that ultimately festers and poisons the culture as a whole.

Fourthly, development and healing come from within us, but can only take place where the environment makes that possible. The neuroscientist Steven Rose describes a similar process he calls "autopoesis" in his book *Twentieth Century Brain*.[7] Psychodynamic psychology makes an impressive contribution to our understanding of the interaction between genetics and environment. However, it courts the danger, especially in turning that understanding into concepts of 'health', of becoming prescriptive, and in so doing of foreclosing on possibilities of variation and richness—with consequences that may be inimical both to the individual and society. For example, Winnicott, clearly troubled that William Shakespeare's sexuality might not measure up to some psychoanalytic developmental ideal, wrestles with this dilemma and tries to resolve it by allotting "health" second place after "richness", and by arguing that "health" includes the toleration, and indeed enjoyment, of difference. The tone is one of graciously making exceptions for historically gifted individuals, a Michelangelo, perhaps, or a Leonardo, or a Newton, or a Keynes, or a host of others. But all of us, whether we have had a benign or a malign beginning in life, or whether we would fare well or poorly on some scale of health or maturity, struggle to create a way of surviving and thriving in our environment. Sometimes this works brilliantly and brings us fame and fortune and fulfilment; in other cases, it works in part and we succeed in one area only to fail in another. Sometimes it fails overall, as in psychosis, for psychotic delusions, as Jung once observed, though notably creative, sadly oblige the individual to live apart from the community. Such tragic outcomes are fortunately not widespread, and the earlier chapters illustrated the often moving attempts by individuals to make something of themselves out of the varied strands of their life experience, and their search for help when in one area or another they find themselves stuck. Often very creative individuals fear they will lose their creativity, but this is usually unfounded, and the impulse is recovered. It is akin, in many ways, to mourning, which, if we can allow it to happen, leads eventually to signs of new or resumed life. For Melanie Klein and her followers, in fact, mourning and creativity, in its widest sense, are intimately connected. Indeed, it is a matter of common experience that grief usually opens up

7   Steven Rose, *The 21st-century Brain, Explaining, Mending and Manipulating the Mind* (London: Jonathan Cape, 2005).

a heightened sensitivity to the feelings of others, an increased ability to put one's self in their place and to imagine how others might see and feel about the world. All schools record this, though the terms in which they do so may differ; some talk, for example, of the withdrawal of projections or use concepts such as 'mentalisation', but the phenomenon they describe is the same—the growth, in fact, of humanism.

Fifthly, that the nurture of humanism depends on far-reaching, psychologically-informed change.

7. Conclusion

"Where there is no vision, the people perish".

Proverbs 29:18

The psychoanalytic movement was, as we have seen, deeply committed to the creation of a more humane society and the erection of barriers against any relapse into barbarism in the four or five decades just before and after the Second World War. Forays into the socio-political field, however, had begun as early as 1908 with Sigmund Freud's paper on "Civilized Sexual Morality and Modern Nervousness" in which he linked the neurotic problems for which his patients sought help with the repressive attitudes towards sexuality of the culture in which he had grown up. Although the language Freud uses is rather grandiose, the essay reflects his deepening conviction that helping individuals had its limits and that profound change was needed in society as a whole. This interest in the wider implications of his work preoccupied Freud more and more in the last decades of his life, but it became a matter of urgency for the psychoanalytic movement in general with the rise of fascism. This was widely perceived as bewilderingly irrational, and many wondered if its leading figures might be mad. Unsurprisingly, governments turned to a psychology that focussed on the irrational and doctors who treated the insane in the hope that they might throw some light on it. Analysts themselves, on the other hand, found their minds rather concentrated on the real as opposed to the internal world when the Nazi regime singled out psychoanalysis as "Jewish science" and publicly consigned Freud's books to a bonfire. Whether one is interested in that context or not, thinking about the wider implications of what practitioners were learning from their patients took place around issues that people at the time found deeply troubling. It was not, therefore, simply theoretical or

     https://doi.org/10.11647/OBP.0416.07

academic; it emerged in profound and urgent existential crises, and was part of a life-or-death struggle for survival.

Opinions about the social and political implications of psychoanalysis, however, have varied as widely as opinions about the social and political implications of Christianity. For some, psychoanalysis is a psychology that implies quietism. As Philip Rieff puts it in *Freud, the Mind of the Moralist* (1961):

> It undercuts the whole problem of the freedom of the individual in any society, emphasising instead the theme of the anti-political individual seeking self-perfection in a context as far from the communal as possible.[1]

Others, such as Erich Fromm, took the opposite view and argued that we can only expect to be healthy in mind if the society in which we live is itself sane. For some, it appeared to provide the psychological justification for capitalism or for a liberal democracy, whilst for others— such as Wilhelm Reich and Herbert Marcuse—its implications were as revolutionary as Marxism and the two should ideally be married off.

Diverse and even conflicting inferences might well be drawn from Freud's creation, but can they all, equally, claim legitimacy? Henry Dicks confronted this issue in his paper "In Search of our Proper Ethic", which was originally his address on becoming chairman of the British Psychological Society in 1950. "It is my impression that there is some sort of shyness when it comes to the verbalisation of values," he writes. The subject causes "tense silence" and "an anxious defensiveness", followed by relief when the talk turns to more concrete matters. "Yet it is ludicrous," he adds "for any of us to pretend that we are neutral, desiccated scientists to whom all ideas are equal and to deceive ourselves that our sole value goal is the disinterested search for truth." The proper end of psychotherapy, he tells us, is integration, a bringing together of different aspects of ourselves, aspects that our culture may well have deemed deviant, or taught us to think of as opposites. It resembles Carl Jung's "individuation" and in effect harmonises Freudian and Jungian views. Therapists are mediators in a creative process and catalyse a reconciliation of conflicting parts of ourselves, parts that we have split

---

1   Philip Rieff, *Freud: The Mind of a Moralist* (Chicago: University of Chicago Press, 1959), 256.

off. Two other goals that have had wide currency in psychotherapy he discards: "self-realisation" is close to integration, but it is "an introverted value with considerable narcissistic under-tones", while "adjustment" is very flawed because societies themselves can be sick; adjustment implies intolerance of deviation and puts pressure on people to conform to what may well be collective psychopathology. Whether conscious or unconscious, it is pernicious, and therapists are very misguided if they allow themselves to collude with it in individual therapy or as an aim for society as a whole.[2]

Jung, for example, was accused, fairly or unfairly, of collaborating with the Nazi regime, and the controversy about that continues; but the concern Dicks voices was less about an allegedly blemished war record than about a subtler betrayal of values and a collusion that was careless or unwitting. Watchfulness about this was widespread in the post-war years, but vigilance now seems to have given way to complacency, which does not, of course, mean that it is no longer justified. For example, the picture that Jacques Lacan paints of the paternal role is disconcertingly close to that which Reich, Erik Erikson, Fromm, Dicks and many others identified as the psychological seed bed of the authoritarian personality. Fromm in *The Fear of Freedom* argues that it leads to the formation of a sado-masochistic personality structure, while Dicks, describing the typical patriarchal family, writes:

> It is my contention that this widespread pattern of authoritarianism
> in state and home was inimical to the growing of strong and self-
> regulating "democratic" personalities.[3]

Nothing could be further from my mind than to suggest that Lacan and his followers had fascist sympathies; I am puzzled, rather, that they commend a particular configuration of family relationships that others have held to be malign, and that they appear to be blithely unaware of these widely disseminated views. Bruce Fink, one of those followers, in his book *A Clinical Introduction to Lacanian Psychoanalysis* (1999), writes as follows on homosexuality in a chapter on "Perversion":

---

2   Henry V. Dicks, "In Search of Our Proper Ethic", *British Journal of Medical Psychology* 23(1 & 2), 1950, 1–14.

3   Henry V. Dicks, *Licensed Mass Murder* (London: Heinemann for Sussex University Press, 1972), 35.

To return to the question of why one boy might agree to give up pleasure while another might refuse, we see that in cases where there is a very close bond between mother and son, a father—in order to bring about separation—has to be quite forceful in his threats and/or quite convincing in his promises of esteem and recognition. But the very fact that such a close bond has been able to form suggests that the father either is incapable of fulfilling the paternal function or does not care to interfere (perhaps happy to be left alone by his wife, who is now preoccupied with her son).

A little later Fink adds:

It seems to me that we have to shift our focus from the kind of father Freud often seems to have *presumed* to exist—that is, the father who forcefully enunciates his will to separate his son from the boy's mother (the pervert being the son who obstinately refuses)—to the all-too-common contemporary father who is a much weaker figure and is often confused about his role.

It is, claims Fink, an indication of "the inadequacy of the paternal function."[4] The language has sinister echoes of negative, stigmatizing stereotyping: "The Jew...", or "The Negro...", or "The Arab" and so on. At best these are pathologizing generalisations, at worst they form the core of Norman Cohn's categories of human beings regarded as incarnations of evil or agents of corruption. Sexuality is portrayed as a matter of choice, and strangely there is no mention of the father's love for his son and the son's need to feel that love, a lack that too many young (and older) men complain of in therapy. Were there no "perverts" or homosexuals in Freud's Vienna? Perhaps the ones Freud encountered and wrote about were just day-trippers.

In *Jacques Lacan: Outline of a Life. History of a System of Thought* (1997), the French analyst Elizabeth Roudinesco writes: "Hating as he did anything that resembled fascism, Nazism or anti-Semitism [Lacan] had no illusions about Marshall Petain's intentions regarding the Jews". Later she adds: "Though [Lacan] was never a Petainist he had little sympathy for the Resistance either. He hated oppression but was

---

4   Bruce Fink, *A Clinical Introduction to Lacanian Psychoanalysis* (London: Harvard University Press, 1999), 173.

scornful of heroism."[5] Where others joined the Underground or fled and enlisted perhaps in the Free French Army, Lacan elected to stay and try, with as much integrity as possible, to survive. According to John Forrester: "At the end of the war, Lacan made a journey to England in search of a moral climate that owed its strength to a war spent in defence and struggle rather than in capitulation and deception".[6]

The relationship between ethics and psychoanalysis, however, was one that had long interested Lacan. They were intimately and intricately related to each other, he believed, but they are not the same: mental health may provide the groundwork for ethical behaviour, but health and goodness differ. An example would be Donald Winnicott's argument that delinquency is a sign of health and hope; what the delinquent does may be wrong and we may find it trying, if not despicable, but compliance can signify deadness. Nor did Lacan share Money-Kyrle's view that successful psychoanalysis brings about humanism. Humanism was a term with which Lacan had no wish to associate himself, but his anti-humanism should not be taken to imply that he was indifferent to, or indeed enjoyed, human suffering: it stemmed rather from his opposition to the Enlightenment belief that human beings are essentially rational and benign. Psychoanalysis and ethical behaviour are not necessarily the same thing because we have free will; not as much as Jean-Paul Sartre and his fellow existentialists liked to imagine, but enough. You can analyse for ever, but there comes a point when the patient has to decide for themselves whether to choose right or wrong. What might guide them? Lacan's answer is Immanuel Kant's categorical imperative, often simplified to the injunction to treat other people as ends in themselves, not as means to our own ends: it is wrong to harm someone else because it is wrong. There is no other reason.

Lacan cites Antigone in the play by Sophocles as an example of ethical action. Antigone chooses to bury her dead brother knowing that in defying Creon's decree she will be punished by death. Her resolve is to obey not Creon, but "the holiest laws of heaven", according to which the dead must be interred. Her cold defiance of the state is her moral

5   Elizabeth Roudinesco, *Jacques Lacan: Outline of a Life. History a System of Thought* (New York: Columbia University Press. Translated by Barbara Bray, 1997), 158.
6   John Forrester, *The Seductions of Psychoanalysis* (Cambridge: Cambridge University Press, 1990), 105.

choice, and it is out of such choices that we create our selves. Antigone's decision is also, Lacan claims, an example of the death instinct, but most of us, I think, would recognise both her determination to see that her brother's mortal remains are treated with due respect and the wish to join him simply as very human marks of mourning.

One of Lacan's followers, Uri Hadar, professor of psychology at Tel Aviv University, tries to highlight the relevance of Lacan's "existential perspective", as he calls it, to the Israeli-Palestinian conflict, where violence smoulders on year after year only to flare up periodically in conflagrations of obscene brutality. How can this cycle of death and destruction be brought to an end? Hadar advocates "social activism": groups of individuals joining together, giving their time unpaid to fight injustices, challenge abuses, take up the causes of persecuted individuals or communities, act as good Samaritans, and create bonds of friendship and trust. One of these, the Palestinian-Israeli orchestra set up by the pianist and conductor Daniel Barenboim, is well known. Such overtures are admirable, but they are only possible in a society that tolerates them: non-Jews attempting to befriend Jews in Nazi Germany would have placed themselves in great danger, as indeed do those who try to help homosexuals in societies that are virulently homophobic. And that kind of reaching out is really only a drop in the ocean of grievance and counter-grievance that constantly engulfs any faint hopes of a peace process.

Although Hadar names Lacan as one of the authors of these ideas, there are countless gestures of this kind around the world where there is raw need or violent conflict, some inspired by the shared values of Judaism, Christianity, Buddhism, Islam or other religious faiths, others simply by humanitarian concern. Hadar acknowledges Lacan's debt to Kant and the categorical imperative, yet "moral universalism as per Kant," he concedes, "may issue in the abuse of power no less than Nietzschean nihilism."[7] It is not, however, the universalism that Kantian ethics advocates that is the problem, but its patriarchal, authoritarian character, the dynamics of which I described in Chapter 3. Authoritarian rule may, some would claim, appear to be the only hope of holding hostile communities together in certain parts of the world, but it can

---

7   Uri Hadar, *Psychoanalysis and Social Involvement. Interpretation and Action* (London: Palgrave Macmillan, 2013), 168.

never be more than a short-term solution because it engenders alienation and ultimately spawns violence.

In his paper "Kant/Sade", Lacan contrasts these two figures, Kant standing for the law, and de Sade for desire. But the contrast, Lacan argues, is more apparent than real, for the sadist and the masochist play out roles in which the sadist punishes in the name of the law whilst the masochist wants to be punished for disobeying it. Sado-masochistic dramas, whether in the form of fantasy or acted out, make sense, however, less as a search for the 'law' than as a search for a part of themselves, or a relationship that the sadist and the masochist each feel they lack, rather as in Plato's myth about the attraction of male and female. The sadist splits off and projects the part of the self symbolised by the masochist, and the masochist splits off and projects the part of the self represented by the sadist. The splitting derives from hate: their longing or desire is guilt-loaded because they feel that love can only be expressed if it is suffused with hate. Guilt about the hate leaves them feeling they deserve punishment. For example, the French philosopher Michel Foucault was someone whose interest in sado-masochism was well known, and it is also no secret that he hated his father, a rich surgeon and, by all accounts, a bully who tried to force his son to follow in his medical footsteps. To this end, Paul, his father, would, apparently, oblige him to watch orthopaedic operations, an experience that was also supposed to "make a man of him". If he identified with the aggressor, or with the victim of an aggressor in erotic play, was this to facilitate the healing and development that his father's 'loi' had failed to bring about, or was he stuck in a trauma deriving from his relationship with his authoritarian father in which he was trying to find a way through conflicts about power and powerlessness, desire and hatred, guilt and the need for punishment, all inextricably entwined?

Hadar argues that the activist morality he advocates is "always a relative morality", but moral relativism, if that is what he means, raises serious problems. If the morality of one group of people allows and perhaps encourages them to kill, torture and rape those who do not share their faith, beliefs or ideals, it is no different from the moral codes that have caused immense suffering in the recent past and very publicly continue to do so in the present. I imagine that Hadar does not mean that, but that the kind of activism he commends needs to be culturally sensitive. It also, however, needs to be based on an ethics that is inclusive. Yet inclusiveness is not a quality one readily associates with Lacan: at the level of theory, Lacanian ethics is very exclusive, intelligible only to an intellectual elite; and his views have also been very divisive. A lot of people may have been (and still are) interested in them because, at a time when so much attention was very rightly being paid to the neglected mother-child relationship, he seemed to be saying "don't forget the significance of fathers"; yet fathers, as I showed, were not forgotten. The part he writes for them, however, is far too schematic, and it is hard not to be troubled by the shady company it keeps and its association with characters whose intentions are far from benign.

Lacan's use of the term anti-humanism is unfortunate because of the very negative connotations it carries in the English-speaking world. The Oxford English Dictionary (2009) offers several definitions of humanism, the most relevant for our purposes being "Sympathetic concern with human needs, interests, and welfare; humaneness". One does not get the impression that Lacan is opposed to these values. Psychodynamic psychology, as I tried to illustrate in earlier chapters, consistently teaches us that love and desire, belonging and meaning, identity and identification with others, guilt and shame, envy and jealousy, anger and hate, fear and grief and a host of other feelings are more powerful than reason: in the English speaking world we would describe such a psychology as humanistic, not anti-humanist, and it is the humanism of the psychology that is surely the deepest source of its appeal. It is why we find case material and stories of the lives of others so engaging. Despair in the face of our endemic stupidity, violence and cruelty easily leads to the conviction that human nature is not benign, although that is not necessarily an anti-humanist position unless, like Freud (and Lacan as his interpreter) we attribute this dark side of ourselves to an instinct, perceive instincts as all-powerful, and hypothesize that there are only two of them. Just as Freud in his early period felt compelled to argue that repressive sexual mores had a malign effect on our mental and physical health, so the later Freud finds himself wondering, as he does in *Civilisation and its Discontents* (1930), if "civilisation" does not ask too much. Echoing Friedrich Nietzsche, he plays with anti-humanism and finds himself in an agonising dilemma because his humanism was heartfelt; but the dilemma was one that he created for himself. The reality is surely that we have a light side as well as a dark side: we may be stupid, violent, selfish, competitive, cruel and warlike, but we can also be wise, intelligent, compassionate, co-operative, self-sacrificing and peace-loving. Whether the dark or the light side of ourselves predominates depends on circumstances rather than on the strength of an inborn instinct. In the Palestinian-Israeli conflict, nothing would be gained by positing a death instinct as part of any explanation of its virulence. Its origins lie in the unshakeable determination of the Israelis not to be the victims of a murderous programme to exterminate the Jewish people ever again, and the determination of the Palestinians not to be deprived of their land and livelihoods because the Israelis have decided that the key to their safety is to regain the territory they lost two thousand years ago and create an impregnable state of their own. Both these positions are rooted in the patriarchal cultures and the patriarchal values which, as James Gilligan described, govern the way both Palestinians and Israelis react to each other. Trying to decide whether human beings are basically good or bad is an irrelevance; for anyone practically working to bring about a peace process it is an academic exercise. A widely held view amongst political philosophers is that, historically, the idea that we are basically good and that the dark side of ourselves only exists because of destructive institutions has provided the underpinning for some very despotic regimes. Deciding whether human nature is bad or good may matter to them, but negotiators and mediators or anyone whose task it is to try to defuse conflict, and reconcile armed or rearming factions, will have more practical questions in mind, questions about the grievances that divide those factions, the history of those grievances, the values and aspirations that influence them, the misperceptions that need to be corrected, the extent to which the hostile sides have any freedom of manoeuvre, their ability to take their supporters with them if they can come to any agreement with their opponents, and so on: down-to-earth considerations that are of the deepest significance if there is to be any hope of easing any specific dispute, however bloody it may have become.

In the nineteen-thirties, forties and fifties the dark forces that threatened us were the tyrannical ideologies and regimes that were responsible for mass starvation, mass murder and cruelty on a stupefying scale. The conditions in which democracies might thrive, therefore, became the focus of serious study. Freud himself, increasingly pessimistic about the prospects for peace, was unconvinced that democracy was the answer, and in his reply to a letter from Albert Einstein, "Why War?" (1932), expressed the view that too many of us hanker after forceful, if not despotic, leadership, and that the best we can hope for is the rule of a wise elite.[8] He seems, however, to have been alone in this Platonic conclusion: much more in evidence was the view that the craving for the guidance of the 'great man' or woman cried out for explanation. Winnicott, for example, published a paper in 1950 in the journal *Human Relations* called "Some Thoughts on the Meaning of the Word 'Democracy'".[9] After apologising for any note of naivety that might derive from lack of familiarity with the language of political philosophy, he argued that democratic institutions, in any community, reflect the prevailing level of psychological health or maturity, the most serious threat to which lies in mass disturbance of the mother-infant relationship. Two groups of people, he argued will either hinder the development of democracy or, where it has been established, threaten it: those who are pro-social, but anti-individual, and those who are pro-individual but anti-society. By the former, Winnicott presumably meant those of an authoritarian mindset, the "authoritarian personality", as it used to be called, whereas the latter would include (but not necessarily be confined to) those who are anti-social in the sense of criminal. Although they appear to be opposites and we might, on the face of it, expect them to be hostile to one another, as indeed they usually are, they may in certain circumstances have a dangerous tendency to fuse and use each other for their own nefarious ends. All communities, whether we are thinking about a school or a hospital or society at large, have to struggle with such anti-democratic elements, but it is important for us to recognise that they may form a threat too powerful to be contained.

Fromm's "Sane Society", which was also published in 1951, argued that the pathological forces in society might be undermined and the healthier elements strengthened by extending democracy to industry.[10] Fromm's thinking anticipates rather remarkably the problems we face

---

8   Sigmund Freud, "Why War?", reply to letter from Albert Einstein (1932), *Standard Edition of the Collected Works, Vol. 23* (London: The Hogarth Press, 1964).

9   D.W. Winnicott, "Some Thoughts on the Meaning of the Word Democracy", reprinted in *Home Is Where We Start From* (London: Penguin Books, 1990).

10   Erich Fromm, *The Sane Society* (London: Routledge, 1963).

today, for the "bonus culture" could be seen as an example of the failure of governments to manage the pro-individual, anti-social elements in society. Those who share Fromm's views might well conclude that the problem only exists because we do not believe in industrial democracy: we are in thrall instead to the fantasy that there are immensely talented individuals who have the ability to transform the fortunes of a firm or an institution and should therefore be paid any ransom that might secure their services. An element in the fantasy is incredulity at, if not explicit rejection of, any notion that employees might have any ideas to contribute to the running of the organisation in which they work, an implicit disparagement that might remind one, in other contexts, of racism. However, the psychologist Daniel Kahneman, in research that won him the Nobel prize for Economics in 2002, has shown that the claim that the performance of fund managers and investment advisors reflects exceptional skill rather than luck is a "cognitive illusion". Their success cannot reflect any more skill than the throw of a dice. Perhaps this is why some banks now talk of "retention" rather than "performance" bonuses. The evidence that "high-quality" chief executives have a positive influence on the performance of companies is scarcely any better, but, as with other cognitive illusions, we go on believing them.[11] Those who work in these areas know they are sustaining a myth, but, dishonestly, they continue to subscribe to it.

This post-war period also saw the emergence of a number of subtle and sophisticated studies of the psychodynamics of companies, hospitals, schools and other institutions. Although they were produced in response to requests for help with specific problems, psychoanalytic counsel has generally been to urge managements to consult and listen carefully to their employees because those who do the work are likely to be an invaluable source of wisdom. Initiatives towards democratic management, however, have been pursued quite independently of psychodynamic thinking, for, as Richard Wilkinson and Kate Pickett point out, they have often originated in the dire circumstances of employees trying to rescue an ailing company in an effort to save jobs. The Tower Colliery in Wales is a frequently quoted example of a venture where this worked very successfully. At other

---

11   Daniel Kahneman, *Thinking Fast and Slow* (London: Allen Lane, 2011), 216.

times, democratically structured enterprises have sprung up anew, as with the Mondragon Corporation in the Basque region of Northern Spain. "Mondragon co-operatives," Wilkinson points out, "are twice as profitable as other Spanish firms and have the highest labour productivity in the country".[12] A large number of studies, however, indicate that participation in management and ownership need to go hand in hand: industrial democracy, for various reasons, does not work without shared ownership. Yet the full-hearted backing of any of the political parties is lacking, even when we are faced with the grotesque abuse of companies being bought and sold over the heads of their employees as in the recent British Home Stores fiasco: we have grown so accustomed to such operations that we are inured to the contempt such deals convey. That industrial democracy has never seriously figured in the programmes of the major political parties may also stem from the reaction to the 1977 Bullock report, whose recommendations for something like the German form of it met with opposition from vested interests on both sides of industry. But that was nearly fifty years ago and it is time now, surely, for the issue to be re-visited.

Saving and creating jobs clearly plays a very important part in ensuring mental and physical wellbeing. Yet, for writers like Fromm, the case for democracy in industry lies less in any contribution it might make to the efficiency, prosperity and survival of an enterprise than in its role in affirming respect and strengthening the sense of control members are able to feel over their lives. In any democracy, however, it is essential for people to be fully and accurately informed: without an honest sharing of the facts, consultation and participation at any level are a charade. Winnicott, Fromm and others warn us of the danger of "false democracy", a sign of which, argued Winnicott, is a "frantic bolstering up of the democratic facade".[13] A free press is universally considered a fundamental of democracy, yet if the press and other sources of information in a country are largely in the hands of vested interests, is that not the ultimate gesture of disrespect? (See Appendix A).

Daniel Pick has recently given a much fuller account of psychodynamic thinking about socio-political issues in *The Pursuit of the Nazi Mind*

---

12   Richard G. Wilkinson, *The Impact of Inequality: How to Make Sick Societies Healthier* (Oxfordshire: Routledge, 2005), 306.

13   D.W. Winnicott, op. cit. 245.

(2012).[14] The study, which lays no claim to being exhaustive, traces the way in which interest in these problems has waxed and waned over the years. At times it has been massive, at others less than marginal. It is a reflection, perhaps, of the extraordinary socio-political convulsions that have overwhelmed us over the last century and the stranglehold that the ideology of capitalism has come to exert over our thinking. A psychology whose special field was perceived as the study of the irrational was relegated to a very peripheral role in a picture of the world that has given star status to rationality. Rationality is a point of pride for males in a patriarchal system because males, so the stereotype goes, do not understand feeling: it is almost a badge of virility not to pay it much heed. The blinkered view that results prevents us seeing the dangers just outside our field of vision, leaving us with control as our sole means for coping with anger, resentment, dissatisfaction, demoralisation and so on. Control may include, as it has included, not just the neglect of insight, but attempts to relegate or supplant it. It is the slippery slope to authoritarianism, and its rehabilitation in 'managerialism' is one indication of how far and how recklessly we have slithered down it.

The Allies fought and won a world war against the authoritarian regimes of Adolf Hitler and Benito Mussolini—and this victory, together with the remarkable implosion of the Soviet Union and its satellites in Eastern Europe, have left a triumphant capitalism. With fascism defeated and communism discredited, economists tell us that capitalism is now "the only game in town". If we are shocked by aspects of it that seem ugly and unacceptable, there is only talk of another kind of capitalism: "progressive capitalism" or "capitalism with an acceptable face", "more caring" or "more carefully regulated", less "predatory", "more moral", "more responsible", "reformed" or at least somehow different. For two hundred years, however, observers have wrung their hands over capitalism's pathogenic tendencies: that it treats human beings as objects and creates societies in which people are valued in terms of their material possessions; that it is prone to periodic crises; and that it generates massive inequalities of wealth. One definition of capitalism, in fact, is that it is a system based on the competitive pursuit of material gain. Communism and fascism, moreover, were both reactions to, if not

---

14 Daniel Pick, *The Pursuit of the Nazi Mind. Hitler, Hess and the Analysts* (Oxford: Oxford University Press, 2012).

offspring of capitalism. *Das Kapital* originated in Karl Marx's anger at the misery it appeared to engender, and typical crises in the capitalist system provided opportunities for communists to seize power. Similarly, fascist ideologies were an attempt to find a middle way between the amoral materialism of capitalism and the amoral materialism of communism and, once again, crises in capitalism played a crucial role in helping fascists grab control of the apparatus of government.

The assumption that there is no serious alternative to capitalism is clearly exemplified in the economist Paul Ormerod's contribution to a conference called "The Politics of Attachment", which was sponsored by the Tavistock Clinic in 1995. The papers were published in a book with the same name, and in it Ormerod writes:

> Capitalism is by far the most successful form of economic organisation invented. Yet it only exists by virtue of what might be thought of as qualities of attachment. As an economic system, it is distinguished from all others primarily because of its capacity to innovate. And innovation, if it is to flourish, requires both a stable and secure overall framework in which the innovators can realise the private gains of their activities, and a willingness and confidence amongst the population to explore, to try new techniques and new methods of working. An important postulate of attachment theory is that security facilitates the development of qualities such as initiative, self-restraint and trust, which are exactly those required for the operation of a capitalist economy.[15]

Ormerod may well be right in arguing that initiative, self-restraint and trust are important in the way he describes, but capitalist systems do not, by their very nature, offer the kind of environment that might nurture them. A degree of security, for instance, is only attained if these systems are regulated. One of the very rich businessmen who funded the Brexit campaign in the UK explained that he did so because he believed that leaving the European Community would make it possible to reduce the security of employees, and that this would drive them to work harder and make the country much more prosperous. Economic Man, once again. A more insecure workforce, however, cannot guarantee the security for children that attachment theory sees as fundamental to healthy physical

---

15   Paul Ormerod, "You Pays Your Money: Models of Capitalism" in *The Politics of Attachment: Towards a Secure Society* ed. Sebastian Kraemer and Jane Roberts (London: Free Association Books, 1996), 178–79.

and emotional growth. Employees who face ever-present anxiety about their jobs are forced to give priority to their work, and the more anxious they become, the more their ability to balance their responsibility for their physical and psychological needs and those of their children with their responsibility to their employers is undermined. Marx wrote about the contradictions of capitalism: there could not be a clearer example of what he meant.

One camp believes that a greater sense of control over one's life and a solid sense of security is fundamental to mental and physical health; the other is convinced that insecurity makes folk work harder, ignoring, or unaware of, the implications that this approach carries for physical and mental health. What does the research tell us?

Two successive secretaries of state for health commissioned Sir Michael Marmot, MRC professor of medical epidemiology at University College, London, to review the evidence on the social determinants of physical and mental health. Marmot was chosen in part because he had conducted a similar review for the World Health Organisation. Heart problems, cancers, diseases related to drugs, alcohol, smoking, poor nutrition and obesity, accidental and violent deaths, and mental illness, Marmot informs us, are the afflictions that bring lives in this country to a premature close, rather than those associated with absolute destitution. Furthermore, levels of morbidity are much less pronounced than they are in many other parts of the world, although they are still cause for deep concern. Rigorous and extensive studies carried out by teams of investigators reveal that people living in the poorest neighbourhoods will, on average, die seven years earlier than people living in the richest neighbourhoods. That is the average, but the contrasts in particular places are deeply shocking. For example, in one ward in Kensington-Chelsea, the wealthiest part of London, a man can expect to live to eighty-eight; in Tottenham Green, less than ten miles away, male life expectancy is seventy-one: a difference in life expectancy of 17 years. Marmot tells us in his review:

> The Commission on Social Determinants of Health concluded that social inequalities in health arise because of inequalities in the conditions of daily life and the fundamental drives that give rise to them: inequities in power, money and resources.

These social and economic inequalities underpin the determinants of health: the range of interacting factors that shape health and well-being. These include: material circumstances, the social environment, psychosocial factors, behaviours, and biological factors. In turn, these factors are influenced by social position, itself shaped by education, income, gender, ethnicity and race. All these influences are affected by the socio-political and cultural and social context in which they sit.

Marmot adds:

> These serious health inequalities do not arise by chance, and they cannot be attributed simply to genetic makeup, 'bad', unhealthy behaviour or difficulties in access to medical care, important as those factors may be. Social and economic differences in health status reflect, and are caused by, social and economic inequalities in society.[16]

These inequalities mean that those in the lower levels of unequal societies feel much less control over their lives, which are lived under constant threat, and it is this heightened degree of insecurity that is so undermining of mental and physical health. Inequality is above all a moral issue, argues Marmot, a matter of social justice, and as such it has important implications for economic policy. As he puts it in his conclusion to the world-wide WHO Commission on Social Determinants of Health: "social injustice is killing on a grand scale". Killing on a grand scale, of course, is what the Columbus Centre, the Centre for Research in Collective Psychopathology, was committed to investigating, though in the Centre's case the killing on which it focussed was mostly deliberate, whereas that which comes about through inequality is not intentional and has only recently begun to be understood. Marmot heads the review with a quotation from the Chilean poet Pablo Neruda: "Rise up with me against the organisation of misery".

A free-market system is widely seen as a defining characteristic of capitalism, if not a synonym for it—the well-spring, along with innovation, of its fertility in generating economic dynamism. On the face of it, there need be no contradiction between such a system and the values of humanism: after all, free markets have usually been seen as the handmaid of free speech. But there may be tensions and

---

16   Sir Michael Marmot, *Fair Society, Healthy Lives: Strategic Review of Health Inequalities in England Post 2010* (London: Institute of Health Equity, 2010), 16.

conflicts between the two in significant areas. Where medical services are provided by commercial companies, for example, the interests of patients and shareholders may be inherently incongruent, if not actually in conflict with each other. Equally, talk of the "labour market" in the field of employment stems from a mindset in which men and women are viewed as commodities.

Ormerod's argument might lead us to infer that a capitalist system is one in which the healthiest rise to the top, but apart from the evidence before our eyes, that is psychologically questionable. Those winning the most glittering prizes in a system based on the competitive pursuit of material gain may be driven by a variety of motives, including a sense of inner poverty that no amount of money can ever satisfy. John Maynard Keynes is supposed to have described capitalism as a system in which the nastiest of people for the nastiest of motives take control. Whether that is fair or not, we only have to look around us to see that, while their activities are often beneficial in creating jobs or funding philanthropy, they may also do great harm to people and the environment. Capitalism is an ideology, a powerful cluster of ideas, that fails to give primacy to human needs; its many defenders assume that those needs will be met almost as a by-product of its regular functioning, an idea that receives lucid expression in the now-discredited 'trickle-down' theory. Logically, there cannot be any significant trickle-down, otherwise differentials would not be preserved. As a system, therefore, capitalism has toxic tendencies. Writing in the first half of the twentieth century, Keynes was very much aware of these, and of the darker forces that could drive out rational calculation of interest. These tendencies have to be managed. Optimists believe this is perfectly possible, but their effectiveness is often undermined in practice by fear of creating an environment that is unfriendly to enterprise. It goes without saying that such a situation would be undesirable; at the same time, it should also be unnecessary to say that the maintenance of an enterprise-friendly environment cannot be at the expense of human mental and physical health. Or indeed lives. We may all agree that we need a police force, but who wants a police state? We may be convinced that we need the protection of armed forces, but who wants a military dictatorship?

I have made brief references from time to time to sketches for another system based on psychodynamic ideas. One such sketch, which Roger Money-Kyrle traces out in *Man's Picture of His World* (1961), lies in the tradition of essays on the 'good' or 'just' society.[17] Money-Kyrle noted the vices of capitalism as I have described them, and tried to envisage something more psychologically grounded. For him, that meant grounded in the thinking of Melanie Klein. Such exercises, however, face a number of problems. If the 'good' or 'just' society is the mentally healthy society, who defines 'health' or 'justice'? And what kind of legitimacy can these ideas claim? If we seek to alleviate suffering, moreover, the findings of other disciplines such as medical epidemiology, which I mentioned above, are highly relevant. So are those of neuroscience. For example, Simon Baron-Cohen, in his book *Zero Degrees of Empathy* (2011), defines empathy as "our ability to identify what someone else is thinking and feeling, and to respond to their thoughts and feelings with an appropriate emotion".[18] He describes the capacity for empathy as an "internal pot of gold", arguing that it has both biological and social roots: "There are", writes Baron-Cohen, "genes for empathy". He goes on to explain that these are "*not* genes for empathy per se, but are genes for proteins expressed in the brain that—through many small steps—are linked to empathy." Empathy is also, however, the legacy of parental love or, in the language of attachment theory, with which Baron-Cohen links his findings, "early secure attachment".[19] The roots of empathy are both genetic and environmental, he insists, and its presence in individuals varies from individual to individual. If lack of empathy is a permanent trait, there is probably little we can do to increase it; if the potential for empathy is there, however, fluctuations may only be temporary.

Baron-Cohen's book does not refer to the experience and reflections of people like Dicks, Cohn and Money-Kyrle, even though his research engages with the same issues of our tendency to demonise and dehumanise, and even though the insights of these authors into splitting and schizoid states appear to be highly relevant. The medical epidemiologists, on the other hand, draw directly or indirectly on

---

17   Roger Money-Kyrle, *Man's Picture of His World* (New York: International Universities Press, 1961).
18   Simon Baron-Cohen, *Zero Degrees of Empathy* (London: Allen Lane, 2011), 11.
19   Ibid. 102.

psychological insights. One example I have mentioned several times is the association between violence and the family of feelings linked with shame. Another example is the theory that a lack of control over one's life might explain the vulnerability of those at the bottom of the heap to cardio-vascular problems: the persistent sense of threat ensures that adrenaline is constantly being poured into the heart, which, along with the manufacture of the clotting agent fibrinogen, means that their physical symptoms are a physiological reaction to feelings of being chronically under stress. Different disciplines focus on different facets of the same problem. They may not actually be in dialogue with each other, but their findings are largely complementary and leave the impression of a growing scientific consensus. (See Appendix B).

For the religious, the barbaric acts that writers such as Baron-Cohen struggle to comprehend are "evil". The word allows us to express our revulsion at these deeds, but is also the kind of language that drives us back to explanations that they are the work of Satan or the Devil, which thwarts the development of a theory of human cruelty. The ultimate effect of such language is that it forecloses on our efforts to prevent or diminish it except through exhortation and the threat of divine punishment. The death instinct is a psychological version of this. Changing the terms of enquiry to focus on empathy, argues Baron-Cohen, allows us to investigate the sources of empathy, and to carry out research into how and why it might or might not develop, and how, therefore, our "internal pot of gold"—and society's—might be increased. It would only be fair, however, to point out that just this lies at the very heart of the great world religions, having, as they do, the cultivation of compassion and the dissolving of self at their core. The problem is that they lend themselves so easily to capture by the very forces they set out to oppose, and mythical traditions and practices that are supposed to affirm and feed those aspirations are replaced by rules and doctrines that are used and abused to licence the very oppression they avowedly abhor. Examples abound, but doctor and medical anthropologist Paul Farmer provides a very vivid illustration in his book *Pathologies of Power: Health, Human Rights, and the New War on the Poor* (2003), in which he makes extensive use of the concept of "structural violence". Rather than attempt a neat definition of this notion, Farmer describes many instances of what Amartya Sen in his foreword to the work calls "a kind of quiet brutality" that can dominate and devastate the lives of the poor and the powerless.[20] Farmer says that the origins of the concept of structural violence lay in liberation theology: priests who were inspired by it believed they were following the teaching of the New Testament, yet they have often been faced with persecution at the hands of the Catholic hierarchy.

Some commentators, in consequence, have hoped to find a sort of secular spirituality in the psychological traditions that derive from Freud and Jung, but their value, as I argued in the last chapter, lies more modestly in the rich web of connections or 'insights' they offer. Psychology is not, of course, the only source of these: throughout recorded history, the arts—literature in particular—have kept a sense of humanity alive and nurtured it even in the darkest of circumstances. And we tend to place a high value on drama, novels and poetry that do not simply divide the world into heroes and villains, good or evil, but which explore subtleties and complexities of character and theme, broadening our sympathies and deepening our understanding of one another.

The insights to which I refer do not amount to another ideology to which we might convert—they simply offer us a choice: a choice between ideologies on the one hand, and on the other, humanistic policies derived from the best available evidence. We could see such policies as contributions towards the formation of a human ecology. In practice, this would mean that we give priority to protecting people from violence from within or without, and aim at securing physical and mental well-being through the kinds of measures that Gilligan, Marmot and others have spelt out. Clearly, some of the qualities we might wish to encourage, such as autonomy and creativity, would be in harmony with the forces economists have identified as vital to a vibrant economy; whilst others, such as those that would favour the reinforcement of a competitive, materialistic value system and the furthering of inequality, would need to be jettisoned. A health service providing universal care would play a key role in complementing such a preventive programme. The widespread belief that health services are only affordable for rich countries has been challenged by the Nobel prize-winning economist Amartya Sen. Healthcare is labour intensive, and labour in poor countries

---

20   Paul Farmer, *Pathologies of Power: Health, Human Rights, and the New War on the Poor* (London: University of California Press, 2003).

is cheap. As Sen reports, a considerable number now have such services, including Thailand, Kerala and other Indian states, Mexico, Brazil, China, Sri Lanka, Costa Rica, Cuba, Rwanda and many more. How they function and the provision they offer varies, but there is no clash between the care they extend and prosperity. They are not a drain on resources and they do not undermine the will to work. As common sense would suggest, the opposite is the case. There is plenty of evidence, argues Sen, to indicate that there is a "positive interdependence" between the two:

> Not only does universal healthcare powerfully enhance the health of people, its rewards go well beyond health. There is, indeed, a strong relationship between health and economic performance.[21]

Kerala, Sen tells us, offers us a brilliant illustration of this. Proposals to set up state-supported health care for all some four decades ago were greeted with derision because Kerala was one of the poorest states in India, but its advocates refused to be daunted. Despite its poverty, the government went ahead and established a system that has worked so well that Kerala can now claim, amongst other things, the longest life expectancy in India, and the lowest rates of infant and child mortality. And in place of their earlier poverty, Kerala's citizens now enjoy the highest per capita income among all the states on the subcontinent.

Health services, however, treat the sick, whereas the major killer diseases of the nineteenth century, certainly in this country—diseases such as cholera, typhoid, diphtheria and tuberculosis—were largely wiped out not by the kind of health services described by Sen, which then, of course, did not exist, or by miracle-working drugs, as is widely supposed, but by prevention. Ill-health was not so much cured as prevented: prevented by improving social conditions, by better housing, nutrition, sanitation, contraception and so on. It is prevention that is the message of the Marmot review. In the nineteenth and early twentieth centuries, knowledge of the links between ill-health and social conditions was not as surely established as it is today, but the evidence is now massive and Marmot identifies six domains in which progress could and should be made. Any government committed to the mental and physical well-being of those it governs, Marmot says, must:

---

21   Amartya Sen, "Universal Healthcare: the Affordable Dream", *The Guardian*, 6 January 2015.

- give every child the best start in life
- enable all children, young people and adults to maximise their capabilities and have control over their lives
- create fair employment and good work for all
- ensure a healthy standard of living for all
- create and develop healthy and sustainable places and communities
- strengthen the role of ill-health prevention

The review spells out what these policy objectives would mean for each life stage from childhood to old age. For adults, for example, they entail employment that is "sustainable", that is, jobs that pay a decent living wage, and are not dead-end, but provide for the possibility of development; employment conditions that allow people to balance work and family life, that promote mental and physical health and protect employees against pressures and practices that put their health at risk. And, in each age group, the review repeats the need to shield people from the harmful consequences of climate change. Pickett and Wilkinson, who drew on the research of Marmot and that of Gilligan on violence, also put forward practical suggestions and recommendations as to how humanistic policies could be implemented in their book *The Spirit Level* (2009). That such evidence can be ignored can only be attributed to the 'cognitive illusion' or ideology of Economic Man, and the vested interests it serves.

How may we conclude? I began this chapter by briefly outlining and commenting on psychoanalytic thinking as to how we might create and maintain a more humane society, the upshot of which, if that is our concern, is that we need to extricate ourselves from the vicious circle of ideologies that are intimately related and feed off, and into, each other. Whilst their beneficiaries might paint them as benign, each of these ideologies has deeply pathological features, though their vices may be more glaring in one case than another; each of them entrenches destructive values and vested interests; and each demonises different groups, whether Jews, 'degenerates', 'undesirables', the 'bourgeoisie', immigrants, 'welfare scroungers', 'skivers' as opposed to 'strivers', the disabled, the disadvantaged or the poor. The portrayal of programmes and policies that reflect any concern for a more humane society as roads to the serfdom of communism or fascism originates in these destructive values and vested interests, for those roads begin with capitalism and the assumptions about human nature, or *homo economicus*, on which it rests. They lead to a sort of malevolent, ideological merry-go-round on which we are all invited to be taken for a ride, yet violence inevitably accompanies the experience, violence which—in the absence of a socio-political understanding of the underlying psychology—can then only be contained by authoritarian means. The question is whether we can find a way to step off without putting lives in jeopardy, or whether we are fated to the apocalyptic scenario foreseen by Marx.

This book has been concerned with the challenge to those assumptions about human nature, or *homo economicus*, posed by psychodynamic psychology. It has been based on work that resembles that of the conservationist who, for example, tries to clean the oil from the feathers of a bird caught up in an oil slick, or fights to protect the habitat of an endangered species. Like the conservationist, psychotherapists have amassed a body of knowledge about the way we relate to each other, and the conditions we need if we are to survive and thrive. For those who might protest that such a different model of human motivation is too bewilderingly complex to form any basis for policy, I have pointed out that much of it is based on understanding that most of us possess. I have also tried to link it with the accumulating evidence from other branches of psychology, from medical epidemiology, from neuroscience, from economists who study health, and from others who do not subscribe to the prevailing economic orthodoxy. One of them, E. F. Schumacher, wrote a book some years ago called *Small is Beautiful* (1973). The subtitle of this widely admired work was *A Study of Economics as though People Mattered*, a disturbing acknowledgement that it is so often pursued as if we do not. These contributors write from different perspectives, and, in some cases, decades apart, but their work is a plea for a society that meets our needs together with some simple and practical strategies for bringing that about. How we are to conceive of those needs is ever open to discussion, but in the seclusion of the settings I tried to evoke in my various examples, there is a learning that can deepen and enrich our understanding of them. The image of sleepwalking was used by Christopher Clark in his 2012 account of how Europe went to war in

1914, but somnambulism appears once again to have us fastened in its hypnotic grip. In this unquiet, dream-like state, we are both participants and onlookers; lost and set on a path to disaster, yet fearful of waking. Faced with urgent warnings about the dangers of climate change, we push on unheeding; troubled by the self-serving actions of vested interests, we are ventriloquized, perversely, by their values. A perennial accompaniment of the March of Folly is the cry that there is no alternative. The poignancy of our situation, however, is that, as in a Greek tragedy, there is a steady gathering of thoughtful and humane voices that might help us find our way.

Appendix A

Psychoanalysis and Democracy

The relationship between psychoanalysis and democracy is a more complex one than might appear at first sight. Psychoanalysis suffered at the hands of the totalitarian regimes of the 1930s in Nazi Germany and in the former Soviet Union, and practitioners contributed to the fight against fascism, as I have shown in earlier chapters. There are aspects of psychoanalysis, moreover, that seem inherently democratic, firstly because psychoanalytic theory is derived from listening to people, and secondly because it bases itself on the belief that there are powerful internal forces that we ignore at our peril. These forces render delusory the idea that we can be moulded like wax or clay into any shape a despotic regime or ideology pleases. In practice, moreover, Erich Fromm was hardly alone in the psychotherapy world in championing industrial democracy. Yet, psychoanalysis has been conducted at times in a tone and a manner that is decidedly authoritarian, and it has concepts that are distinctly totalitarian in their implications.

But what do we mean by totalitarianism? "Psychoanalysis in the Age of Totalitarianism" (2016) is a collection of papers edited by Daniel Pick and Matt Ffytche that sympathetically explores aspects of the relationship between psychoanalysis and totalitarianism. The volume contains an article, "Totalitarianism: a Sketch", by Joel Isaac in which the author reflects on the term. Isaac writes that totalitarianism "was linked to something like the total penetration of the human subject by the state or party." He adds: "A strong link exists between fascist rule and the making and unmaking of subjectivity or personality." And on the following page:

    https://doi.org/10.11647/OBP.0416.08

Totalitarianism was a doctrine of political order that reached into the psychological constitution and the mental lives of its subjects. It went hand in hand with the denial of a realm of social value open to conscience and individual discretion.[1]

I suppose that, for most of us, totalitarianism, whether of the right or of the left, means an ideology or political philosophy that compels compliance by every means at its disposal, by controlling all sources of information, by creating an education system and other institutions that reflect that ideology or political philosophy, and by suppressing all other, dissident views, if necessary, by force. Right-wing forms of it invariably secure power by exploiting feelings of humiliation, shame and loss of control, whilst left-wing versions tend to trivialise and disparage psychological ideas as "bourgeois ideology". With the Behaviourists, they appear to share an assumption that we are basically like clay and can be moulded into any form our rulers wish. Compliance may be the aim, but as any psychotherapist knows the (healthy) schizoid defence against that is to comply in order not to comply, rather like the vicar of Bray in the song of the same name.

Psychoanalysis, however, also has totalitarian ideas built into it, most notably in the concept of resistance. I am not for one moment suggesting that there is no such thing. "Clare" in Chapter 4 is a very clear example of someone who was aware of her own resistance, but the term suggests that the analyst or therapist is the sole source of truth and that psychoanalytic theory is beyond criticism or refutation, rather as in a totalitarian society truth is defined by officials of the party or state. Essentially, practitioners are trying to conceptualise their experience that patients may find change difficult because the patterns of relationship we have developed, the compromises we have unconsciously made to meet our basic needs, are familiar to us. They may not work very well, but change and re-consolidation involve a plunge into the unknown and all the anxiety that entails. As the well-known saying has it: "Always hold on tight to nurse for fear of someone worse". But how do we find a language that is not redolent of the tyrannies that plagued us in the twentieth century? Unfortunately, it is not just a question of terminology:

---

1   Joel Isaac, "Totalitarianism: A Sketch" in *Psychoanalysis in the Age of Totalitarianism*, ed. Matt Ffytche and Daniel Pick (Abingdon: Routledge, 2016).

for much of its history, psychoanalysis has had criteria of truth associated with it according to which theoretical disputes between practitioners, or differences of opinion about interpretation, are resolved by appeals to authority: the authority of those who were analysed by Sigmund Freud. To what extent this is still the case I do not know, but one is reminded of the Roman Catholic Church and the Apostolic succession; the claim that its authority as exclusive guardian of the truth derives from Christ's words to the disciple Peter, recorded in Matthew 16:18: "Thou art Peter and upon this rock I will build my Church".

In Chapter 6 I cited Harry Guntrip's paper on his experience of therapy with Ronald Fairbairn and Donald Winnicott. In a letter written a little before his death he enclosed a copy and said that he had recently read it at the Institute of Psychanalysis in London—"the first 'outside' lecture; Kleinian students forbidden by their training analysts to attend". In an earlier letter he refers to Winnicott's objection to Fairbairn on the grounds that he criticised Freud. If these reports are accurate, they intimate a climate of intolerance of anyone ploughing a different furrow to that laid down by the 'leader', as indeed does Melanie Klein's retention of the death instinct to avoid the accusation of deviance.

The existence of controversies and splits is not in itself evidence that psychoanalysis is unscientific: they exist, so scientists tell me, in a number of other scientific fields. To a sympathetic outside observer, a significant part of the problem may be that the psychoanalytic movement lacks any agreed way of resolving theoretical disputes. Close examination of a key controversy such as that between the Kleinians and the Freudians over the early origins of the Oedipus Complex, for example, reveals that while each side makes constant reference to the clinical evidence, both sides, with equal constancy, fail to produce any. Neuroscience might help settle some important issues. As I point out in Appendix B, it supports the views of John Bowlby and Fairbairn that we fundamentally seek relationship rather than instinctual gratification, but it does not support the idea of a death instinct. Earlier this year, however, I attended a conference on the death drive in which the three speakers, a Kleinian analyst, a Lacanian analyst and a relational psychotherapist, all simply took its existence for granted – and continued to defend it even when challenged. The danger is that psychoanalysis becomes a political religion, where the most important thing is to make clear whose side one is on by saying the right thing and displaying other identifying symbols of loyalty. Sadly this alienates many who might otherwise consider its findings valuable.

I made extensive use of Henry Dicks's contribution to the fight against fascism, but one of the papers in this volume, Peter Mandler's "Cultural Relativism and the Neo-Freudians", calls for comment, because he takes the view that the "pathologising language" used by Dicks and others was generated for propaganda purposes. Mandler quotes examples of the "stigmatising" terminology Dicks employed, and the reasons for the author's use of such terminology would make an interesting study, but to perceive it as propaganda suggests that he imagines that the War Office employed Dicks to hurl psychiatric abuse at the enemy rather as the ancient Britons hoped to intimidate and repel the invading Roman armies by shouting curses at them. How was this propaganda to be used? Was it to be dropped in the form of pamphlets behind enemy lines? Or broadcast on the radio? Or used to raise the morale of Allied troops? In fact, the paper in question by Dicks and similar papers by others were reports to the authorities at the time or published in professional journals after the war. "Personality Traits and National Socialist Ideology", though written during the war, was not published until 1950, and Walter Langer's book *The Mind of Adolf Hitler* was not brought out until 1972 because it had been commissioned by the Office for Strategic Studies (a forerunner of the CIA) and for three decades had remained classified as secret. When Langer's book appeared, Hugh Trevor Roper, then Regius Professor of History at Oxford, gave it a withering review as exemplifying all the faults of psychohistory. But psychohistory it was not: it was a psychological profile. As such, it resembled psychological profiles and artists' impressions requested by the police when hunting for an unknown murderer, rather as the police force employed Arthur Hyatt Williams, an internationally recognised authority on the dynamics of murder, to help them understand the kind of person they should be looking for in what became known as the "Yorkshire Ripper" case. The papers Dicks wrote were similarly psychological profiles, written either for the eyes of the authorities or, in the case of *Licensed Mass Murder*, for the Columbus Centre as part of the Centre's mission to understand "collective psychopathology" and learn lessons as to how its spread might be forestalled. Dicks analyses the psychopathology of Nazism in terms of national character and patriarchal values. The former is misguided, as Mandler rightly argues, but the latter goes to the heart of fascist ideology and, as I observed, links with feminism and the findings of James Gilligan, which I cited in Chapter 5. Can it be that Oxbridge professors really do not understand the differences between propaganda, psychohistory, psychological profiling or a psychiatric assessment? Or are we into territory wars?

Perhaps the most important initiative to secure democracy and prevent the spread of authoritarianism was the foundation of the European Union, but the 2016 debate about whether Britain should stay or leave was very divisive and for many people deeply disturbing. The key issue was control. Some of the 'remainers' might concede that there was a 'democratic deficit', others argued that the Union was democratic because those who occupied important positions in it had been elected. But crucially, people did not feel that. It is rather as if, intriguingly, in setting it up, the founding fathers had unconsciously replicated the pattern of the patriarchal family, the pattern so vividly depicted by Erik Erikson, Dicks and others, in which the authority lies with a paternal figure who might be benign or malign, but is invariably remote. People were presented with a choice between leave or remain; there were very few voices proposing that the country should continue to be a member, but work for its reform. The former Greek Finance Minister, Yanis Varoufakis, was a notable exception, arguing in his book *And The Weak Suffer What They Must?* (2016) that flaws in its design have been responsible for the fragmentation of the Union and the resurgence of racism across the continent. A different model was needed, not a top-down model of integration, but one based on respect for the autonomy of its constituent members, a recognition that any authority the Union might claim derived from them, and a commitment to pursue policies that would affirm and enhance the aspiration and desire we all have to feel in control of our lives.

Fears about immigration, of course, lay at the heart of that debate, and they currently represent the most dangerous and growing threat to democracy because they are so easily manipulated and exploited by authoritarian forces. The psychodynamic psychotherapeutic approach is not to dismiss those fears or suppress discussion of them, but to take them seriously and patiently address them; to bring to light anxieties that are obscure or that are felt to be too shameful to voice. People's worries about losing their jobs may be quite overt, and more understandable in some places than others, but other concerns, for example, that culture and community will be undermined, may be vaguer and indeed more veiled. They may well be more obscure, but no less powerful for that because they take us into the deepest psychological waters – the waters of our primitive jealousies and ambivalence towards siblings, and beyond that of transitional objects which, as Winnicott argued, lie at the root of culture, and therefore of identity for both the migrant and those we hope might find it in their hearts to make them welcome. Putting these fears into words, however, creates an opportunity for us to develop policies that might effectively alleviate them. One possibility would be for the countries of Europe, whether members of the Union or outside it, to create and fund a European peace force, which asylum seekers and other would-be migrants could join as an alternative to other legal routes. Such a force would provide refuge and protection, education and training, medical care and work opportunities for those fleeing from persecution and violence, including the violence of poverty and destitution. Those who have skills could be posted to places where their skills might be in short supply, and those who do not could be helped to acquire them, or to form or contribute to task forces where labour is lacking for harvesting, or the management of emergencies, disasters, and so on. They would not be competing for jobs, but meeting a need which the local population is unable to supply. The recruits for such a force would not count in the immigration figures of any individual member country because they would be part of a pan-continental protectorate, but it could also be open to young nationals of the participating European states who might be seeking adventure, the offer of further learning or training, and the experience of working in different countries with people from other parts of the world. The Conservative party floated the idea of introducing conscription before the 2024 election, but this, by contrast, would be an international, and purely voluntary service. I do not know if such an idea would be feasible, but if we do not try to find creative solutions for a problem that is desperately crying out for them, paranoid fantasies like the great displacement theory will insidiously extend their grip and the hope of a humane response to those who are utterly desperate will slip from our grasp.

'Putting these fears into words', however, may also run into another current threat to democracy: the growing 'cancel culture' and the attempt to supress opinion we may disagree with in the name of morality, which of course has been the subject of this book. It is exactly the phenomenon that Dicks had in mind when he observed that one of the dangers of authoritarianism is its tendency to provoke an authoritarian response—a sort of mirror-image fascism that is increasingly infecting institutions, including professional bodies representing psychotherapists. If the price of freedom is eternal vigilance, we need to make sure that those who vie to keep watch over us do not suffer from their own moralistic or, indeed, defective vision.

Appendix B

Psychoanalysis and Science

Sooner or later, whenever practitioners try to speak or write about the application of psychodynamic thinking to socio-political issues, past or present, the objection is raised that psychoanalysis, from which it derives, is unscientific. It is difficult to know how to respond to such a judgement because it is sweeping and dismissive, and needs to be unpacked. What is the critic saying? And what is meant by psychoanalysis? The issue is very complicated, and it is hard to do justice to it in an appendix, but there is a need to say something about it.

In his autobiography (1935), Sigmund Freud described psychoanalysis as three things: a method of investigation, a form of treatment and a body of knowledge that was gradually being built up into a science. Freud believed that it was important for his creation to be regarded as a science because it was concerned with dreams, fantasies, feelings, neurotic symptoms and other phenomena that the scientific world at the time would not otherwise have taken seriously. But Freud, as a medical man, was engaged in the empirical study and treatment of the issues with which his patients sought help; he would have been struck, as others had been struck, by the clusters of symptoms they described, or, as they came to be called, hysterical and anxiety states, phobias and obsessional neuroses. In Freud's time these syndromes were the stuff of neurological practice, and most of us would expect that any professional practitioner would learn a lot about the way our minds work from simply listening hour after hour to those who were trying to convey their experience. There are others, however, who cannot imagine that there is any learning to be had. Some psychiatrists take that view—"it's all a matter of chemistry", as one said to me—but

  https://doi.org/10.11647/OBP.0416.09

there are also those who dismiss psychoanalytic findings for other reasons. Talking with one well-known philosopher about R. D. Laing's *Divided Self* (1960), I said that I thought that Laing's descriptions of how his schizoid and schizophrenic patients saw the world was very illuminating. It is not remotely likely that they talked about themselves in some of the existential jargon in which he couched his reports, but it is not uncommon for therapists to hear such patients complain of feelings of falseness and inauthenticity, to confide that they feel they are playing roles, and it is not wildly unjustified to infer that that might be a defence against a fear of invasion and reflect a very fragile sense of self. The philosopher in question said, rather impatiently, "he teaches them to say these things: it's all just suggestion". By contrast, another philosopher, Karl Popper, the person who originally made the claim that psychoanalysis is unscientific, goes on to say that he nevertheless does not doubt the truth of much of what Freud claimed. Freud had presented his findings in terms of the interaction of impersonal forces because the prevailing philosophy of science, mechanistic materialism, dictated just that. Ironically, it bears some responsibility, together with the jargon into which Freud's writings have been translated, for the impression that it is pseudoscience. Popper's encounter with psychoanalysis drove him to re-think the nature of science, to reject mechanistic materialism, and argue that a field can only be described as scientific if one can make inferences from it that are open to falsification.

Popper's claim that psychoanalysis is unscientific was based on his view that it contains concepts like "resistance" that mean that it cannot be falsified: if a practitioner makes an interpretation to a patient and they reject it, the rejection can be dismissed as a reflection of their pathology. This presupposes a rather top down, authoritarian way of doing therapy. A different way of picturing it is that one person, the therapist, helps another, the patient, to explore the issues that have led her or him to seek help, and that it is that very process of exploration, if carried out sensitively and with empathy, that builds trust, and is, in itself, therapeutic because it makes it possible for the patient to re-integrate parts of the self that have become split off and repressed. Connections may be suggested by the therapist, derived, perhaps, from their life experience, their training, and bits of theory that seem relevant, but they may also be put forward by the patient. A body of knowledge is created that may confirm the findings of other practitioners, qualify, or extend them; and ideas from that body of knowledge may appear to offer illuminating ways of looking at issues in other contexts.

A good example of this way of working is the "conversational" model of psychotherapy described by R. F. Hobson, in his book *Forms of Feeling: The Heart of Psychotherapy* (1985). Hobson, a Jungian analyst who became Reader in Psychotherapy at Manchester University, urged his trainees to respond to what their patients were saying with tentative statements to check that they have properly understood what their patient is trying to convey. Those statements may then be modified by the patient, or confirmed, or refuted.

Some practitioners just ignore the controversy and talk about "scientific meetings" or refer to psychodynamic psychology as science, as David Malan does in the title of his book *Individual Psychotherapy and the Science of Psychodynamics*. These claims and counter claims have bedevilled the history of the psychoanalytic movement because they hook us into a controversy and beg questions such as why the scientific standing of the psychology should matter and what such a science might be for. Whether it matters or not depends, in fact, on the relationship in which we want to be heeded, rather as Thomas Kuhn argues that scientific work is done with a specific audience of other scientists and their shared values in mind. For instance, how might the scientific standing of psychodynamic psychology be relevant in the relationship between a therapist and a patient? To take an imaginary example, 'scientific' studies of psychodynamic hypotheses usually yield results such as: "69% of the sample tested showed oedipal jealousy at the age of 5", or it might be 53% or 71%, or whatever, but if a patient rejects the interpretation that he was jealous of his father's relationship with his mother and projects his hostility to his father on to him, how could any therapist know that the patient is one of the 69% or the 53% or the 71%? And how would quoting the statistics to him help the patient accept the interpretation? Such an exchange would be very remote from the way in which therapy is practised and the tentative, provisional way in which interpretations are offered.

An example might help. Several years ago, I was asked to see a man in his late forties who had had a breakdown. When I asked him to tell me a little more about what had happened he said that he had woken up in terror that his wife was terminally ill, although in fact she was in good health and able to reassure him that there was nothing for him to worry about. Amongst several other symptoms he described was a bizarre but equally panicky conviction that the police cars sounding their sirens going over the nearby bridge were actually coming to arrest him, although the rational part of himself knew full well that he had done nothing wrong. I learnt that Kit, as he liked to be called, had been brought up on an estate in North London and had been a carer for his mother, who was chronically sick. She had cancer, which had been diagnosed just before Kit was born. Her doctors explained to her that treatment at that point would kill the baby, so she decided to reject it. Kit was her only child and she was determined to be the best mother she could to him. Mother and father, however, did not get on, and his father left when Kit was four. He remembered feeling glad about that because his father had been abusive towards his mother. His father, who worked as a school caretaker, rarely, if ever, paid maintenance, so Kit and his mother lived on benefits and faced perpetual anxiety about money. For Kit there were frequent trips to hospital with his mother and ever-present anxiety about her health, so much so that he slept poorly and would play the BBC World service throughout the night because he was always on the alert for a crisis.

Fortunately, the comprehensive school he attended was excellent, and the headmaster did all he could to help him. He was interested in music and the school had an orchestra so a cello was acquired for him and lessons arranged. When he was seventeen or eighteen he won a place at a London music college, and after graduation auditioned successfully for a position in a world-famous orchestra. But the poverty and anxiety he had experienced earlier in his life were buried not very deeply inside him, like an unexploded mine. He remembered his mother walking regularly with her head down in the hope of finding a lost coin, and on one occasion he said he had been out for a stroll with his wife and had tripped on a root and half torn off the sole of his shoe. He had been deeply upset. When his wife wondered why something annoying, but essentially rather trivial, had so deeply disturbed him he said that it plunged him into a memory of a similar mishap when he was a child: he was re-living the distress he then felt when he accidentally ripped a plimsol on a rough path and dreaded telling his mother because there was no money to buy him another pair. When, two or three sessions later, he returned to his fear that the police were about to arrest him I said that I wondered if he'd felt rather triumphant as a child that he had driven his father out and now had his mother to himself. He hadn't, of course, driven his father out, but if that was how he'd understood his leaving there might be some unconscious guilt about the part he imagined he had played in it—another case of a child feeling guilty about something they could not possibly be responsible for, which I noted in Chapter 4. "I wonder if your fear that the police cars are coming to arrest you is a fantasy that father figures are about to take their revenge," I said. "I can't do anything with that", he replied. And we left it there because we were close to the end of the session.

It is hard to imagine any therapist responding to this with a comment such as, "well, there are many studies showing that children want to get rid of the parent of the opposite sex in order to have the mother or father to themselves". The invariable response would be to wait and see what followed. In fact, Kit came in two or three weeks later and said that he'd had a strange dream: he was in a young offenders' unit, but he didn't know why he was there. His only visitor was his father and he believed his father knew the nature of his offence. They had a long talk, but he couldn't remember what they talked about. I asked him if he had any inkling of what he might have done wrong, but he couldn't think of anything. Eventually I reminded him of my original interpretation, and I was left with the impression that he could see it might make sense.

In a relationship between a psychoanalytically trained consultant and an institution such as a doctor's surgery, staff do not ask whether or not the consultant's insights are scientific: they judge them by whether or not they are helpful and throw new light on the problems they face. One of the best-known examples of this was the study by the Tavistock Institute of the training of nurses in a London teaching hospital. A third or more would drop out and the Tavistock was invited to look into why this loss might be happening. In her paper entitled "Social Systems as a Defence Against Anxiety", Isobel Menzies Lyth argued that patterns of relationship or "social structures" had grown up to try to manage the anxieties evoked by the nature of the nurses' work. There was a diffusion of responsibility, for example, and the de-personalisation or dehumanisation of patients, who might be referred to as "the liver in number 10", or "the pneumonia in bed 15". Nursing became a series of tasks to be performed, or a set of skills, rather than a caring relationship with a person. The author's argument is that the culture of the hospital had taken this form in order to help the nursing staff avoid anxiety, guilt, doubt and uncertainty, but it failed, and it left trained nurses and trainees feeling unsatisfied and uncared-for. The study does not tell us if those who commissioned it worried about whether or not it was scientific: what mattered was that it clearly confirmed that the established 'social system' was harmful, and that becoming more conscious of the anxieties it attempted to contain was the key to finding better ways of managing them.

In a different relationship, that between practitioner and legislator, the credibility of what practitioners have found in a specific area might be much more important, and that credibility would usually take the form of statistical evidence of the kind produced by James Gilligan. As I said, Gilligan's evidence derives quite explicitly from his therapeutic work with prisoners, but his theories are tested against extensive research on the figures relating to violence from countries throughout the world, including countries like Sweden and Japan, whose social systems differ very considerably from each other. The conclusions of the Marmot reviews do not stem so directly from psychotherapeutic practice, but the importance of a sense of control over our lives that emerges from them matches and supports what we learn when we listen to people who seek professional help with mental health issues. Studies of the kind reported by Gilligan, or reviewed by Michael Marmot, Kate Pickett and Richard Wilkinson, use the language legislators respect; they are evidence-based and they are open to revision and refutation. They render arguments as to whether psychodynamic psychology is or is not scientific largely academic.

Whether psychoanalysis is a science or better described as a humanity, it needs to be in conversation with science, both informing it and being informed by it. Mark Solms is a neuroscientist and a psychoanalyst who has written extensively on these issues in recent years and it is worth citing his conclusions. Neuroscience, he argues, supports the core claims on which psychoanalysis is founded. These are that:

1. The human infant is not a blank slate, like all other species, we are born with a set of innate needs.

2. The main task of mental development is to learn how to meet these needs in the world, which implies that mental disorder arises from failures to achieve this task.

3. Most of our methods of meeting our emotional needs are executed unconsciously, which requires us to return them to consciousness in order to change them.

These core claims, Solms continues, could also be regarded as foundational premises, but it is important to recognise that they are scientific premises, because they are testable and falsifiable.[1]

It is important, Solms goes on to say, to distinguish between these core claims and individual details. A forest is still a forest, one might say, even if its owners decide to replace the old chestnut trees with oaks or conifers. Thus neuroscience supports Freud's claim that we are all bisexual, but rejects the concept of a death drive or instinct. Our innate needs are experienced as feelings; they represent unsatisfied needs; psychoanalysis and psychodynamic psychotherapy are about those feelings and helping people to find better ways of managing them, and better ways, therefore, of meeting their needs. This involves a process of re-consolidation, which may be difficult, and does not always work; the evidence, however, is that psychoanalytic psychotherapy in general is "a highly effective form of treatment".[2]

---

1   p. 2. M. Solms, "The Neurobiological Underpinnings of Psychoanalytic Theory and Therapy", *Frontiers in Behavioural Neuroscience* 12 (2018), https://doi.org/10.3389/fnbeh.2018.00294
2   Ibid.

Postscript

Two or three years before he died, Norman Cohn told me, as I gather he had told others, that he had ceased to believe that psychological hypotheses were needed to explain the Holocaust: it could all be accounted for, he said, by the efficiency of the German bureaucracy and the reliability of the country's railways. It was a case of what Hannah Arendt had called the banality of evil. It is hard to imagine that this was his final, considered view on the subject because it would have invalidated the greater part of his life's work. Moreover, he also said that he stood by everything he had ever written. This is very puzzling, but perhaps the key to it lies in the forward to the third edition of *Warrant for Genocide* (2005) where he endorses and affirms the value of psychoanalytic theory in shedding light on such disturbing, paranoid fantasies as the Protocols of the Elders of Zion, but confesses that "given the increasing sophistication of psychoanalytic thinking, my interpretation now appears somewhat primitive."

That may be what Cohn felt in his early nineties, but the re-emergence in the past few years of movements fired by lethal, moralistic zealotry has led to a renewed interest in psychoanalytic thinking on the subject. Some of that thinking is little known, or unknown, or forgotten, and some of it is hard for lay people to understand because it is it is complex and couched in theory or jargon that many find impenetrable. I wanted both to draw attention to it and try, so far as possible, to convey and consider it in clear, intelligible English. Although I have written particularly about the issues that preoccupied the Institute for Research in Collective Psychopathology more than half a century ago, the key ideas that emerged at that time are highly relevant to any understanding of the unspeakable inhumanity of humans to other humans that we see around us at the present.

 https://doi.org/10.11647/OBP.0416.10

In my Appendix B on Psychoanalysis as Science I quoted the neuroscientist and psychoanalyst Mark Solms as stressing that psychotherapy is about feeling. The main lesson we might learn from a psychology derived from its practice, therefore, is emotional literacy, being able to imagine the thoughts and feelings of others, or empathy. We acquire this, in so far as we do, from parent figures; mothers and fathers play a crucial role in it, although the role of fathers is often not appreciated, and where it is, has become controversial. Contrast the views of Henry Dicks and Donald Winnicott on the one hand with those of Jacques Lacan on the other. Amongst those whose learning is poor or patchy, some may end up in therapy, or in psychiatric hospitals; some, however, become delinquent, whilst others, many others, resolve their maturational problems by developing authoritarian personality traits. Emotional intelligence in men in patriarchal cultures is disparaged and discouraged, and young males may identify with fathers who embody such a model. But it is also, as I said, reinforced by the culture in which they grow up. If boys show any sensitivity to feeling early on, they are supposed to grow out of it. The comic writer Robert Webb, in his autobiographical *How Not to be a Boy*, has given a vivid account of this in his own background, and the Jungian analyst Joy Schaverien, in her book *The Boarding School Syndrome*, has described how the boarding school experience similarly undermines the development of emotional maturity in young people from a different part of society, one from which our leading politicians, lawyers and civil servants are drawn. In my fifth chapter, on Guilt and Shame, I quoted James Gilligan's description of the same taboo in American prisons, where, he reports, the only permissible emotions are anger and hate. In fact, even anger and hate are seen as indicating vulnerability, so the message is "don't get mad, get even", and if you do not avenge a slight, if you do not respond with violence to humiliation or being disrespected, you are regarded as being gay. Homophobia underlies the value system that Webb and Schaverien depict, as Webb explicitly says; in the prison system, it manifests itself in a particularly virulent form. We worry about the recent cult of toxic masculinity, though it clearly appeals to boys who are struggling with just these issues.

But if individuals have to struggle with them, so do societies, because those who are in charge of them have to manage groups who have found different solutions to these maturational problems, whether those solutions work or, in some way or other, make life difficult for them. This is particularly hard with those who are anti-social or authoritarian. We are only too familiar with the harshness those of an authoritarian bent habitually display towards those who are delinquent, but they may also, contrarily, have a menacing tendency to join forces, the criminal admiring the authoritarian, the strong man or woman, and the latter, whether male or female, manipulating the antisocial for their own demonising, dehumanising ends. The storming of the U.S. Congress after the election of President Biden in January 2021 is just one of many examples.

The two most important contributions that psychodynamic psychology can make to preventing such developments are to urge governments to protect and nurture the conditions that are known to be vital for the growth of emotional intelligence, and for governments and their advisors to prevent the dehumanising and demonising elements, who lack it, gaining power. The key is for governments and their advisors to avoid policies and reject proposals that impair fundamental human needs. Affects, the neuroscientist Mark Solms pointed out, make us aware of those needs. The crucial importance for us of some sense of control over our lives is a point I have made several times. The absence of control is not only damaging to mental and physical health but, by displacement, lies behind the appeal of populist slogans promising to take it back. Belonging is similarly important because, as I argued earlier, not belonging puts us at the mercy of predators, as migrants and asylum seekers know only too well. It also affects who we trust and who we do not trust and, therefore, what we are willing to accept as evidence, or dismiss as "fake news". Shame and humiliation are directly related to belonging, because the values of the community we belong to, or aspire to belong to, determine what may and may not be seen. But the psychology of shame and humiliation, and how it operates in societies where patriarchal values predominate, is vital for understanding the roots of violence. Diplomats understand that and, in trying to resolve disputes, try to find solutions that avoid either party losing face. But governments do not always show such wisdom. The Treaty of Versailles shamed and humiliated Germany, unfairly blaming the country for causing the First World War, and, as is well known, John Maynard

Keynes, soon after it was signed, warned against the consequences of imposing such a settlement. Later, after the Second World War, the Norwegian peace activist Johan Galtung argued that the rise of Adolf Hitler and the Holocaust might actually have been averted if the Treaty had been rescinded in the 1920s and Germany given help with its economic difficulties. The victors, however, preferred vengeance.

Similarly, in my Introduction I related the claim of David Stuckler and Sanjay Basu that the "shock therapy" visited on Russia after the implosion of the former Soviet Union was directly responsible for the death of ten million people. The figure is hotly disputed and the truth of the matter has now disappeared into a quagmire of technicalities, but many witnesses testify to the fact that it created widespread destitution, deprived many of any vestige of control they might have had had over their lives, and exposed millions to shame and humiliation. Shock therapy in Russia paved the path to Vladimir Putin because he was able to bring order to a chaotic situation, and a people who had suffered a traumatic loss of respect could identify with someone who would champion the restoration of their country to its former glory. The problem was compounded by the failure of Western politicians to grasp another emotion: fear—his fear of NATO.

By contrast, the implementation of policies that reflect a high degree of awareness of their emotional consequences, policies that are psychologically informed, may imply far-reaching change, but by their very nature, they do not entail violent upheaval. It is very hard to imagine that anyone could seriously believe that putting the recommendations of the Marmot reports into practice would be dangerous because it could bring about some twenty-first-century version of the storming of the Bastille or the Winter Palace, or a regime of terror in which categories of people designated as evil would be sought out and killed. On the contrary, it is policies and programmes that lack, are indifferent to, or disparage emotional intelligence that promote the spread of the "scourge"; apocalyptic thinking and utopian ideas are simply symptoms, whether harmless or harmful, of the devastation and the suffering they create.

Bibliography

Alderdice, John, Lord, "Understanding Terrorism: The Inner Word and the Wider World", *British Journal of Psychotherapy* 21 (4), 2005, http://dx.doi.org/10.1111/j.1752-0118.2005.tb00247.x

Aristotle, *The Nicomachean Ethics*, translated by H. Rackham (Cambridge: Harvard University Press, 1968).

Astor, David, 'Towards a Study of the Scourge', *Encounter*, August 1962.

Baron-Cohen, Simon *Zero Degrees of Empathy: A New Theory of Human Cruelty* (London: Allen Lane, 2011), https://doi.org/10.1192/bjp.bp.111.098434

Blundell, Susanne, "Fatherless Sons", in *The Importance of Fathers: A Psychoanalytic Re-evaluation*, ed. Judith Trowell and Alicia Etchegoyan (Hove: Brunner-Routledge, 2002), https://doi.org/10.4324/9780203013946

Briant, M.G. *Fact and Value in Psychoanalysis*. Unpublished Ph.D. thesis. London University, 1973.

Camus, Albert, *The Plague,* translated by Stuart Gilbert (London: Penguin Books, 1960).

Clark, Christopher, *The Sleepwalkers. How Europe Went to War in 1914* (London: Allen Lane, 2012).

Cohn, Norman, *Europe's Inner Demons* (London: Pimlico, 1993).

—, The Pursuit of the Millennium (London: Pimlico, 2004).

—, *Warrant for Genocide* (London: Serif, 2005).

Dante, *The Divine Comedy*, translated by Clive James (London: Picador, 2013).

Dicks, H.V., "In Search of Our Proper Ethic", *Human Relations* 23 (1 & 2), 1950.

—, *Licensed Mass Murder* (London: Heinemann for Sussex University Press, 1972).

—, *Marital Tensions* (London: Karnac, 1993).

—, "Personality Traits and National Socialist Ideology: A War-Time Study of German Prisoners of War", *Human Relations* 3, 1950.

Eliot, T.S., *Collected Poems, 1909-62* (London: Faber & Faber, 1963).

Erikson, Erik, *Childhood and Society* (London: Penguin, 1965).

Evans, Richard J., *The Coming of the Third Reich* (London: Allen Lane, 2003).

Fairbairn, W.R.D., *Psychoanalytic Studies of the Personality* (London: Routledge and Kegan Paul, 1952).

—, *From Instinct to Self: Selected Papers of W.R.D. Fairbairn*, Vol. 11. *Applications and Early Contributions*, ed. Eleanor Birtles Fairbairn and David Scharff (New York: Jason Aronson Inc., 1994).

Farmer, Paul, Pathologies of Power: Health, Human Rights, and the New War on the Poor (London: University of California Press, 2003).

Farrington, David P. and West, Donald J., *The Cambridge Study in Delinquent Development: Long-Term Follow Up: Final Report to the Home Office* (Cambridge: Institute of Criminology, University of Cambridge, 1988).

Ferrari, Lorenzo, *Norman Cohn e Il Lato Oscuro della Storia* (Milan: Franco Angeli, Biblioteca della Storia, 2023).

Ffytche, Matt and Pick, Daniel, *Psychoanalysis in the Age of Totalitarianism* (Abingdon: Routledge, 2016), https://doi.org/10.4324/9781315760773

Fink, Bruce, *A Clinical Introduction to Lacanian Psychoanalysis* (London: Harvard University Press, 1999).

Forrester, J., *The Seductions of Psychoanalysis: Freud, Lacan and Derrida* (Cambridge: Cambridge University Press, 1990).

Freud, Sigmund, *An Autobiographical Study*, (1935), *Standard Edition of the Collected Works*, Vol. 20 (London: The Hogarth Press, 1959).

—, *Civilisation and its Discontents*, (1930), *Standard Edition of the Collected Works*, Vol. 21 (London: The Hogarth Press, 1964).

—, *Civilised Sexual Morality and Modern Nervous Illness* (1908), *Standard Edition of the Collected Works*, Vol. 9 (London: The Hogarth Press, 1959).

—, *The Economic Problem of Masochism* (1924), *Standard Edition of the Collected Works*, Vol. 19 (London: The Hogarth Press, 1961).

—, *The Ego and the Id* (1923), *Standard Edition of the Collected Works*, Vol. 19 (London: The Hogarth Press, 1961).

—, *An Outline of Psychoanalysis* (1938), *Standard Edition of the Collected Works*, Vol. 23 (London: The Hogarth Press, 1964).

—, *Why War?* Reply to letter from Albert Einstein (1932), *Standard Edition of the Collected Works*, Vol. 22 (London: The Hogarth Press, 1960).

Fromm, Erich, *The Fear of Freedom* (London: Routledge and Kegan Paul, 1960).

—, *The Sane Society* (London: Routledge, 1963).

Gay, Peter, *Freud, A Life for Our Time* (London: Dent, 1988).

Gellner, Ernest, *The Psychoanalytic Movement* (London: Paladin, 1985).

Gilligan, James, *Preventing Violence* (London: Thames and Hudson, 2001).

Gray, John, Black Mass: Apocalyptic Religion and the Death of Utopia (London: Allen Lane, 2007).

Guntrip, H.J.S., "What Does Psychoanalytic Therapy Really Accomplish? My Experience of Analysis with Fairbairn and Winnicott", *International Review of Pycho-analysis* 2, 1975.

Hadar, Uri, *Psychoanalysis and Social Involvement: Interpretation and Action* (London: Palgrave Macmillan, 2013), https://doi.org/10.1057/9781137301093

Hampshire Stuart, *Spinoza* (London: Penguin Books, 1953).

Hobson, R.F., *Forms of Feeling: The Heart of Psychotherapy* (Abingdon: Routledge, 1985).

Jones, Ernest, *Sigmund Freud, Life and Work* (London: The Hogarth Press, 1955).

Jung, Carl Gustav,*Memories, Dreams and Reflections* (London: Collins and Routledge and Kegan Paul, 1963).

—, *The Practice of Psychotherapy* (London: Routledge and Kegan Paul, 1966).

Kant, Immanuel, *Groundwork for the Metaphysics of Morals* (1785), translated by Allen W. Wood (New Haven: Yale University Press, 2002).

Lacan, Jacques, *The Ethics of Psychoanalysis, 1959–1960; The Seminar of Jacques Lacan: Book VII*, translated by Dennis Porter (London: Routledge, 1992).

Laing, R.D., *The Divided Self* (London: Penguin, 1960).

Langer, Walter, *The Mind of Adolf Hitler* (New York: Basic Books Inc., 1972).

Leonardo da Vinci, *Notebooks* (Oxford: Oxford University Press, 1980).

Machin, Stephen, and Meghir, Costas, "Does Crime Pay Better?", *CentrePiece, The Magazine of Economic Performance* 4(3), 1999, 25–27.

Malan, David, *Individual Psychotherapy and the Science of Psychodynamics* (London: Butterworths, 1979).

Marcuse, Herbert, *One Dimensional Man: Studies in the Ideology of Advanced Industrial Society* (Boston: Beacon, 1964).

Marmot, Sir Michael, *Fair Society, Healthy Lives: Strategic Review of Health Inequalities in England Post 2010* (London: Institute of Health Equity, 2010).

Miller, James, *The Passion of Michel Foucault* (London: Harper Collins, 1993).

Milton, John, *Paradise Lost*. Oxford World Classics (Oxford: Oxford University Press, 2004).

Mollon, Phil, *Shame and Jealousy: The Hidden Turmoils* (London: Karnac, 2002), https://doi.org/10.4324/9780429480102

Money-Kyrle, Roger, *Man's Picture of His World* (New York: International Universities Press, 1961).

—, "Psychoanalysis and Ethics" in *New Directions in Psychoanalysis,* ed. Melanie Klein, Paula Heimann and Roger Money-Kyrle (London: Tavistock Publications, 1977).

Muller, Knuth, "Psychoanalysis and American Intelligence since 1940" in *Psychoanalysis in the Age of Totalitarianism,* ed. Matt Ffytche and Daniel Pick (Abingdon: Routledge, 2016), https://doi.org/10.4324/9781315760773

Menzies Lyth, I.E.P., "Social Systems as a Defence against Anxiety: An Empirical Study of the Nursing Service of a General Hospital" in Trist, E. and Murray, H. (eds.) *The Social Engagement of Social Science, Volume 1: The Socio-Psychological Perspective* (London: Free Association Books, 1990).

Nadler, Steven, *Spinoza, A Life* (Cambridge: Cambridge University Press, 1999).

Nietzsche, *Friedrich, The Genealogy of Morals,* translated by Francis Golffing (New York: Doubleday, 1956).

Ormerod, Paul, "You Pays Your Money: Models of Capitalism" in *The Politics of Attachment,* ed. Sebastian Kramer and Jane Roberts (London: Free Association Books, 1996).

Pascal, Blaise, *Pensées,* ed. Leon Braunscvig (Paris: Editions Cluny, 1934).

Pick, Daniel, *The Pursuit of the Nazi Mind, Hitler Hess and the Analysts* (Oxford: Oxford University Press, 2012).

Popper, Karl R., in *British Philosophy in the Mid-Century,* edited by C. A. Mace (New York: The Macmillan Company, 1957).

Raworth, Kate, *Doughnut Economics: Seven Ways to Think like a 21st-Century Economist* (London: Random House Business Books, 2017).

Rees, Jonathan, *The Case of Rudolf Hess: A Problem in Diagnosis and Forensic Psychiatry* (London: Heinemann, 1947).

Reich, Wilhelm, *The Mass Psychology of Fascism* (New York: Farrar, Strauss and Giroux, 1969).

Rieff, Philip, *Freud, The Mind of a Moralist* (New York: Viking Press, 1961).

Rose, Steven, *The 21st-Century Brain: Explaining, Mending and Manipulating the Mind* (London: Jonathan Cape, 2005).

Roudinesco, Elizabeth, *Jacques Lacan: Outline of a Life, History of a System of Thought,* translated by Barbara Bray (New York: Columbia University Press, 1997).

Rycroft, Charles, *A Critical Dictionary of Psychoanalysis* (London: Nelson, 1968).

Saint Augustine, *Confessions* (Harmondsworth: Penguin, 1961).

Sands, Phillippe, *East West Street* (London: Weidenfeld and Nicholson, 2016).

Schaverien, Joy, *The Boarding School Syndrome* (London: Routledge, 2015).

Schumacher, E.F., *Small is Beautiful: A Study of Economics as if People Mattered* (London: Blond and Briggs, 1973).

Schweitzer, Albert, *The Quest of the Historical Jesus* (London: A. & C. Black, 1910).

Sen, Amartya, "Universal Health Care: The Affordable Dream", *The Guardian*, 6 January 2015.

Sereny, Gita, *Into That Darkness* (London: Pimlico, 1995).

Shakespeare, William, *King Lear* (London: The Arden Shakespeare, Routledge, 1991).

—, *The Tempest* (London: The Arden Shakespeare, Methuen, 1954).

—, *King Richard III* (London: The Arden Shakespeare, Methuen, 1987).

Solms, Mark Leonard, "The Neurobiological Underpinnings of Psychoanalytic Theory and Therapy", *Frontiers in Behavioural Neuroscience*, December 2018, https://doi.org/10.3389/fnbeh.2018.00294

Spinoza, Benedictus de, *Ethics* (London: Dent, 1993).

Stewart, Matthew, *The Courtier and the Heretic: Leibniz, Spinoza, and the Fate of God in the Modern World* (London: Yale University Press, 2005).

Stuckler, David and Basu, Sanjay, *The Body Economic: Why Austerity Kills* (London: Allen Lane, 2013).

Symington, Neville, *The Analytic Experience* (New York: St. Martin's Press, 1986).

Victoria, Brian Daizen, *Zen at War* (New York: Weatherill, 1997).

Varoufakis, Y., *And The Weak Suffer What They Must? Europe, Austerity and the Threat to Global Stability* (London: Vintage, 2016).

Webb, Robert, *How Not to be a Boy* (Edinburgh: Canongate, 2017).

Wilkinson, Richard G., *The Impact of Inequality: How to Make Sick Societies Healthier* (Abingdon: Routledge, 2005).

Wilkinson, R. and Picket, K., *The Spirit Level* (London: Allen Lane, 2009).

Williams, Arthur Hyatt, *Cruelty, Violence and Murder: Understanding the Criminal Mind* (London: Karnac Books, 1998).

Williams, Bernard, *Shame and Necessity* (London: University of California Press, 1994).

Winnicott, D.W., *Home is Where We Start From* (London: Penguin Books, 1990).

—, *The Maturational Processes and the Facilitating Environment* (London: The Hogarth Press, 1965).

Index

About the Team

Alessandra Tosi was the managing editor for this book.

Lucy Barnes proof-read this manuscript and compiled the index; Annie Hine provided editorial assistance.

Jeevanjot Kaur Nagpal designed the cover. The cover was produced in InDesign using the Fontin font.

Cameron Craig typeset the book in InDesign and produced the paperback and hardback editions. The main text font is Tex Gyre Pagella and the heading font is Californian FB.

Cameron also produced the PDF and HTML editions. The conversion was performed with open-source software and other tools freely available on our GitHub page at https://github.com/OpenBookPublishers.

Jeremy Bowman created the EPUB.

Raegan Allen was in charge of marketing.

This book was peer-reviewed by Prof. Timo Storck, Psychologische Hochschule Berlin, and an anonymous referee. Experts in their field, these readers give their time freely to help ensure the academic rigour of our books. We are grateful for their generous and invaluable contributions.

This book need not end here...

Share

All our books — including the one you have just read — are free to access
online so that students, researchers and members of the public who can't
afford a printed edition will have access to the same ideas. This title will be
accessed online by hundreds of readers each month across the globe:
why not share the link so that someone you know is one of them?

This book and additional content is available at
https://doi.org/10.11647/OBP.0416

Donate

Open Book Publishers is an award-winning, scholar-led, not-for-profit press
making knowledge freely available one book at a time. We don't charge
authors to publish with us: instead, our work is supported by our library
members and by donations from people who believe that research
shouldn't be locked behind paywalls.

Join the effort to free knowledge by supporting us at
https://www.openbookpublishers.com/support-us

We invite you to connect with us on our socials!

BLUESKY
@openbookpublish
.bsky.social

MASTODON
@OpenBookPublish
@hcommons.social

LINKEDIN
open-book-publishers

Read more at the Open Book Publishers Blog

https://blogs.openbookpublishers.com